Slough Library Services

Please return this book on or before the date shown on your receipt.

To renew go to:
Website: www.slough.gov.uk/libraries
Phone: 01753 535166

Slough
Borough Council
www.slough.gov.uk

D1426396

34 4124 0006 6701

THE GREATEST ALBUMS
YOU'LL NEVER HEAR

General Editor
Bruno MacDonald

THE GREATEST ALBUMS YOU'LL NEVER HEAR

Aurum
Press

First published in the United Kingdom in 2014 by
Aurum Press Limited
74-77 White Lion Street
London N1 9PF
www.aurumpress.co.uk

Copyright © 2014 Quintessence Editions Ltd.

All rights reserved. No part of this book may be reproduced or utilised in any form or
by any means, electronic or mechanical, including photocopying, recording or by any
information storage and retrieval system, without permission in writing from Aurum
Press Ltd.

Every effort has been made to contact the copyright holders of material in this
book. However, where an omission has occurred, the publisher will gladly include
acknowledgement in any future edition.

The album covers that accompany each entry in this book have been created by
contemporary designers to convey to the reader a fictional interpretation of how such
a cover might have looked. These are merely creative interpretations of 'what might
have been'. Where the names of real-life individuals or organisations appear, there is
no intention to denote that such individuals or organisations would have proceeded
with involvement in the albums as depicted in these fictional covers.

A catalogue record for this book is available from the British Library.

ISBN 978 1 78131 219 3

10 9 8 7 6 5 4 3 2 1
2018 2017 2016 2015 2014

This book was designed and produced by
Quintessence
The Old Brewery
6 Blundell Street
London N7 9BH

Project Editor	Juliet Lough
Designer	Sarah Holland
Picture Researchers	Sarah Holland, Juliet Lough, Bruno MacDonald
Production Manager	Anna Pauletti
Editorial Director	Jane Laing
Publisher	Mark Fletcher

Colour reproduction by ChromaGraphics Pte Ltd.

Printed and bound in China by 10/10 Printing International Ltd.

p2: The Beatles with producer George Martin, circa 1963.

CONTENTS

INTRODUCTION

The *Greatest Albums You'll Never Hear In Quite The Way The Artists Intended At The Time* was never going to fit on the cover. Some of these you *will* hear if you have no objection to bootlegging. Others you may eventually have the opportunity to purchase because, as the music business scrabbles at the soil to keep from falling into its own grave, everything that can be reissued will be. Bob Dylan's original *Blood on the Tracks* (p78) and The Smashing Pumpkins' *Machina II* (p190) may even be out by the time you read this. However, the tales of these albums failing to make it to market at the time provide insight into why rock stars are rarely allowed to pilot planes or teach children: questionable judgment, disregard of deadlines, too many drugs.

Even albums that *did* find their way into stores provide cautionary lessons. Don't, for example, assume that a big-name producer will necessarily enhance your career. Brian Eno helming Television's *Marquee Moon* was a creative cocktail that might have redefined art rock. However, complained guitarist Tom Verlaine, 'He recorded us very cold and brittle – no resonance.' (Verlaine ended up doing it himself, with Andy Johns – whose brother Glyn graces our chapters on The Beatles [p24], The Who [p44], and The Clash [p116].) And when Jim Steinman steered a first shot at Def Leppard's *Hysteria,* the results, singer Joe Elliott shuddered to *Classic Rock,* were 'the worst bootleg you've ever heard. Those tapes are locked away in my library – and that's where they'll stay.'

A seemingly inspired decision to pair post-punk visionary Andy Partridge of XTC with Blur on *Modern Life Is Rubbish* didn't pan out as expected. 'The man from the record company, Dave Balfe, really wasn't happy,' Partridge told the *Independent.* 'They got him stoned one night and he heard some rough mixes and of course he was floating around going, "Urr, you're George Martin and they're The Beatles! It's fantastic, man!" And then two days later, when he heard the finished mixes, he was like, "Well, this is really shit, Andy."'

Two producers could be even worse. George Martin thought he was in sole charge of The Beatles' *Let It Be*, and was thus 'considerably shaken' when the album – a descendant of *Get Back* (p24) – was released with additional input from Phil Spector. The absence of a producer can be equally calamitous. Unimpressed with Rick Rubin's hands-off approach, U2 parted ways with him, only to create *No Line on the Horizon,* their most ho-hum album – hence, in part, the tortuous decline of *Songs of Ascent* (p232). And although Joy Division's Peter Hook dismissed Martin Hannett's contribution to *Unknown Pleasures* as 'he added some salt and pepper and some herbs and served up the dish,' we're willing to bet the version recorded *without* one of the 1980s' most maverick producers wouldn't often find its way into all-time great lists.

Then there are the albums that *did* get released, but to such limited circles that history overlooks them. Examples include Eminem's *Infinite* ('Me trying to figure out how I wanted my rap style to be,' said Mr Mathers), Nickelback's *Hesher* ('I'm trying to bury that album,' front man Chad Kroeger confessed), and Jimmy Page's soundtrack for Kenneth Anger's *Lucifer Rising* (unhelpfully issued on vinyl only, via Page's website, forty years after the movie's completion). In 2001, sixteen-year-old Katy Perry made a Christian rock album under her real name, Katy Hudson. Sadly, even a positive review by *Christianity Today* couldn't push its sales beyond a reported 100 copies. This tale of woe echoed that of Tori Amos, whose debut *Y Kant Tori Read* was rarely discussed and never reissued when she became a star; a scenario repeated by Jewel's *Save the Linoleum,* produced by Neil Young's pedal steel guitarist Ben Keith and featuring a formative version of her breakthrough hit, 'Who Will Save Your Soul?' Bucking the trend, Alanis Morissette scored two top forty albums in 1991 and 1992 . . . but only in her native Canada, enabling 1995's *Jagged Little Pill* to be marketed elsewhere, with staggering success, as her debut.

The quintessential 'lost' album is the KLF's *1987 (What the Fuck Is Going On?).* Credited to the duo's first incarnation The Justified Ancients of Mu Mu, it shot into Britain's indie chart in 1987. But when Abba objected to its sampling of 'Dancing Queen', all unsold copies were ordered destroyed. Mu-men Bill Drummond and Jimmy Cauty dumped some in the North Sea, burned others in a Swedish field, and auctioned their final five copies for £1,000 each.

A rarer phenomenon finds releases *almost* making it to record stores before plugs get pulled. Witness the Stones' *American Tour '72* (p56), John Fogerty's *Hoodoo* (p84), Duff McKagan's *Beautiful Disease* (p176), and 50 Cent's bullet-strewn *Power of the Dollar* (p184). Brian Eno (p148) and Cat Power both requested that albums be shelved to make way for preferred efforts, while the Sisters of Mercy's Andrew Eldritch, in a bid to annoy his record company, made an album (p168) that he correctly considered near-unreleasable.

Many albums that *did* make it looked as if they might not. Pink Floyd's *Dark Side of the Moon* was widely toured as the underwhelming *Eclipse (A Piece for Assorted Lunatics).* Courtney Love mooted, for years, *How Dirty Girls Get Clean,* before transforming it into the Hole album *Nobody's Daughter.* George Harrison toiled for a year on *Somewhere in England,* only for Warner Bros to veto four of its songs and even its artwork. Julian Cope was obliged to 'water down' *Jehovahkill* to meet Island's request for a more commercial product.

Sometimes pressure comes from within. Axl Rose tinkered at length on Guns N' Roses' *Use Your Illusion* albums. 'I left the studio with a mix of them that was simple and raw,' Slash wrote in his autobiography, 'before any synths and horns or backup vocal tracks were layered on. . . . I wish that I still had a copy of them, or that they were floating around the internet somewhere. . . . They were entirely different beasts altogether from the versions that got released.' At the angst-ridden end of the spectrum, My Chemical Romance created *Conventional Weapons,* only to release it as a series of singles – after which humiliating climb-down they split up. Other examples of gruelling creative enterprises have happier endings, such as *Who's Next* (p44), *Young Americans* (p72), *The Final Cut* (p120), *Nebraska* (p126), and *Sign 'o' the Times* (p136).

Some albums never make it that far. A sequel to *Layla and Other Assorted Love Songs* by Derek and the Dominos 'broke down halfway through,' reported Eric Clapton, 'because of the paranoia and tension.' Other acts have been spanked and sent to their rooms by record companies, as the red cheeks of Kiss (p50), The Bee Gees (p58), Public Enemy (p172), The Smashing Pumpkins (p190), David Bowie (p194), and Duran Duran (p226) will attest.

Some albums that *weren't* made became as much part of their makers' tapestry as ones that were. Frank Zappa (p96), Bruce Springsteen (p106), Neil Young (p18, 60, 80, and 90), and Ryan Adams (p222) could have filled this book on their own. And Brian Wilson's life might have been different if he had finished *Smile* (p12) or – scarily – rapped his way back to success (p150).

Also of note are two reclusive Brits. Prefab Sprout's Paddy McAloon, in the wilderness years after 1990's *Jordan: The Comeback,* conceived multiple follies with titles like *Earth: The Story So Far, The Atomic Hymnbook,* and *Zorro the Fox.* Most intriguing was *Behind the Veil,* a concept album about Michael Jackson that drew in Princess Diana and wound up on a desert island. McAloon revived bits of these abandoned projects for later albums, in contrast to The The's Matt Johnson, who has reportedly amassed an unreleased catalogue of equal proportions to his actual output but who has kept a strict leash on the likes of 1982's *The Pornography of Despair* and 1997's *Gun Sluts.*

Circumstances beyond an act's control can send schedules spiralling into the unknown. Usher's *All About U* was delayed twice when some of its tracks were leaked online. 'I didn't want that to be the way my record was remembered,' he complained. When a set titled *8701* emerged instead, a defensive publicist maintained that it was 'practically a new album'. Indisputably a new album was *American Idiot,* created when – if you believe Green Day (and, spoiler alert, the editor of this book doesn't) – its precursor was stolen (p206).

One might have thought there could be no greater obstacle to an unfinished album's release than the death of its maker. However, as 2Pac's posthumous output proves, that is very much not the case. Meanwhile, demos for an album by Jeff Buckley (p164) appeared with eyebrow-raising haste after his demise.

In one instance, the gestation of an album was terminated by that of a child. Wu-Tang Clan associate Blue Raspberry's 1999 solo album was canned when – as producer RZA explained with an uncharacteristic lack of chivalry – 'She got pregnant and went through that whole bullshit and fucked my shit up.'

In conclusion, then, if you don't want to appear in revised editions of this book, don't take drugs, don't expect record companies to agree that art is preferable to hits, don't annoy Abba, and, well, don't get pregnant.

WITH THANKS TO MARK BENNETT, ANDREW GREENAWAY, MATTHEW HORTON, AND JOHNNY LAW

Chapter 1

The Beatles   Get Back

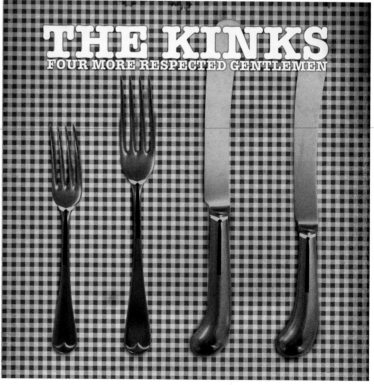

THE KINKS
FOUR MORE RESPECTED GENTLEMEN

Cover: Dean Martin

SMILE

Artist The Beach Boys **Year** 1967 **Country** US **Genre** Psychedelic surf **Label** Capitol
What The original Greatest Album You'll Never Hear

On 20 February 2004, Brian Wilson stepped off stage at London's Royal Festival Hall in a state of stunned jubilation. He had just received a ten-minute standing ovation for a performance of re-worked tracks from his masterpiece-that-never-was: the lost Beach Boys album, *Smile.* It was thirty-seven years after the project had ground to a standstill owing to Wilson's fragile state of mind and only three since he had said, 'I don't really ever want to put out the *Smile* stuff. It's just not appropriate music. [It] scared me.' Now he was frightened for a whole different reason: his fans' adulation. 'It's almost scary . . .' he told biographer Peter Ames Carlin. 'I couldn't believe they could like it so much.' After a successful run of five shows in London, Wilson and his backing band The Wondermints toured Britain and Europe. Back in the US in the spring, they set to work recording a studio version of the completed *Smile* songs. When that album hit stores and reviewers' desks, the response was overwhelmingly positive: it went on to receive three Grammy nominations. However, not everyone was ecstatic about the revival. 'Some of *Smile*'s majesty is its mystery,' noted Jeff Turrentine on slate.com. 'To return to this now-mythic collection of songs is to gild the rarest, wildest lily in pop music.'

ANGELIC FIGURES

To fully understand that mysterious majesty, we must return to the summer of 1966, in the aftermath of The Beach Boys' classic *Pet Sounds*. That album heralded a departure for the band, being more introspective and sophisticated than their previous surfboards, girls, and cars fare. 'It was just so much more than a record,' Wilson's bandmate and brother Carl reflected. 'It had such a spiritual quality. It wasn't going in and doing another top ten. It had so much more meaning than that.' It was also the first album for which Brian Wilson worked predominantly with an outsider. Lyricist Tony Asher helped him write songs for the album while the rest of the band fulfilled their touring commitments – something Wilson was no longer willing nor able to do.

One track slated for *Pet Sounds* was 'Good Vibrations.' Having begun life as a sort of R&B track, it gained layers of instrumentation: harpsichord, cello, Jew's harp, tack piano, flutes, chromatic harmonica, and Brian's crowning

BRIAN WILSON
Wilson's mooted magnum opus ultimately contributed to his isolation from the group he helped make famous. And while this most fractious of acts were hardly united in support of *Smile,* at least one member was enthusiastic. 'In my opinion,' Dennis Wilson told *NME,* 'it makes *Pet Sounds* stink – that's how good it is.'

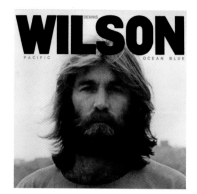

WILSON

PACIFIC   OCEAN BLUE

BAMBUZLED

Dennis Wilson was the first Beach Boy to release a solo album, with 1976's *Pacific Ocean Blue* (above). While recording that release, he also worked on songs for its planned follow-up, *Bambu*. A combination of money struggles, drug problems, and Beach Boy commitments meant it was never finished. Wilson claimed *Bambu* was 'a hundred times better than *Pacific Ocean Blue*.' A 2008 reissue of the latter, including tracks from the former, provides an opportunity to verify that claim.

HEROES AND VILLAINS

Opposite *Top* Al Jardine and Mike Love. *Bottom* Brian Wilson at work. Although Mike Love was often at loggerheads with his talented cousin, he told *Mojo* that he had 'zero, nothing' to do with '*Smile* not coming out at that time. That was Brian.'

touch, a type of Theremin. Realizing the song didn't fit with the moodier feel of *Pet Sounds*, Wilson considered bequeathing it to a soul singer such as Wilson Pickett. Ultimately, however, he decided to keep it for himself – and, as he revisited it again and again, a grander plan emerged. He began to envisage 'Good Vibrations' as a single-sized, psychedelic version of George Gershwin's 'Rhapsody in Blue' – a piece with which he had been obsessed since childhood. His own song, Wilson declared, was a 'little pocket symphony.'

The birthing process was lengthy: as well as recording different sections in different studios for their differing tones, Wilson was also rearranging various sections in an intricate process that stretched to twenty-two sessions over seven months. The song would eventually cost a staggering $50,000 to record. The sound, structure, and length of 'Good Vibrations' all became controversial within the band. 'There was a lot of, "Oh, you can't do this – that's too modern," or, "That's going to be too long a record,"' Wilson told *Rolling Stone* in 1976. 'I said, "No, it's not going to be too long a record – it's going to be just right."'

In fact, Wilson was so alive to pop's myriad possibilities that he envisioned an album that would be even more ambitious. This would use the same modular approach, with individual sections, songs, and movements, to create what he described as 'A teenage symphony to God.' Sitting at his piano late at night, his creativity fuelled by amphetamines, he would see small, angelic figures moving through the air above him. Figuring they were heavenly figures delivering the music to him, he began to call the proposed album *Dumb Angel*.

A new collaborator appeared in the form of the esoteric, punning lyricist Van Dyke Parks. Wilson initially asked Parks to finish his incomplete lyrics to 'Good Vibrations' – an invitation he graciously declined. Instead, the pair set to work on completely new material. At Wilson's house in Beverly Hills, inspiration flowed thick and fast. First to be completed was the Old West allegory 'Heroes and Villains'. 'We had the whole thing, apart from one section, in one sitting,' Parks recalled. 'That was the enthusiasm. And that gave ignition to the process. The engine had started. It was very much ad hoc. Seat of the pants.'

WACKY IDEAS

'Good Vibrations' rocketed to the top of the US and UK charts, but it seemed that The Beach Boys' label and even some of the band members regarded it as little more than a fluke. Sheltering from criticism of his best work by his nearest and dearest, Brian Wilson buried himself in the music for the new album – which he had rechristened *Smile,* to reflect the difference in tone from *Pet Sounds.* As he told *Sounds* in 1976, 'That is a concept in humour. Laughing is a very spiritual state of mind and I regard it as a high thing.' (Carl Wilson emphasized the spiritual aspect in a 1967 interview with *Rave:* 'At present our influences are of a religious nature – not any specific religion but an idea based upon that of Universal Consciousness. The concept of spreading goodwill, good thoughts, and happiness is nothing new. It is an idea which religious teachers and philosophers have been handing down for centuries, but it is also our hope. The ideas are there in 'God Only Knows', 'Good Vibrations', 'Heroes and Villains' . . . and it is why the new LP is called *Smile.*')

LOCKED DOWN
In 1969, the Beach Boys, needing to fulfil their contract with Capitol, began recording new tracks. The label wasn't impressed and instead released *Live in London* (initially in the UK only – it appeared six years later at home). After *Sunflower* (above) – the first album for their new label Warner/Reprise – performed worse than expected, many of the studio tracks were resurrected for an album provisionally titled *Landlocked.* The band's new label also rejected the tracks. However, many *did* appear on what is considered one of the greatest Beach Boys albums: 1971's *Surf's Up* – named after the title track, a *Smile* outtake.

The notion of humour as an ideal seemed to infect Wilson's mind as much as the copious drugs he was taking during the creation of the album. ('Brian said in his book, "Boy, Van Dyke really loved those amphetamines!,"' Parks observed to writer Barney Hoskyns. 'But those were *his* amphetamines; they were in *his* medicine cabinet!') Stories abound of the wacky ideas Brian had at the time. Wanting to feel the beach beneath his feet while writing, he had a sandbox built around his grand piano; he sent a young reporter around Los Angeles to record water sounds; and he orchestrated guests at his dinner table to tap their cutlery in complex rhythms, hinting they would end up on the album.

But that didn't mean the band wasn't part of the writing process. One of the album's greatest songs is the elegiac 'Surf's Up', the last verse and title of which were incomplete until Dennis Wilson returned from the UK with tales of how Brits had laughed at the band's striped shirts. The story touched Parks deeply and the mood of sophistication turned to cynicism that they were trying to achieve in the song was set, as was the title.

INCOMPREHENSIBLE FREAK OUT
The album's theme had expanded to being a symphony for the great frontier land of America. 'Cabin-Essence' and 'Do You Like Worms' referred, respectively, to the coming of the railroad and the Europeans sailing to Plymouth Rock. 'Cool, Cool Water' and 'Wind Chimes' hymned the beauty of the natural world, while 'Child Is the Father of the Man' sought God in the face of decadence. Musically, Wilson contrasted traditional American sounds with symphonic arrangements and modern electric instruments. He was also repeating a process that had begun with 'Good Vibrations': taking acetates of the day's recordings and playing the sections in different orders to identify the

> *'Everyone was high but me. It was like being trapped in an insane asylum.'*
>
> Al Jardine

most logical sequence. But while that had worked with the single, it served only to make compiling *Smile* even more complex.

The challenge of working his way out of this musical maze was to have a catastrophic effect on Wilson's already somewhat precarious frame of mind. After the recording session for the 'Fire' section of an 'Elements' suite – during which he had tasked an assistant to set light to kindling in a bucket so the musicians could smell smoke as they played – the composer noticed a spike in the number of fires around Los Angeles. Concerned that his music might be cursed, Wilson destroyed his copy of the master tape and vowed it would never be heard in public. In another instance that has become part of *Smile* lore, on viewing the sci-fi horror movie *Seconds,* he became convinced that a character called 'Wilson' was part of a conspiracy by director John Frankenheimer and record producer Phil Spector – the latter of whom had nothing whatsoever to do with the film – to 'mess with my head.'

Just as worrying was animosity he was feeling from bandmates who resented his role as figurehead and the frequent hailing of him as a genius. 'Brian would go through tremendous paranoia before he'd get into the studio,' observed friend and producer David Anderle, 'knowing he was going to have to face an argument.' There were also concerns that his avant-garde leanings would alienate the band's fans and cost them record sales (especially as *Pet Sounds* had only scraped into the US top ten). 'As far as lyrics are concerned, you can put me down as saying I'm a stickler for words,' Wilson's bandmate and cousin Mike Love told *Rave* in 1967. 'More seriously, you might say that we like to communicate. This incomprehensible "freak out" scene is not for me.'

REALLY DRUGGED FEELING

Things came to a head during a session for 'Cabin-Essence', when Love demanded to know what the lyrics he was supposed to sing actually meant. Confronting Van Dyke Parks, he pointed to, 'Over and over the crow flies / uncover the cornfield / Over and over the thresher and hover the wheat field ...' Parks could not provide an explanation and, as Love scoffed at the absurdity, he made his excuses and left. 'One of the failures of the *Smile* period . . .' the lyricist later confessed to *Rolling Stone*, 'was the fact that the words were maybe too important or something. Or were given unnecessary importance.'

Parks ultimately returned, though the rift was never healed. Meanwhile, work continued, but Wilson could feel all sides collapsing in on him. He and The Beach Boys were battling their record company Capitol over alleged non-payment of royalties – and, in Parks's view, 'that litigious environment destroyed the project. No common citizen could possibly comprehend the enormity of grief that such a lawsuit can inflict unless he's read *Bleak House*. It can consume a life and still the most expressive creative spirit.'

Meanwhile, the sessions descended into mayhem. 'Everyone was high but me,' Al Jardine marvelled to *Goldmine*. 'It was like being trapped in an insane asylum.' Wilson subsequently concurred. 'We didn't realize, but the music was getting too influenced by (drugs),' he admitted to *Rolling Stone*. 'The music had a really drugged feeling. I mean, we had to lay down on the floor with the microphones next to our mouths to do the vocals. We didn't have any energy.'

As his increasing amounts of music made decreasing amounts of sense, Wilson became ever more depressed. On 18 May 1967, he failed to turn up for a studio session and it was cancelled. The fight to bring *Smile* to fruition was over, leaving Wilson punch-drunk on the canvas. **DC**

WHAT HAPPENED NEXT . . .
Needing to release something after *Smile*'s collapse, the band rushed out the childishly-titled *Smiley Smile,* which included shortened, simplified versions of 'Heroes and Villains', 'Wonderful', 'Wind Chimes', and 'Vege-Tables'. Other *Smile* tracks resurfaced on *20/20* ('Cabinessence'), *Sunflower* ('Cool Cool Water'), and of course *Surf's Up*. But perhaps the most significant legacy of *Smile* and Brian's retreat from the creative hub was to afford his bandmates an opportunity to record their own tracks, and also to deepen the rift in the band between the Wilson brothers and Mike Love, Al Jardine, and Bruce Johnston.

WILL IT EVER HAPPEN?

3/10 You could argue that, with the release of 2004's *Brian Wilson Presents Smile* and 2011's *Smile Sessions* (original takes from 1966–67), it already has. However, no-one can tell how – with so many different, transient sections – a finished version from 1967 would have ended up sounding (least of all Brian Wilson). *Brian Wilson Presents Smile* provides a blueprint and a track listing – but it ain't The Beach Boys.

STAMPEDE

Artist Buffalo Springfield **Year** 1967 **Country** US **Genre** Country rock **Label** Atco
What Buffalo boys roam while record label jumps the gun

STEPHEN STILLS
'I conceived a certain group making a certain defined, and what I considered rather beautiful, sound,' Stephen Stills (above, centre) told *Disc & Music Echo* about Buffalo Springfield (clockwise from top left: Dewey Martin, Neil Young, Bruce Palmer, and Richie Furay). 'In the end, we blew it. But while it lasted I suppose it was the nearest thing to an American version of The Beatles. Not in fame and acclaim, but simply in musical terms.'

According to the lucky few who saw Buffalo Springfield live and in the flesh, none of the three albums they released in the mid-1960s ever got close to reproducing the chemistry created by the West Coast outfit on stage. If *Stampede,* the follow-up to their self-titled 1966 debut album, had made it to record stores, it might have best captured the sound they were trying to achieve on vinyl. But while their record company had a title and even a cover ready to go, the band were on a different page entirely.

TWO OLD LADIES
The first Buffalo Springfield album, remarked Robert Plant, 'was great, because it was the kind of music you could hare around to or you could sit down and dig . . . I thought, "This is what an audience wants – this is what *I* want to listen to."' However, guitarists Stephen Stills, Neil Young, and Richie Furay, drummer Dewey Martin, and bassist Bruce Palmer were frustrated that it didn't represent what *Rolling Stone* characterised as their 'inspired, if idiosyncratic, rock 'n' roll.' 'The real core of the group was the three Canadians – me, Bruce Palmer, and Dewey Martin,' Young told writer Nick Kent. 'We played in such a way that the three of us were basically huddled together behind while Stills and Furay were always out front. 'Cos we'd get so into the groove of the thing, that's all we really cared about. But when we got into the studio, the groove just wasn't the same. And we couldn't figure out why. This was the major frustration for me as a young musician. It fucked me up so much.'

Despite their status as one of the most innovative and exciting bands during a golden period for American West Coast music, their early aims were simple. 'All we need,' declared Young, 'is what we've always tried to get . . . a smash record.' Yet the restlessness and speed of development in the band – particularly that of Stills and Young, the strongest creative talents – refused to be channelled into the record sales and chart positions expected of them.

Stampede might just have been the record that nailed the rawness the band wanted the wider world to hear. As it turned out, experimental recording sessions at Atlantic Records' studio in New York and Sound Recorders, Gold Star, and Sunset Sound in Los Angeles failed to satisfy them. Well-documented

stampede • buffalo springfield

Cover: Simon Halfon

PHOTO COPY

With Bruce Palmer out of the band, *Stampede's* cover depicts Stills, Furay, Martin, and Young behind stand-in Dick Davis, his face hidden by a hat. (Road manager Davis was a sort of sixth Springfield. 'Steve [Stills] moved next door and ruined Dickie's eardrums with the aid of a powerful amp,' ran an early profile. 'When the Buffalo formed, Dickie was sort of adopted. He couldn't hear anything else anyway.') When the Springfield-loving Long Ryders wanted a cover for their *Native Sons* (1984), they channelled *Stampede*. Conveniently, their line-up numbered just four, so there was no need to disguise a fifth.

tensions were also taking hold. 'Things got pretty hot on stage,' remarked Martin, 'and, when Neil and Stephen got into the dressing room, they started swinging at each other with their guitars. It was like two old ladies goin' at it with their purses.' In the studio, Young and Stills were taking control by producing their own tracks and, not for the last time, the former was about to leave the band. 'My nerves wouldn't handle the trip,' he told Nick Kent. 'It wasn't me scheming for a solo career. It wasn't anything but my nerves.'

UNFORTUNATE TRUTH

What the Atco label envisaged releasing, and what the band were attempting to create in spring 1967, were entirely different stories. The Springfield, unconcerned by deadlines and record company business, spent hours in the studio experimenting with new songs and new personnel, not necessarily intending to release what they were recording. ('We didn't know what we were doing,' Young later confessed. 'We didn't have the kind of direction we needed and didn't have the production assistance we needed.') Atco, in contrast, had assigned a catalogue number and had an album cover ready. The Wild West-style group photograph, shot in the Hollywood Hills, masked an unfortunate truth: at

*'When Neil and Stephen got into the dressing room,
they started swinging at each other . . .'*

Dewey Martin

that point, Bruce Palmer was out of the band. Unreliability, fuelled by copious drugs, had led to him being busted and deported back to his native Canada.

In the studio, Ken Koblun (a veteran of Young's Canadian band The Squires and the first, then-unnamed incarnation of the Springfield), Love's Ken Forsi, future Blood, Sweat & Tears bassist Jim Fielder, and Monkees session man Bob West filled in. (The Monkees link neither began nor ended there. Stills, having flunked an audition for that band prior to the launch of Buffalo Springfield, graced their 1968 soundtrack *Head,* as did Dewey Martin and Neil Young.)

Atco had so much faith that *Stampede* would be a Buffalo Springfield release that they printed almost 100,000 sleeves before they had any albums to slip inside. This burst of activity might have had something to do with the group enjoying their first hit around this time, as Stills's 'For What It's Worth' rose to number seven on the *Billboard* Hot 100. With no actual product to accompany the packaging, the redundant covers were eventually given away as promotion for the band's actual second album, *Buffalo Springfield Again,* later in 1967.

RAW, THRILLING

A *Stampede* bootleg, complete with the original cover, began to circulate in the 1970s. As the band never finalised a track listing, this shouldn't be taken as representative of what they might have released. However, it does contain live cuts – Stills's 'Pay the Price' and 'Rock 'n' Roll Woman', Furay's 'Nobody's Fool' and 'My Kind of Love', and Young's 'Nowadays Clancy Can't Even Sing' – from a summer 1967 gig in Los Angeles that hint at their raw, thrilling concert sound (albeit minus Young, who was out of the band at the time).

The majority of the bootleg was made up of tracks from sessions in New York, jams, and outtakes from their 1966 debut: Stills's 'Baby Don't Scold Me', 'Neighbor Don't You Worry', 'We'll See', and 'Come On', Young's 'Down to the Wire', 'Do I Have to Come Right Out and Say It', 'Give Me One More Sign', and 'There Goes My Baby', Furay's 'My Kind of Love', two raga instrumentals, and a song of unknown provenance, 'Ringing Bells'.

Back in 1967, the Springfield played the iconic Monterey festival, with Daily Flash guitarist Doug Hastings deputising for Young (then working in London with Jack Nitzsche and Andrew Loog Oldham), and guest vocalist David Crosby, then of The Byrds. (Previously unreleased takes of songs from this era appear on 2001's *Buffalo Springfield* box set.) But with the advent of a Beatles classic and the return of Young, *Stampede* was lost, forever, in the rush. **DR**

WILL IT EVER HAPPEN?

3/10 The bootleg proves that fuzzy, raw recordings exist of the studio and live tracks recorded at the time *Stampede* was being touted by Atco. As the members of Buffalo Springfield never envisaged these as the *Stampede* album, it would be inappropriate to package everything up and release the bootleg officially. However, the cover is designed, ready and waiting if anyone *does* decide to go ahead . . .

WHAT HAPPENED NEXT . . .

By the end of a rollercoaster 1967, *Buffalo Springfield Again* had emerged. Bar the same catalogue number, this featured little that the band had rehearsed and recorded in the early part of the year when Atco were readying *Stampede*. When the Springfield's writers – Stills, Furay, and, in particular, Young – heard *Sgt. Pepper,* released in June, their country rock took on a much broader psychedelic perspective. And just as pop's possibilities suddenly appeared limitless, so the future of this band also looked different. Bruce Palmer sneaked back over the US border to briefly rejoin and Young returned to contribute 'Mr Soul', 'Expecting to Fly', and the Beatlesque 'Broken Arrow'. These and Stills's 'Bluebird' were created by two musicians constricted by a band environment.

After a self-explanatorily titled third album, *Last Time Around,* in 1968, Young sought the freedom of a solo career. His began that year with *Neil Young,* while Stills's rich vein of writing found a perfect place to flourish in Crosby, Stills & Nash, whose debut sprang forth a year later.

Richie Furay, meanwhile, stuck with pure country rock and formed Poco with latter-day Springfield bassist Jim Messina. Poco's debut album was poignantly titled *Pickin' Up The Pieces,* a reference to the Springfield's disintegration.

FOUR MORE RESPECTED GENTLEMEN

Artist The Kinks **Year** 1968 **Country** UK **Genre** Proto-Britpop **Label** Reprise **What** Kinks kiboshed

RAY DAVIES

'It was going to be an album about manners and things,' Ray Davies (above, in yellow, with Pete Quaife, Dave Davies, and Mick Avory) told *NME* about this lost Kinks klassic. 'Table manners. What a joke all that is.' A joke indeed – *Four More Respected Gentlemen* in fact appeared to have nothing to do with table manners.

Even by the diminished standards of the frequently fractious Kinks, 1968 was not a good year. Chief songwriter Ray Davies was bored and feeling trapped; he wanted to be somewhere else. The malaise was creeping into their live sets, as they often played to half-full venues. 'It was a chore,' bassist Pete Quaife admitted. 'Very dull, boring, and straightforward.' When 'Wonderboy' became their first single in four years to fall short of the British top twenty, Quaife was damning: 'It sounded like Herman's Hermits wanking. Jesus, it was bad. I hated it.' ('It should never have been released,' Davies conceded at the time.) But while the band struggled, Davies had in mind a concept of an idyllic English past, which typified his desire for escape and provided a means to move the band forward. It was based on a track they had recorded a year earlier: the Bach-inspired 'Village Green'.

SCREAMING MATCH

Recorded around the same time as 'Wonderboy' were the tracks 'Phenomenal Cat', 'Mr Songbird', and 'Berkeley Mews'. Davies also composed a series of character sketches ('Do You Remember Walter', 'Monica', and 'Johnny Thunder') and a trilogy of nostalgic songs ('Pictures in the Sand', 'People Take Pictures of Each Other', and 'Picture Book') for his mooted concept album.

Davies raced to get the piece finished, to take advantage of the small vestiges of commercial clout The Kinks retained. But before he could knock it into shape, the band's US record label, Reprise, came calling, demanding a new album. Under duress, Davies submitted fifteen tracks, comprising songs destined for *The Kinks Are The Village Green Preservation Society*, singles, and offcuts. 'I tried,' he noted, 'to put as many songs on one album as possible.'

Thinking the album – which Reprise provisionally titled *Four More Respected Gentleman* – would be released in tandem with a UK-only, twelve-track *Village Green* album, Davies gave the label songs that were less parochial than those intended for his cherished English concept. These included his heartfelt 'Days', a song that brought tensions in the group to a head. During the recording session, an incensed Davies thought he saw Quaife writing 'Daze' on the tape box. A row ensued. As Davies admitted in his autobiographical *X-Ray,*

Cover: Damian Jaques

WHAT HAPPENED NEXT . . .
The pastoral *The Kinks Are the Village Green Preservation Society* was released as a fifteen-track LP on both sides of the Atlantic (although, adding to the confusion, the initial British release contained only twelve songs), including five from *Four More Respected Gentlemen*: 'Monica', 'Johnny Thunder', 'Animal Farm', 'Picture Book', and 'Phenomenal Cat'. A flop at the time, failing to chart in either the U.K or US, it has since been reappraised as *the* quintessential Kinks album.

'My work had become too precious to me. I was literally in an emotional daze about where I was, who I was, and who I wanted to be with.' (The label's official biography of the band at the time admitted that the composer 'has very definite ideas about almost everything, and enjoys an occasional sulk.')

Davies may have been unsure of himself, but Reprise were certain they didn't want a fifteen-track album and dropped four songs: 'Autumn Almanac', 'Did You See His Name', and the Dave Davies-penned 'There Is No Life Without Love' and 'Susannah's Still Alive'. This left:

Side 1: She's Got Everything · Monica · Mr Songbird · Johnny Thunder · Polly · Days
Side 2: Animal Farm · Berkeley Mews · Picture Book · Phenomenal Cat · Misty Water

Although acetates were prepared for the record company, legend has it that no actual test pressings were made of the album, owing to Ray Davies's obstinate prevarication over the final artwork. 'The album got mixed in with *Village Green*,' he told *NME,* 'and we decided to finish *Village Green* instead.' Reprise had already assigned it a catalogue number but the album – doubtless to Davies's relief – dropped off the schedule, never to return. **DC**

WILL IT EVER HAPPEN?

3/10 All the tracks have been released on *The Kinks Are the Village Green Preservation Society, The Kink Kronikles,* and *The Great Lost Kinks Album.* Reprise have no reason to release the album as recorded, and the prickly relationship between Ray and Dave Davies means it won't be re-recorded. 'You can't be glued in the '60s,' the latter declared to *Radio Times.*

The Beatles

Get Back

Cover: Herita MacDonald (*Let It Be* photography by Ethan Russell and design by John Kosh)

GET BACK

Artist The Beatles **Year** 1969 **Country** UK **Genre** Rock **Label** Apple **What** The Fab Four get back to basics then let it be

On 1 June 1967, The Beatles unleashed their masterpiece and the soundtrack to the Summer of Love: *Sgt. Pepper's Lonely Hearts Club Band.* Having quit touring the previous year, the band set out to prove to the world that they were capable of honing and harnessing skills learnt on the road to produce a great, succinct work of art in the studio. *Pepper* was an extraordinary success: it spent thirty weeks at No. 1 in Australia, twenty-seven in the UK, and fifteen in the US, and became the best-selling album of the decade. However, it arguably heralded the beginning of the end. 'The Beatles made it, stopped touring, had all the money and fame they wanted, and found out they had nothing,' remarked John Lennon. 'And then we started on our various LSD trips, the Maharishi, and all the other mad things we did. . . . We have exactly the same paranoias as everybody else, the same petty thoughts – everything goes just the same for us. We have no super answers.'

GEORGE HARRISON & JOHN LENNON
Work had barely begun before Harrison (left) and Lennon (right) were at odds. 'The little bunny rabbits' batteries were running down,' reflected Paul McCartney of The Beatles' final year. 'We were all fraught with each other and just about everything else. We were probably all on the verge of nervous breakdowns.'

GLORIOUS MESS
Their next studio album saw the lads increasingly working in isolation, with long-time producer George Martin being needed less and less. That it featured all four performing together on just over half of its thirty tracks says much about the glorious mess that is *The Beatles,* better known as 'The White Album'.

The planned sequel was a television show featuring performances of tracks from that double set. This transmuted into the creation of a new collection of songs for a televised concert. 'Nobody would have heard the material before,' Martin told the BBC, 'and it would have all the atmosphere and so on. But we couldn't get a large enough audience. The Beatles by this time were too famous to go into the Hammersmith Odeon (in London), and we thought about going to the Forum in Los Angeles, but that would have cost too much because of the royalties in America. And then we thought of taking it to Tunisia, but then it would have been difficult to get the crowds there – it was in the middle of winter, by the way – and we couldn't do it in England in the open air, so we finished up in Twickenham Film Studios, with no audience.'

They decided to film their rehearsals for this new music, so fans could see the songs develop. 'We had camera teams looking over our shoulders all

LIGHT FANTASTIC

Despite the *Anthology* and *Live at the BBC* releases, there remains one Beatles recording that fans would dearly love to see officially released: their near fifteen-minute experimental piece, 'Carnival of Light'.

In December 1966, Paul McCartney was asked by underground writer Barry Miles to contribute a free-form recording for a festival promoting electronic music at the Roundhouse in London. So, during sessions for 'Penny Lane', the bassist – as he recollected to rockingvicar.com – said to his bandmates, '"We've got half an hour before the session officially starts: would you mind terribly if I did this thing?" And they all just fell in with the spirit of it.' The tape was then played at The Million Volt Light and Sound Rave (sometimes referred to as The Carnival of Light Rave) on 28 January and 4 February 1967. Designer and festival organiser David Vaughan confessed that he thought McCartney 'would make more of it than he did.'

Beatles chronicler Mark Lewisohn writes that the song includes 'distorted, hypnotic drum and organ sounds, various effects, and Lennon and McCartney screaming dementedly and bawling aloud random phrases like "Are you alright?" and "Barcelona!"' At its conclusion, reported engineer Geoff Emerick, George Martin (right, with McCartney) told him, 'This is ridiculous – we've got to get our teeth into something more constructive.' The bassist, his tongue hovering near his cheek, now claims it's 'the coolest piece of music since sliced bread!'

LET IT BEARD

For *Get Back*'s artwork, Lennon suggested the hirsute 1969-style Beatles replicating the cover of their 1963 debut, *Please Please Me*. The result, featuring the four gazing down the stairwell of EMI's offices in London's Manchester Square, wound up on 1973's compilation *1967–1970*.

the time,' Martin shuddered. 'It was an awful mess.' As Lennon grumbled to *Rolling Stone*, '(McCartney) had these ideas that we'll rehearse and then make the album. And, of course, we're lazy fuckers. . . . We're grown men, we're not going to sit around rehearsing. I'm not, anyway. It was a dreadful, dreadful feeling in Twickenham Studios. . . . I just wanted to go away. You couldn't make music at eight in the morning, or ten or whatever it was, in a strange place with people filming you, and the coloured lights.'

The intended denouement to this project was a return to live-without-a-net performance. 'We were wondering where we could go,' recalled Ringo Starr. '"Oh, the (London) Palladium or the Sahara." But we would have had to take all the stuff, so we decided, "Let's get up on the roof."' The roof in question was that of their record label Apple's office at 3 Savile Row, London. 'Nobody had ever done that,' George Harrison noted, 'so it would be interesting to see what happened when we started playing up there. It was a nice little social study.'

Get Back was to have been the title for the resultant television show and album – arising from McCartney's notion to 'get back' to the band's rock 'n' roll roots. 'I would have liked The Beatles never to have broken up,' the bassist told *Playboy*. 'I wanted to get us back on the road doing small places, then move up to our previous form, and then go and play.' (At the time, Lennon didn't rule out a return to the stage. 'It's not out of the question,' he remarked, 'it's just a big responsibility. There is such a mystique about The Beatles that they'll be expecting God to perform.')

WEIRD VIBES

The *Get Back* sessions witnessed the band's second temporary walk-out. Starr had briefly quit midway through work on 'The White Album', following a spat with McCartney over the drum track for 'Back in the U.S.S.R'. This time it was

Harrison who felt the band were being sidelined by Lennon's fixation on his new squeeze, Yoko Ono. 'It was a very tense period,' McCartney told writer Barry Miles. 'John was with Yoko, and had escalated to heroin and all the accompanying paranoias and he was putting himself out on a limb.'

On 10 January 1969, Harrison – at twenty-five, the most junior of the four – told Lennon he was leaving the band immediately. 'It was just weird vibes,' the guitarist told *Crawdaddy.* 'I found I was starting to be able to enjoy being a musician but, the moment I got back with The Beatles, it was just too difficult. There were just too many limitations based upon our being together for so long. Everybody was sort of pigeonholed. It was frustrating.'

'If he doesn't come back . . .' Lennon sneered, 'we get Clapton.' But a week later, Harrison agreed to return, on two conditions: that they stop filming at the 'dreary Twickenham Studios', and that they not play another concert abroad. (Their terrifying exit from the Philippines in 1966, having unintentionally snubbed the nation's first lady Imelda Marcos and been shot at, had scarred Harrison. This and the outcry that greeted Lennon's 'more popular than Jesus' remark in the US were key contributors to their decision to stop touring.)

'The quiet one' returned to the fold, bringing organist Billy Preston along to provide morale, just as Eric Clapton had done for the taping of 'While My Guitar Gently Weeps' the year before. 'It helped, because the others would have to control themselves a bit more,' said Harrison. 'John and Paul mainly – because they had to, you know, act more handsomely.' (Lennon and McCartney did however argue between themselves about whether or not to engage Preston as a full-time band member. In the end, the keyboard player received co-billing only on the internationally chart-topping April 1969 single that paired 'Get Back' with 'Don't Let Me Down.')

Despite Preston's elevating presence, sessions at the band's new Apple Studio in Savile Row ran far from smoothly. McCartney's drive to keep things going couldn't compete with Lennon's stoned isolation, Harrison's increasing disinterest in working on anyone's songs but his own, and Starr's pursuit of film work (having appeared in 1968's *Candy,* the drummer starred in another

TWO OF THEM
Although her relationship with Lennon added to tension during the *Get Back* sessions, Yoko Ono told *Rolling Stone,* 'It wasn't that bitter. The press wanted to sensationalize it, because afterward the group was over. But it was a creative time . . . It was not a commercial situation, where the producer was saying, 'Do this.''

PRIMAL? SCREAM!

In May 1968, at Harrison's home in Surrey, The Beatles demoed twenty-seven songs – some still works-in-progress – that had largely been conceived in Rishikesh, where they undertook a transcendental meditation course with Maharishi Mahesh Yogi. An album called *Primal Colours* was apparently mooted, containing some of these demos, plus early takes for what became 'The White Album'. But, judging by the opening 'Brian Epstein Blues' – an unfunny improvisation captured during sessions for 'Sexy Sadie' – it seems inconceivable the band would have sanctioned such a ramshackle release.

Seven of the demos ('Happiness Is a Warm Gun', 'Mean Mr. Mustard', 'Polythene Pam', 'Glass Onion', 'Junk', 'Piggies', and 'Honey Pie') graced *Anthology 3* (1996). The *Anthology* albums were double-disc compilations of outtakes and rarities, which McCartney joked he and Harrison were thinking of calling 'Scraping The Bottom Of The Barrel'. But had they released *Primal Colours,* the public would certainly have had far worse things to say.

adaptation of a Terry Southern book – *The Magic Christian,* with Peter Sellers – the following year). Finally, what Lennon described as 'all the traumas and paranoia – all the different things that happen . . . when you try and make a record' took their toll. Although hours of new material were committed to tape by the end of January 1969, the album was effectively abandoned.

FALSE STARTS

At McCartney's behest, the four agreed to put their differences to one side and make a brand new album. George Martin insisted on playing a greater role, and together they conjured *Abbey Road,* the most polished and cohesive album of their career – possibly thanks to all four suspecting this might be their swan song. 'We split up after *Abbey Road,* and weren't really thinking about splitting on the one before,' Starr remarked. 'It's all very strange.' Aptly, the album opens with Lennon's 'Come Together' and closes with McCartney's 'The End'. 'I don't think there's a bad track on it,' the bassist remarked. 'Very abstract,' decided Harrison, 'but it all gels and fits.'

Meanwhile, throughout the making of *Abbey Road,* engineer/producer Glyn Johns attempted to salvage something from the *Get Back* tapes. 'I originally put together an album of rehearsals,' he told the BBC, 'with chat and jokes and bits of general conversation in between the tracks . . . breakdowns, false starts.' 'There were some good songs on it,' remarked George Martin, 'but I

WONDERFUL CHRISTMAS TIME

From 1963 to 1969, The Beatles produced seven 'not for sale' Christmas flexi-singles, issued free to their UK fan club members. These were the brainchild of press officer Tony Barrow, who foresaw a PR disaster as the club struggled to cope with mountains of mail being sent to the band.

The boys loved this damage limitation exercise, and asked Barrow to prepare a script for the spoken-word selections. Manager Brian Epstein, however, was concerned that, as the fan club was a non-profit-making affair, he would have to subsidise such a venture. To keep costs down, Barrow approached Lyntone Records, who produced promotional flexi-discs for *Reader's Digest.* With Epstein appeased, the discs included messages of thanks to loyal Beatle 'peedles' (a mispronunciation from their Hamburg days), skits, carols, and, latterly, original compositions. Stateside fan club members only received the messages from 1966, and initially as even cheaper 'postcard' records. Barrow says he and Lyntone founder Paul S. Lynton hurriedly edited the boys' initial greeting in 1963 with a pair of scissors, and ponders the value of pieces of tape that littered the studio floor, never to be heard again.

None have been widely released, although an uninterrupted version of 'Christmas Time (Is Here Again)', extracted from the 1967 flexi-disc, graced the B-side of 1995's 'Free as a Bird', concluding with a smidge of dialogue from the previous year's festive single. (Starr recorded his own version of the song for the1999 album *I Wanna Be Santa Claus,* adding a guitar solo by Aerosmith's Joe Perry.)

In December 1970, the club issued *From Them to You,* a compilation of all seven recordings (repackaged in the US as *The Beatles' Christmas Album,* but not sent out until the spring of 1971). It was mastered from the original flexi-discs, the master tapes having gone astray.

The Official Beatles FAN CLUB
45 R.P.M.
Another Beatles Christmas Record

WHAT HAPPENED NEXT . . .

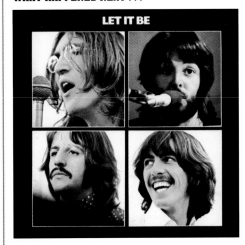

In March 1970, the Apple tapes were handed to producer Phil Spector, who created yet another new version of *Get Back* (including the versions of 'Across the Universe' and 'I Me Mine' from Johns' final attempt). This was finally released in May 1970 as *Let It Be,* ostensibly the soundtrack for the engrossingly depressing motion picture of the same name. Three George Martin-produced songs from the sessions had already been issued on singles: 'Get Back' with 'Don't Let Me Down', and 'Let It Be'. 'Get Back' and the title track were remixed for the album, while Spector simply discarded Lennon's 'Don't Let Me Down'.

McCartney was bitterly unhappy with Spector's work, especially on his songs – notably 'The Long and Winding Road', which he envisaged as a simple piano ballad, but onto which the producer overdubbed an orchestra and female vocals. 'I was sent a re-mixed version . . .' the composer marvelled. 'No one had asked me what I thought. I couldn't believe it.' Lennon, though, defended Spector in *Rolling Stone,* declaring that the producer had been given 'shit . . . and he made something of it.'

wasn't crazy about it, although it was what John wanted.' The ramshackle collection certainly played to Lennon's self-confessed disinterest in production. 'All that, "Get the bass right, get the drums right," that's a drag to me,' he grumbled. 'All I want to do is get my guitar out and sing songs.'

Johns edited together a number of composite albums, the last of which featured a 1968 version of 'Across the Universe' as well as a January 1970 rendition of Harrison's 'I Me Mine' recorded without Lennon, who by then had unofficially quit the band. Although Johns claimed the band 'really liked' this final configuration, all of his proposals were ultimately rejected. 'It was all done over my head,' rued McCartney, decades later. 'I had an acetate of the final mixes that Glyn Johns had done . . . Today it would sound "Unplugged" because it was very basic, very bare. And I thought, "This is good – really good. We're reduced to just bare bones. There's something great about it. Something very compelling." But (then-manager) Allen Klein stuck his oar in, and he said, "Look, I don't think it's right," and he made a lot of decisions. I think it was his decision to bring Phil Spector in. We were all sort of feeling that we had come to the end.' *Get Back* was gone. **AG**

WILL IT EVER HAPPEN?

1/10 'You know what would be really cool?' McCartney teased to *Beatlefan* in 2002. 'If we put the naked version of the record out . . . It's not announced or anything yet, but that's what's in the pipeline.' The following year duly brought *Let It Be... Naked,* a remixed and edited version of their final offering (which Martin had wanted to see credited as 'Produced by George Martin and overproduced by Phil Spector'). With 'Don't Let Me Down' reinstated to the track listing, *...Naked* sounded very much like the last word, making it highly unlikely that the *Get Back* tapes will be revisited.

THE WHO   LIFEHOUSE

Chapter 2

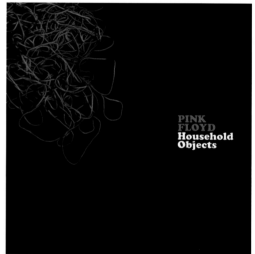

PINK
FLOYD
**Household
Objects**

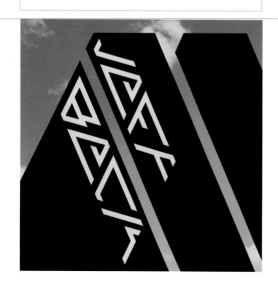

DAVID BOWIE
THE GOUSTER

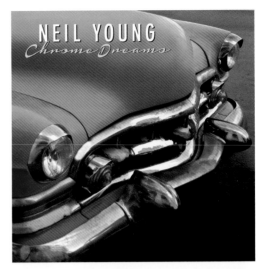

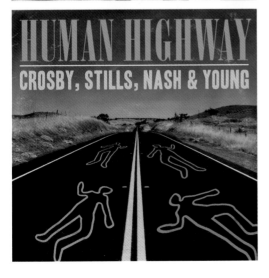

The Seventies

'THE MOTOWN ALBUM'

Artist Jeff Beck **Year** 1970 **Country** UK/US **Genre** Rock **Label** EMI Columbia
What Guitar hero goes to Detroit and gets his 'ears well and truly smacked'

JEFF BECK
'We went downtown and met (label boss) Berry Gordy . . .' the guitarist told *Rolling Stone*. 'He said, "Welcome to Motown. I've got great faith in you. I know what you do. Maybe the session guys don't know, but I know. You've got a great idea here."'

A 'catalogue of disasters' was Jeff Beck's verdict on his attempt to cut an album at Hitsville USA, the headquarters of Berry Gordy's label Motown. Beck regarded the hits that had emerged from the studio for the past decade as 'so musical and so beautifully executed – wonderful pop records,' and was keen to alchemize the same magic. Instead, the sessions created possibly the rarest recordings in this book.

FRACTURED SKULL

The 1960s didn't end well for Beck. Old rival Jimmy Page was conquering the world with Led Zeppelin, while Beck's ambivalence towards live work was proving corrosive to his band. 'Every opportunity (including Woodstock) was there and we blew it by constantly cancelling out tours,' grumbled keyboardist Nicky Hopkins. 'We'd wake up one morning in the States and find Jeff had left the night before and was back in England.' Worse still, in August 1969, Beck was hospitalised with a fractured skull after a car crash. While he was recuperating, Tim Bogert and Carmine Appice – Vanilla Fudge's rhythm section, with whom Beck was plotting a new band – grew tired of waiting and formed their own new outfit. The final straw came when his vocalist Rod Stewart and bassist Ronnie Wood opted to seek fame and fortune with The Faces.

Beck's road to recovery began when his producer, Mickie Most, insisted on a new album to capitalise on the success of *Truth* (1968) and *Beck-Ola* (1969). He duly enlisted drummer Cozy Powell and set sail for Motown. In retrospect, though Powell was 'like a lost brother I never knew', his powerhouse style was hardly the best fit for a studio founded on poppy soul. 'What the hell was I doing,' the guitarist marvelled to *Rolling Stone,* 'taking a rock drummer, with two huge Ludwig bass drums, into Motown?'

The studio's musicians – including legendary bassist James Jamerson – were initially bemused, then assuaged when Powell 'started playing like (influential New Orleans funk band) The Meters'. However, the mood swung back again when the drummer decided to swap the studio's kit for his own. 'They're going berserk,' Beck recalled. 'He has moved the sacred Motown drum kit out of the studio and wheeled this stupid double kit of Ludwigs in. The studio tech came

Cover: Damian Jaques

WHAT HAPPENED NEXT . . .
Despite getting 'our ears well and truly smacked', Beck and Powell's partnership endured for another two albums. The guitarist's relationship with Motown carried on too: in the studio with Stevie Wonder, he helped originate 'Superstition'. However, Berry Gordy refused to allow Beck to record it first. The song soared to No.1 in 1972, making Beck's version of it (on *Beck, Bogert & Appice*, 1973) seem anticlimactic. But, as Beck graciously told the BBC, 'The credit went where it was due, because he wrote it.'

up to me and said, "Didn't you guys come in here for the Motown sound?" "Yeah." "Well, it just went out the door."'

The sessions ultimately yielded 'nine or ten tracks'. However, as Beck conceded to *Mojo,* 'The whole idea was very nebulous. We were going to do instrumentals, get Holland, Dozier, and Holland to write a great tune, and I'd play it. But we completely disrupted the whole Motown session! It was costing a fortune, then we ran out of time and had to get out. It was a total missed opportunity, a catalogue of disasters. We were glad Mickie had the clout to open those doors for us, but once they were open we didn't know what to do.'

The indignity didn't end even when the tapes stopped rolling. 'The same guy who said that thing about the drums?' remarked Beck. 'When we walked out of the studio on the last day with the master, he said, "You're not going to mix here? You just shot yourself twice." I knew. But we'd had enough.' **BM**

WILL IT EVER HAPPEN?

3/10 None of the tracks were ever released. 'I've still got the multi-track,' Beck told *Rolling Stone,* 'although I bet if you put that on the machine now, it will collapse into pieces. I made one copy onto cassette. That's all there is. Talk about collector's item, pal.'

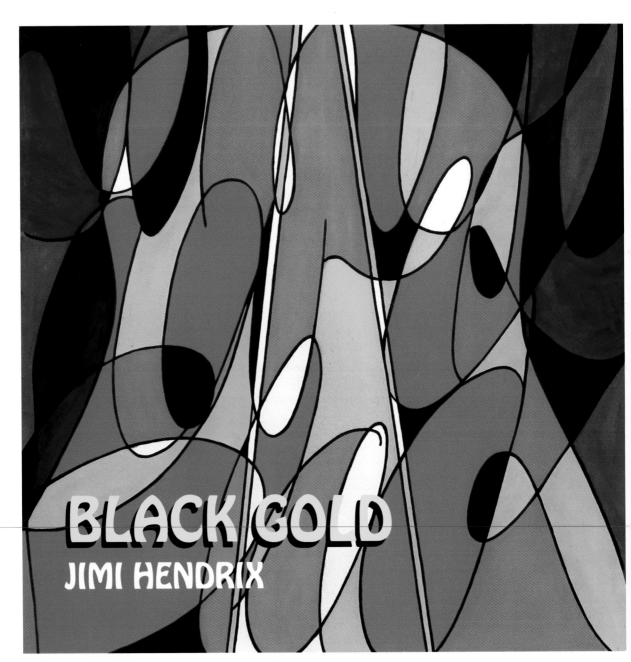

BLACK GOLD

JIMI HENDRIX

Cover: Jayne Evans

BLACK GOLD

Artist Jimi Hendrix **Year** 1970 **Country** US **Genre** Acid rock **Label** Reprise **What** Guitar hero turns superhero

A dust-covered Rembrandt in the attic? An unknown Harry Potter novel lying in a long-disused drawer? Who hasn't daydreamed about something similar? At the point of his untimely death in 1970, Jimi Hendrix's business affairs were a seemingly impenetrable jungle of chaos and contracts. But amid that undergrowth, the story of the proposed *Black Gold* is a still scarcely believable tale of riches lying undiscovered for decades.

STRANGE SCENES
Quoted in Steven Roby's *Black Gold: The Lost Archives of Jimi Hendrix,* fellow guitarist Mike Bloomfield called Hendrix 'a massive chronicler of his own jams' who committed huge amounts of music to tape – according to close associate Deering Howe, around 1500 hours at the time of his death. So when the guitarist handed over a set of cassettes – bound with a headband – to Experience drummer Mitch Mitchell in 1970, their importance was not apparent, either immediately or in the longer term.

As with most things in the Hendrix universe, the existence and content of the tapes has been the subject of much speculation. The man himself provided some pointers. In an interview with *Rolling Stone,* he spoke of 'mostly cartoon material . . . There's one cat who's funny, who goes through all these strange scenes. I can't talk about it now. You could put it to music, I guess.'

Investigations were not helped when producer Alan Douglas revealed in the mid-1980s that the tapes – containing songs that he called 'beautiful' – were stolen during a break-in at Hendrix's apartment, not long after their creator's death. The trail then went cold until 1992, when Mitchell – still assuming that the cassettes would add little to his former bandleader's oeuvre – contacted Hendrix expert Tony Brown. The drummer's view was swiftly corrected.

The clues pointing to a comic-strip-type character washing around Hendrix's kaleidoscopic thoughts had long been there. One of his constant companions for a time was an issue of Marvel's *Spider-Man* comic entitled 'The Birth of a Super-Hero!' This was one of the inspirations for the character of The Powerful Sound King in a self-penned screenplay called *Moondust.* 'The innocent girl comes to visit,' he wrote, 'and tells the player . . . "Please be careful with your power . . . It

JIMI HENDRIX
After the longest period of his shooting star career without an album release, Hendrix saw exciting possibilities in store for 1970. 'With the music we will paint pictures of earth and space, so that the listener can be taken somewhere,' he told *Melody Maker* in an interview published the day before he died. 'Something new has to come and Jimi Hendrix will be there.'

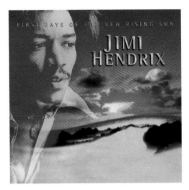

could be dangerous for you and the world" . . . He says, "What power?" and laughs very heavy. She runs away – far away. She runs all day . . . music runs with her . . . the sun sets. The moon comes . . . she feels better. She sings a song . . . the moon slips through the skies and dances with her . . . the sky dances . . . she is trippingly high . . . so is the sky. The sky makes her feel much better because she likes the player more and more.' Being a movie star

> *'With the music we will paint pictures of earth and space, so that the listener can be taken somewhere.'*
>
> Jimi Hendrix

was one of Hendrix's boyhood dreams, but public patience with rock idol screen indulgences had been stretched by The Beatles' *Magical Mystery Tour* (1967). Undeterred, Hendrix simply morphed *Moondust* into a new endeavour. In 1969, he said: 'Here was this cat came around called Black Gold.'

GOLDEN TEARDROPS

Many critics opine that Hendrix in 1970 was a busted flush, at a creative dead end, but the range of projects in various stages of development points to a restless soul searching for a new path. Three weeks before his death, he claimed to have been working on a 'symphony production'. Prior to that, percussionist Juma Sultan spoke of 'different things with horns and keyboards'. As Hendrix said in the final year of his life: 'I'm trying to do too many things at the same time.' He felt cornered by touring obligations to pay off debts, especially as many audiences wanted only the old tracks and stage tricks of

NEW DAWN

Black Gold wasn't the only Hendrix proposition left in limbo in 1970. In 1969, he told *NME* about *The Last Ray of the Morning Sun* – a title subsequently reborn as *First Rays of the New Rising Sun*. 'It's going to give a lot of people the answers to questions they are searching for,' he said. The track listing reached as far as the third side of an intended double album. Many tracks were commandeered for the posthumous *The Cry of Love,* and it wasn't until 1997 that *First Rays of the New Rising Sun* emerged, as a single CD.

'THIS CAT CAME AROUND . . .'

'I don't want to be a clown anymore,' the guitarist told *Rolling Stone* in 1969, 'I don't want to be a "rock 'n' roll star."' Yet this photograph – taken just two weeks before his death – suggests Hendrix was ready to embrace the flamboyant superhero at the heart of *Black Gold.*

which he had grown bored. 'We're going to go out somewhere into the hills . . . ,' he promised *Rolling Stone,* 'to get some new songs.' Instead, it was just Hendrix and his acoustic guitar in early 1970 at his Greenwich Village apartment. Friend and former Animal Eric Burdon said, 'I remember Jimi telling me about his idea for *Black Gold* . . . an autobiographical feature about a black rock star – himself on the road.' ('It was magnificent!' enthused Alan Douglas. 'We were going to do an album from it, and a movie, and so on.') Of the tapes in Mitchell's possession, the *Black Gold* material features on the first:

Suddenly November Morning · Drifting · Captain Midnight 1201 · Local Commotion · Local Commotion Part 2 · Here Comes Black Gold · Black Gold · Stepping Stone · Little Red Velvet Room · The Jungle Is Waiting · Send My Love to Joan of Arc · God Bless the Day · Black Gold · Machine Gun · Here Comes Black Gold · Trash Man · Astro Man Part 1 · Astro Man Part 2 · I've Got a Place to Go

Of these, a few have been brought into the wider world. 'Suddenly November Morning' – a just-as-pretty sister of 'The Wind Cries Mary', in which Hendrix sings of 'drifting in a sea of golden teardrops' – was the final track on a 2010 anthology, *West Coast Seattle Boy.* The star switched into mischievous, cloud-bouncing mood for 'Astro Man' – announcing, 'Here I come to save the day,' on a track that surfaced on 1971's *The Cry of Love.* There was serious intent, though, running through the suppressing fire of 'Machine Gun'. Ernie Isley of The Isley Brothers, for whom Hendrix once played guitar, said the track – which wound up on 1970's *Band of Gypsys* – was 'the closest a human being playing guitar can get to the hands of God.'

As for the rest, we have only Tony Brown's notes from his impressions. 'Here Comes Black Gold' 'was performed in almost a fanfare kind of way'; 'Little Red Velvet Room' stirred the emotions; 'The Jungle Is Waiting' steered into 'very jazz-flamenco' warm waters. But the troubles that stalked Hendrix pervaded 'I've Got a Place to Go', in which he was reaching out and 'still lonely'.

The Hendrix community breathed a collective sigh of relief that the *Black Gold* material had not been lost for ever. Now all that's needed is for it to stop being so close at hand yet still tantalisingly out of reach. **CB**

WHAT HAPPENED NEXT . . .
In the same month that Hendrix said, 'I am not sure I will live to be twenty-eight years old,' his prediction – made more than once – came tragically true. On 18 September 1970, two months shy of his birthday, Hendrix was found dead in a London apartment belonging to sometime girlfriend Monika Dannemann. Coroner Paul Thurston said the cause of death was 'inhalation of vomit due to barbiturate intoxication'. After his funeral (below), the tracks on *Black Gold* and other projects were left in an embryonic state. Barrel scrapings cobbled together for releases would have left the great man – a studio perfectionist – aghast. *War Heroes* (1972), anyone? *Loose Ends* (1974)? *Crash Landing* (1975)? *Nine to the Universe* (1980)?

WILL IT EVER HAPPEN?

8/10   It did – in 1996. Unfortunately, beneath the attention-grabbing *Black Gold* title was an unofficial collection of outtakes, unconnected to the Greenwich Village holy grail. Ironically, this was just after the Experience Hendrix company gained control of the back catalogue, with archivist John McDermott promising to 'reset the posthumous landscape'. That meant a policy of releasing unviolated material – in contrast to Alan Douglas's approach of applying new backing tracks. As keepers of the flame, Experience Hendrix have occasionally proved fallible, but, in a 2010 interview, stepsister and CEO Janie Hendrix promised that the world will hear *Black Gold* before 2020.

SING SLOWLY SISTERS •
THE LONER • THE KID'S NO GOOD

Artist Robin Gibb • Maurice Gibb • Barry Gibb **Year** 1970 **Country** UK **Genre** Pop **Label** Polydor **What** Bee Gees, banjaxed

ROBIN GIBB

'I was getting too hurt . . .,' said Robin, the first of the brothers to jump ship. 'Music to me is an adventure and I can do far more on my own,' he told *NME*. 'It was restricting writing for the Bee Gees but I enjoyed it until they began to judge what I was doing. I'm not going to be judged.'

The Bee Gees had eaten themselves. Success, peaking on both sides of the Atlantic towards the end of the 1960s, gave birth to that twin beast: ambition and jealousy. Those impulses are enough to split any band – in a trio of siblings they wrought destruction. As 1969 came around, the Gibb brothers were still young – Barry twenty-two, Robin and Maurice just nineteen – and woefully incapable of maintaining their position atop the pop tree.

DEPTH OF SORROW

Burgeoning ability or hubris had led the Bee Gees to conjure an epic in the style of The Beatles' self-titled double album or The Beach Boys' uncompleted *Smile* (see page 12). Grand and emotionally stark, March 1969's idiosyncratic *Odessa* was the apotheosis of the Gibbs' pre-disco development, but its power concealed rifts. Chief agitator was Robin, the most recognisable voice and the band's sobbing heart. Like any great talent at a sensitive stage of his career – rubbing against similarly strong, talented characters – Robin felt marginalised. 'I'm not saying (Barry and Maurice) became bigheaded,' he told *NME*, 'but I found the simple things we used to talk about were not happening.'

Robin wasn't getting the leads he believed he warranted and sensed it was very much his older brother's band; *Odessa*'s single 'First of May' – fronted by Barry – being a particular bugbear. There was interference from outsiders, too. 'When the brothers arrived in London (from Australia), they were naive kids,' guitarist Vince Melouney told the *Sydney Morning Herald*. 'Within six months, they were swept up by their own celebrity. They all had their own houses and their own hangers-on who caused problems with bickering and gossip.' Maurice, Barry, and manager Robert Stigwood believed Robin's wife Molly was pushing her husband to chase solo stardom. In the meantime, the brothers' parents attempted to make him a ward of the court, owing to his amphetamine-fuelled instability. Bad blood brewed until Robin decided to leave.

It seemed a good idea at the time. His 'Saved by the Bell' was a UK smash and the ensuing *Robin's Reign* was an ideal showcase for his tremulous voice and melodramatic music. Even Maurice had time for 'Saved by the Bell', telling *NME,* 'I hope it is a hit.' Nonetheless, when the two parties appeared on the

Barry Gibb
The Kid's No Good

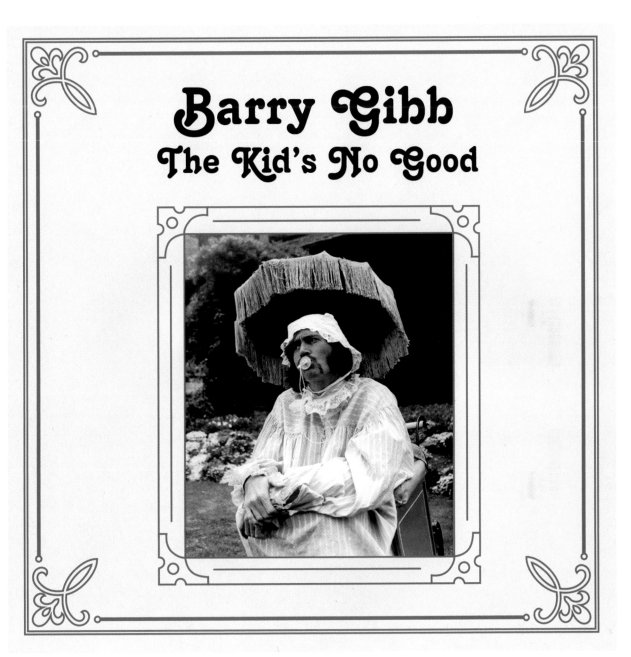

All covers on pages 39–41: Sarah Holland

Barry Gibb, *The Kid's No Good*
Born
One Bad Thing
The Day Your Eyes Meet Mine
Happiness
Peace in My Mind
Clyde O'Reilly
I Just Want to Take Care of You
I'll Kiss Your Memory
The Victim
This Time
What's It All About
Mando Bay

BBC's *Top of the Pops,* they had separate dressing rooms. 'We solemnly didn't talk to each other,' Robin told *Mojo.* 'It was completely ridiculous.'

Barry and Maurice soldiered on with their album and TV movie *Cucumber Castle,* a folly that proved the cost of the split. Robin, however, was buoyed by the promise of his first effort and, in 1970, set to work on *Sing Slowly Sisters,* whose existence he would later deny. It was wreathed in the heartbreak that had become his speciality: songs like 'C'est La Vie Au Revoir' ('You were mine / But you couldn't take the time') speak of a depth of sorrow that threatened to overwhelm a nascent career. (Robin later became *the* tearjerking Bee Gee. 'It was almost like his heart was on the outside,' remarked Roger Daltrey.)

> *'We solemnly didn't talk to each other. It was completely ridiculous.'*
> Robin Gibb

'Avalanche' takes poetic licence with a near-death experience that shook Robin and Molly, when their Alpine cabin was buried by an avalanche while they were on honeymoon. The funereal 'Cold Be My Days', meanwhile, is almost psalm-like. The album occasionally stirs into gear, recalling Jimmy Webb's country-soul on 'Engines and Airplanes' and painting Western vistas on

Robin Gibb, *Sing Slowly Sisters*
A Very Special Day
All's Well That Ends Well
C'est La Vie Au Revoir
Cold Be My Days
Avalanche
Engines and Airplanes
Everything Is How You See Me
Great Caesar's Ghost
I've Been Hurt
Irons in the Fire
Janice
Life
Make Believe
Sing Slowly Sisters
Sky West and Crooked
The Flag That I Flew
You're Going Away

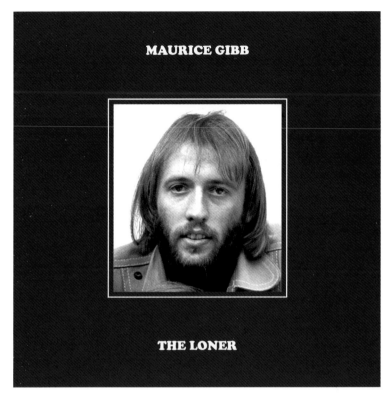

MAURICE GIBB

THE LONER

'Everything Is How You See Me'. Otherwise, it's gorgeously orchestrated dirge after gorgeously orchestrated dirge, with horns sneaking in on the title cut and 'Life' to offer slivers of hope. Whether this was Robin's mood or just where he knew his skills lay is moot, but it makes for a difficult, dramatic, listen.

WHIMSICAL FANCIES
The same year, as their popularity waned steeply, Maurice and Barry exercised their solo whims. Maurice had started work after the close of the _Cucumber Castle_ sessions in October 1969, and by December was in the groove. _The Loner_ – a title that reflected his place in the band, at least before Robin left – gave free rein to his love of blues, country rock, and more whimsical fancies, and was written with his pop star wife Lulu's brother Billy Lawrie. With a band including guitarist Leslie (brother of Alex) Harvey and drummer Geoff Bridgford (who would later join the re-formed Bee Gees), Maurice put together tracks that swung and rolled, in stark contrast to his twin's harrowing ballads.

'Railroad' was a single, albeit a flop in any significant market. A shame, because it's a country strum with attractive honky-tonk piano and sprightly fiddles, and its gently psychedelic B-side 'I've Come Back' is even better. 'The Loner' itself ploughs a gossamer psych furrow with floating woodwind and a touch of Fred Neil, while 'Soldier Johnny' sounds like an outtake from George Harrison's _All Things Must Pass_ and 'She's the One You Love' goes country-funk. If anything, Maurice sounds too laid-back – a whispery presence on the chiming 'Something's Blowing', as he and his band pour their efforts into sounding accomplished yet light as air. Finished by the end of March 1970, the album was mastered six months later, but never released. Nonetheless, Maurice had found a way to ease tension and exercise creative control.

SICK OF FAMILY ARGUMENTS

Barry's solo album, on the other hand, sprang from a state of disillusionment. To have Robin quit the band was one thing; for Maurice to step away from the Bee Gees and into his solo work was the final straw. Sick of family arguments, Barry claimed to be leaving Britain for America, with shares in RSO (Robert Stigwood Organisation) his only financial support. 'As from today I'm solo,' he told the *Daily Express*. 'Whatever Maurice does is his business.'

From December 1969, the Bee Gees were defunct and the world was left with three separate Gibbs, all vying to trump the others. *Cucumber Castle* came out in April 1970, within weeks of Robin's debut *Robin's Reign,* but neither troubled chart compilers. By this time, however, Maurice's album was in the can, and Barry had belatedly wrapped up sessions on *his* solo endeavour.

Not officially titled at the time, *The Kid's No Good* had sprung to life just weeks earlier. Barry took two *Cucumber Castle* outtakes – 'The Day Your Eyes Meet Mine' and 'One Bad Thing' – and built a sturdy set around them with session players and the Bee Gees' orchestral arranger Bill Shepherd. Singer P.P. Arnold graced the Memphis swagger of 'Born', the opener for an album

BROTHERS UP IN ARMS

'It was like three different little worlds,' explained Barry (right). 'Robin and I were always competing to get the most attention as lead singers, and Maurice was in trouble with drinking problems.'

that feels the most realised of the brothers' ill-fated jaunts. It brims with potential singles, although 'I'll Kiss Your Memory' was the only one that squeaked out, to no great fanfare, in May 1970. Had the campaign continued, it might have been followed by 'Happiness', with pointed lyrics ('Don't you leave me here alone') and a tremulous, Robin-style vocal, or the Band-like blues of 'Clyde O'Reilly'. The very Bee Gee-esque 'The Victim' above all gives credence to the suggestion that this is a Gibb brothers album in all but name – certainly ahead of *The Loner, Robin's Reign,* or *Sing Slowly Sisters.* At this point – and arguably forever more – Barry became the voice and exemplar of the band, inseparable.

RIGHT THE WRONGS

Whether Maurice or Barry could have made a success of their solo forays, no one knows, but the signs weren't promising. Robin had enjoyed a bona fide

> *'As from today I'm solo. Whatever Maurice does is his business.'*
>
> Barry Gibb

hit – his brothers barely caused a ripple – but even he came unstuck when tackling long-players. As it was, expedience forced their hands before anyone had to consider release schedules: in the summer of 1970, financial disaster struck when RSO went public. Its projected price was not even in the same ballpark as the cold, hard truth and the Gibbs – who had pretty much every dollar they owned sewn up in the organisation – lost big. Rumors persisted, too, that shady characters came out of the woodwork looking for monies owed. Whatever the facts, the Gibbs were in need of a quick fix. The answer was staring them in the face: time to get the old band back together.

But while cash played a part – a reunion could hardly have done the brothers or the stricken RSO any harm – there was also an opportunity to recapture the magic missing from each solo session. In August 1970, Barry, Maurice, and Robin excluded their lawyers for the first time in months, bridged their rifts, and launched themselves straight back into the studio, ready to right the wrongs of the previous year. The missing albums didn't fit with their new intentions and were shelved – perhaps forever. The brothers would take time to get back to the top of the commercial tree, but they were on the right track. MH

WHAT HAPPENED NEXT . . .

Following a blizzard of intra-band apologies played out in the press, the Bee Gees reconvened as if nothing had happened. The comeback album *2 Years On* was released in double-quick time and performed little better than *Cucumber Castle,* although it did produce an encouraging hit in 'Lonely Days'. However, problems ran deeper. The Bee Gees had an identity, but were behind the curve: more a remnant of the 1960s than a band forging a Technicolor future. There was, as yet, no sign of their second wind, of the phenomenon they would become with a flash of inspiration and, in Arif Mardin, a canny choice of collaborator. Still, they had hope. 'We were okay separately,' Maurice told *Playboy,* 'but together we're something else.'

WILL IT EVER HAPPEN?

6/10 Devotees have pieced together each of the Bee Gees' 1970 solo albums – sometimes with differing track listings or contemporary extras thrown in – and all of them have enjoyed unofficial releases in territories other than the US and the UK. Given the climate for revisiting 'lost' albums in deluxe formats, the need of record companies to capitalise on their assets, and the renewed interest in the Bee Gees' legacy since Robin Gibb's death in 2012, it seems likely these solo efforts *will* see a release in some form or another.

THE WHO

LIFEHOUSE

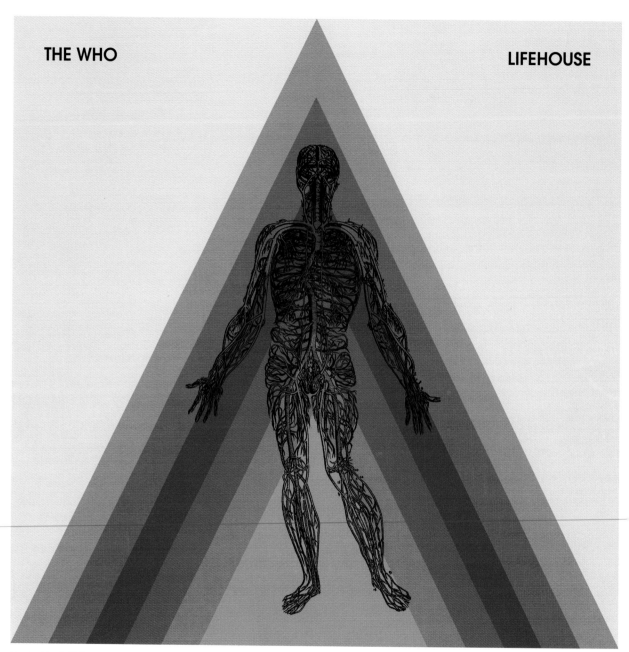

Cover: Heath Killen

LIFEHOUSE

Artist The Who **Year** 1971 **Country** UK **Genre** Rock **Label** Track Record **What** A notion nuttier than *Tommy*

Pretentious, confessed Pete Townshend of the concept that haunted him for three decades, 'is just not a big enough word.' At its heart, his story was straightforward: 'I had goodies and baddies,' he told the BBC. 'The baddies were people who did the entertainment . . . gave us programmes through television and intravenously. The goodies were these savages who'd kept rock 'n' roll as a primitive force and gone to live with it in the woods. And the story was just about those two sides coming together and having a brief battle.' Embellished with an allegory 'about the nature of music and both its power to communicate good ideas and feelings (and) its power as a mystical spiritual force,' the piece spawned an album that became one of the band's best loved – but not by Townshend, to whom *Who's Next* was 'a personal disaster'.

PETE TOWNSHEND
'Probably the biggest waste of time the group's ever got into . . .' The Who's leader conceded to *Crawdaddy* of the doomed *Lifehouse* in 1971. 'I've worked myself on something which you'll never see to the point of, like, nervous breakdown.'

HIPPY NOTION

By August 1970, when they made a second appearance at the Isle of Wight festival, The Who had risen to superstardom, thanks to *Tommy's* slow-burning success and a memorable showing at Woodstock. But a problem arose: what to do next. Initially best known as a singles band, they had toyed with concepts and song cycles for several years, notably 1966's 'mini-opera', 'A Quick One, While He's Away'. None, however, had the commercial impact of their 1969 opus about the deaf, dumb, and blind pinball wizard turned saviour. Consequently, as Townshend noted in *Rolling Stone*, 'The first thing people are going to want to hear after listening to *Tommy* is, of course, *Tommy* again.'

Townshend conjured *Lifehouse*, and took it to rehearsals for an autumn tour in 1970. However, ideas that seemed simple to him were lost in translation. 'Pundits wishing to detract from the possibility that (*Lifehouse*) could ever have worked speak disparagingly about the "one note" idea on which I rested my thesis . . .' Townshend grumbled in his autobiography, 'relating it to the hippy notion of a universal chord, something I hadn't mentioned at all.'

'It had a wonderful core idea . . .' singer Roger Daltrey agreed in *Uncut*. 'If you found the beginning of life, it would be a musical note. It was a very interesting idea, but we all had incredible difficulty with the narrative of it . . . I didn't think it needed to be bogged down in this kind of science-fiction world.'

WHO'S FOR TENNIS?
To fill the void between 1967's *The Who Sell Out* and 1969's *Tommy,* the band's co-manager Kit Lambert (above) proposed a compilation of *Sell Out* offcuts, singles, and new tracks recorded in 1968, entitled *Who's For Tennis?* Unimpressed, the band recorded only a mooted opener, 'Glow Girl', before focusing on *Tommy.* Most of the cuts surfaced on later retrospectives.

That world opened with 'Baba O'Riley', the accompaniment to, Townshend explained, 'rock 'n' roll guys in an old, beaten-up motor-home . . . listening to old rock 'n' roll music.' It closed with 'Song Is Over', which 'tries to describe the atmosphere at the end when the battle is over. There's been a great concert (and) as the enemy approaches, there's a tremendous tension building. They're coming to attack it because it's an unofficial entertainment: it's a rock 'n' roll concert in a time when all entertainment is licenced, approved, censored, and has a real purpose – it's living our lives for us . . . At the moment that the troops arrive and burst in, the band and the audience just completely disappear.'

MARS BAR UP YOUR BUM
The ambitious concept touched on ideas that would eventually come to fruition in genres like cyberpunk and movies like *The Matrix* (Townshend conceded at the time its debt to François Truffaut's 1966 film of Ray Bradbury's *Fahrenheit 451*). But being ahead of its time wasn't the story's sole problem: equally baffling were details like the 'entertainment suits' via which 'the baddies' fed mindless distractions to the masses. 'I could explain it to Roger and John (Entwistle, bassist) and Keith (Moon, drummer),' Townshend despaired to *Q*, 'and they'd say, "Oh, I get it, you put these suits on and you put a penny in the slot and you get wanked off." I'd go, "No, no, it's much bigger than that." "Oh, I get it, you get wanked off and you get a Mars bar shoved up your bum . . ."'

Demos recorded at Townshend's and Entwistle's home studios yielded, the former recalled, 'two reels of songs which related directly or loosely to the film script I had written, or were intended as padding to be replaced by experimental music produced during the Young Vic workshop.' This 'workshop' was an intermittent series of open-door performances at London's newly opened Young Vic theatre from January to March 1971.

'The idea was to get two thousand people, and keep them for six months ...' Townshend said. 'Characters would emerge from them; eventually the group would play a very minor role. Maybe five hundred of the original two thousand would stay during the six months, and we would have filmed all that happened.' However, he rued, 'The first workshop was held during the day, so was

'I just drank bottle after bottle of brandy . . . probably imagining I was showing great self-restraint.'
Pete Townshend

attended only by truants. Also, frightened we would be overrun, we made no announcements at all. So, in fact, no one knew what we were doing.'

With characteristic brevity, Entwistle told *Rolling Stone:* 'I never understood what that was all about.' In the band's defence, however, Daltrey noted, 'It wasn't just (us) who couldn't get to grips with it, it was the whole inner circle – management and everything. No one could see it.' The biggest betrayal, for the composer, was that of co-manager Kit Lambert, whose encouragement had

led Townshend to think beyond three-minute singles to rock operas. Lambert set up meetings with Universal to finance a *Lifehouse* movie, but eased the studio's concerns about the impenetrable narrative by assuring them that Townshend was working his way towards a cinematic adaptation of *Tommy*.

OUT OF CONTROL

In March 1971, The Who decamped to New York's Record Plant to commit *Lifehouse* to tape. Warm-up sessions were helmed by Felix Pappalardi, who had produced Cream before forming his own band Mountain – hence an early version of 'Won't Get Fooled Again' featuring Mountain's Leslie West playing what Townshend described as 'the most extraordinary guitar'. However, a second set of sessions, produced by Lambert, proved disastrous. 'Kit was out of control,' Townshend wrote in 1995. 'At one point during a kicking jam session at the end of "Getting in Tune", he ran out holding a little sign that said "DON'T STOP". Of course, by the time we'd all read his aristocratic but illegible scrawl, we'd lost the magic. He was also disappearing to shoot up all the time. It soon became clear that other people in the team (including Keith Moon) were using hard drugs, too. I just drank bottle after bottle of brandy as usual, probably imagining I was showing great self-restraint.' Something had to give. The Who's official history notes: 'Deeply frustrated, desperately overworked, and at odds with Lambert, Pete suffers his first nervous breakdown.'

ENDLESS WIRE
When Townshend delivered the *Lifehouse* idea, complete with its technology-assisted entertainment suits, 'Roger said, "This'll never work, this film." I said, "Why?" He said, "You could never get that much wire." That kind of thing did send me over the edge.' ('I wasn't being dogmatic for the sake of it,' Daltrey protested. 'I just knew that it wouldn't work.')

ROCK IS DEAD, LONG LIVE ROCK

Among other concepts that Townshend proposed as follow-ups to *Tommy* (such as 'maybe developing "Rael" from *The Who Sell Out*') was an 'album about the history of The Who called *Rock Is Dead – Long Live Rock.*' The title song was later issued as a single (above) and featured on the 1974 compilation *Odds & Sods,* in whose liner notes the composer noted: 'This was featured briefly in the film for which Keith made his acting debut, *That'll Be The Day.* Billy Fury sang it. This is most definitely the definitive version.' The concept itself 'blossomed into *Quadrophenia.*'

After a final *Lifehouse* concert in April 1971, Glyn Johns – who had engineered the band's early singles before producing the likes of Steve Miller, The Rolling Stones, and The Faces – was enlisted to salvage the project. 'We went to Stargroves, which was Mick Jagger's house in the country in those days, a huge old Victorian mansion . . .' the producer told the BBC. 'I said, "I'll come and work with you for a week, and we'll see how we get on. If it doesn't work out, you can have whatever we've done as a present, and we'll call it quits." But it worked really well, so we carried on.'

The boozy Stargrove sessions gave way to 'disciplined and sober' work at Olympic Studios in London, where a double album's worth of material was whittled down. 'Glyn would say, "What have you got now?"' Townshend told *ZigZag.* 'I'd say, "Well, nothing, but I never do at this time of the day," and he'd say, "Well, unless you've got anything now, I think the best thing to do would be to put the album together this way." Of course, halfway through *Tommy,* if he'd asked me the same question, I'd have had to say nothing, 'cause we had nothing – (just) a lot of disconnected songs about a deaf, dumb, and blind boy.'

Among the victims of this cull was 'Pure and Easy', a joyful song that encapsulated the 'one note' concept on which *Lifehouse* was founded. 'We

> ## 'Glyn Johns said, "Pete, I don't understand a fucking word you've been saying." I was unbelievably angry.'
>
> Pete Townshend

recorded it, but it didn't work out very well,' Townshend admitted. 'And also I agreed with Glyn not to include things because they told the story, but to include them only if they worked.' To clarify his concerns, Johns took Townshend out for lunch. 'He sat me down and said, "Tell me about the *Lifehouse* story," so I started to tell him. He let me speak for about an hour and a half, looking quite interested and nodding and going, "Mmmm." And I got to the end and he said, "Pete, I don't understand a fucking word you've been

IT'S ALL TOO MUCH

When *Lifehouse* evolved into *Who's Next,* songs to fall by the wayside included 'Too Much of Anything', a favourite of Daltrey (far right). 'This summed up just what too much of anything could do to a person – too much sex, drink, drugs, even rock and roll or nasty blues music,' Townshend wrote. 'Realising at the last minute how totally hypocritical it would be for a load of face-stuffing, drug-addicted alcoholics like us to put this out, we didn't.'

saying" . . . And I was so unbelievably angry – not with him, but with myself, just for being drawn back into it again and being excited by it again.'

PERSONAL DISASTER

Released in August 1971, the Johns-produced *Who's Next* went gold in a month in the US and became the band's only UK chart-topper. 'It's a wonderful record . . .' Townshend conceded. 'But one of the reasons why it marks The Who's subsequent decline is that it was almost like life was giving me a little ticking off; you know, saying, "Don't get too big for your boots, little rock 'n' roll person: you can make good records, but nothing else." I hated to feel that rock was limited, so for me it was a personal disaster.'

As late as 1978, The Who were, he told *Trouser Press,* 'planning a revival of the *Lifehouse* film. . . . What fell apart with it before was that I actually tried to make this fiction that I'd written happen in reality. . . . This time, it'll be done like a film script.' Daltrey, however, sounded a note of caution: 'I don't think we're actually going to do it. The story's not really strong enough for a major film.' Indeed, two other movie projects reached fruition instead: 1979's excellent *The Kids Are Alright* and the iconic *Quadrophenia*.

Townshend was still harbouring fantasies about *Lifehouse* in 1980: 'A treatment was sent to Ray Bradbury, because I fancied getting someone like him to finish it off,' he told *NME*. 'I'd done a couple of scripts for it, but I can't see the wood for the fucking trees any more. Anyway, he's interested and, if he did the script, then maybe someone like Nic Roeg would probably be a great director for it.' Roeg, however, was not convinced – especially after Townshend made an abortive attempt to steal his girlfriend, actress Theresa Russell (eulogised in The Who's 'Athena'). In 1982, Townshend confessed he was 'still working on' the script and, in 1996, he told writer Ira Robbins, '*Lifehouse* is a going concern. . . . If I could get a story together that really worked, that didn't feel dated – because of virtual reality as a subject having become rather passé – then I think *Lifehouse* would pay off.'

Years after the concept's faltering birth, Townshend remained defiant: 'I was at my most brilliant and my most effective, and when people say I didn't know what the fuck I was talking about, what they're actually doing is revealing their own complete idiocy, because the idea was so fucking simple.' **BM**

WHAT HAPPENED NEXT . . .

Most of the *Lifehouse* songs appeared in one form or another. 'Pure and Easy' and 'Let's See Action' featured on Townshend's 1972 solo album *Who Came First* (below). The Who's version of 'Let's See Action' was issued as a single in 1971, and material recorded at New York's Record Plant and during the Young Vic residency was appended to a deluxe reissue of *Who's Next.* As Townshend observed, 'The music that's been written for the various incarnations of that project, most of which have failed, has always been of the highest quality.'

WILL IT EVER HAPPEN?

4/10 In a sense, it has happened: in 1999, a radio play of *Lifehouse,* written by Townshend, premiered on BBC Radio 3. This appeared alongside Townshend's original demos and related music on the *Lifehouse Chronicles* box set in 2000 – the same year in which Townshend staged a musical version of the piece at London's Sadler's Wells theatre (a performance also issued on CD and DVD). Retrospective sets – often compiled with refreshing intelligence – so greatly outweigh albums of original material in The Who's discography that it is not unthinkable that their versions of the songs will one day be compiled into a 'new' *Lifehouse* set.

WICKED LESTER

Artist Wicked Lester **Year** 1972 **Country** US **Genre** Rock **Label** Epic **What** Kiss begin with a whimper not a bang

GENE SIMMONS & PAUL STANLEY
Simmons, né Gene Klein (left), and
Stanley, né Stanley Eisen, of Kiss, pictured
around the time that a former record
company tried to exhume their past.
The band's new label promptly bought
the rights to the *Wicked Lester* album to
ensure it would stay unreleased.

Immediate dislike was Paul Stanley's first impression of his future Kiss co-pilot Gene Simmons. 'Gene had a very high opinion of himself,' Stanley told *Playgirl.* 'And, at that time, he thought that the only three songwriters were Lennon, McCartney, and himself.' Simmons, similarly unimpressed, rejected Stanley when the guitarist auditioned for a band he was plotting. Ultimately, however, the pair united in a new group. 'We were called Rainbow,' Simmons recalled to *Q,* 'because we did some heavy stuff, some light stuff, some Beatlesque stuff, three-part harmonies, even some country.' This kaleidoscopic cocktail, however, failed to set musical tastebuds tingling – and not even a name change, a Phil Spector songwriter, and a drummer who looked like Geezer Butler could save their first album from indignity.

THIS PECULIAR MIX
Determined to escape his day job as a cab driver, rhythm player Stanley – then known by his birth name, Stanley Eisen – joined bassist Simmons, keyboardist Brooke Ostrander, and guitarist Steve Coronel in the summer of 1970. Drummer Joe Davidson briefly completed Rainbow, before being replaced by Tony Zarrella. 'He was as bright as a tree stump,' recalled Stanley. 'But he looked like (Black Sabbath bassist) Geezer Butler, so we had to have him.'

After months of rehearsals, the band finally secured bookings in the spring of 1971. At their first show, Ostrander told Kisstorian Ken Sharp, 'Paul spoke to the audience with a Cockney accent. I don't remember why.' Equally odd were Simmons' formative writing efforts, including 'Stanley the Parrot' (composed before he met Eisen, and which evolved into Kiss's 'Strutter') and 'Eskimo Sun' ('Kind of Beatley,' remembered Stanley. 'Gene's biggest influence was McCartney, so all the stuff had a tinge of that').

Most significant were two future Kiss classics. For the melancholic 'Goin' Blind', Simmons and Coronel were inspired by Mountain's 'Theme from an Imaginary Western', a Jack Bruce composition embellished with, as Simmons told *Guitar World,* 'a lick in the chorus that I ripped off from "Layla" and played backwards.' The duo also conjured up the swaggering 'She'. 'He starts writing these words about "She walks by moonlight and no one really knows" . . .'

Wicked Lester

Cover: Gerry Fletcher

MAN OF 1,000 FACES

'Gene Simmons told me he submitted a hundred songs for (Kiss's) *Psycho Circus* and they used four,' remarked guitarist Ace Frehley. 'To me that's insanity . . . if you write a hundred songs and not know which one's better.' Nonetheless, Simmons often mooted a box set of unreleased tracks. 'I've always written "outside" stuff, but Kiss is Kiss,' he told Ken Sharp. 'And that means the outside stuff winds up on solo albums, or I keep it in the drawer.'

Among potential inclusions were 'Mongloid Man' ('a very bizarre tune' recorded with Aerosmith's Joe Perry), 'You've Got Nothing to Live For' (the embryo of *Destroyer*'s 'Great Expectations'), and, most temptingly, cuts demoed for *Love Gun* with his protégés Eddie and Alex Van Halen: 'Have Love Will Travel' (later 'Got Love for Sale'), 'Christine Sixteen', and 'Tunnel of Love' (the last of which wound up instead on his 1978 solo album, right).

Originally named *Monster* (a title eventually bequeathed to Kiss's 2012 album), the set was renamed *Alter Ego* and planned for 2009. As of 2014, however, it has yet to appear.

Coronel told legendaryrockinterviews.com. 'He was like, "Yeah, you know, I'm thinking of Pocahontas walking by moonlight on these stepping stones through the forest," and I just look at him and go, "What in the fuck are you talking about?"' Stanley's contributions to this peculiar mix included a self-confessed steal from 'Open My Eyes' by Todd Rundgren's group the Nazz: his 'Love Her All I Can' was later reworked on Kiss's *Dressed to Kill*.

NOTHING EVEN REMOTELY PROFESSIONAL
'The main thrust of the band – that we all thought was real exciting and somehow had never been done before – was that we were doing all original material,' boasted Simmons. 'No Top Forty; nobody's else's material.' Convinced of the strength of their repertoire, Rainbow indeed played only originals at their first show – an inauspicious debut of which Stanley told Ken Sharp, 'The place was literally empty. I don't know if there were ten people there. It was pouring out and the only thing that made the gig memorable for me was I caught crabs in the bathroom.' Better-attended subsequent shows saw the band add a slew of covers, including Jethro Tull's 'Locomotive Breath',

> '*Absolutely nothing was passable and they could only copy what other people were doing.*'
> Ron Johnsen

The Jeff Beck Group's 'Rock My Plimsoul', Neil Young's 'When We Dance', Free's 'All Right Now', and The Rolling Stones' 'Jumpin' Jack Flash'.

Along the way, they discovered another group rejoiced in the name Rainbow (not Ritchie Blackmore's later act). 'Gene says, "I have an idea to change the name of the band to Wicked Lester . . ." remembered Coronel. '"He's this mischievous little guy – a little devil." I was like, "Well, what does that have to do with a great rock band?" . . . I was really surprised that a guy who dreamed as big as Gene and had as big intentions as he did would want to call his band

Wicked Lester.' Stanley and Simmons also began badgering producer Ron Johnsen, the chief engineer at New York's Record Plant studio. 'I caught one of their rehearsals and they were horrible . . .' he marvelled to Curt Gooch and Jeff Suhs, authors of the superb *Kiss Alive Forever.* 'Absolutely nothing was passable and they could only copy what other people were doing. There was nothing about them that was even remotely professional.'

CATCHING A DISEASE

Eventually won over, Johnsen helmed demos that found their way to the Epic label's A&R man Tom Werman (later to prove instrumental in Cheap Trick and Mötley Crüe's success). With Epic's backing, work on Wicked Lester's debut began in late 1971. However, the label, unimpressed by Coronel, demanded the guitarist's ousting. The issue wasn't helped by his low opinion of Johnsen: 'This guy didn't produce Hendrix, he didn't produce Janis Joplin or any of the bands we liked or came up on (and) here he was, taking my song "She" and putting bongos on it and Brooke Ostrander's flute on it.' (Johnsen later helmed the similarly eclectic first and only album by Lyn Christopher, now remembered solely for Simmons' and Stanley's backing vocals.)

As recording dragged on into 1972, Coronel was replaced by guitarist Ron Leejack, who had played with Carmine Appice's band Cactus. 'Ron Johnsen set up one more audition with Epic A&R,' Leejack told KissFAQ.com. 'Ron said he didn't think they were going pass. I said, "Don't worry about it." So when the time came, I put my amp where I thought the A&R man might sit – and I was right. I just cranked it up and overplayed . . . played every trick I knew on guitar. Gene and Stan were looking at me like, "What's he doing?"' Epic, however, were impressed. Wicked Lester's manager Lew Linet duly 'worked out a one-album deal with options and a nice little advance for the boys.'

Other perks included a groupie that the terminally on-the-prowl Simmons summoned to the studio. 'She went into the vocal booth and everybody joined in . . .' Tony Zarrella recalled. 'I remember Ronnie Leejack coming out of the

ALIVE, ALIVE OH . . .

Over a year before Cheap Trick cut their career-making *At Budokan,* Kiss recorded their 2 April 1977 show at the Tokyo Hall for a mooted live set. However, engineer Eddie Kramer's tapes were deemed unfit for release, and the album was shelved. Two cuts – 'I Want You' and 'Beth' – wound up on *Alive II* (above) and the tapes have become much-loved bootlegs.

CROSBY, STILLS & LESTER

Jeff Beck and John Mayall were among the famous names working at the Electric Lady studio while Wicked Lester toiled on their album – as were two superstars making a rare in-studio appearance away from the west coast. 'Stephen Stills (spotlit on the right in the photo) was doing the *Manassas* album,' Wicked Lester keyboardist Brooke Ostrander told writer Ken Sharp. 'Steve actually played a solo on "Sweet Ophelia". It didn't work out real great. We kept it until (guitarist) Ron Leejack joined and then we compared Stills's solo with Ron's solo and we liked Ron's better.'

On another occasion, Steve Coronel told KissArmySpain.com, 'Gene came up behind a guy in a long buckskin jacket while he was playing the grand piano in Studio A. Not knowing who it was, Gene started to clap slowly and loudly when he finished, and said, 'Hey, that was *really* good.' It was David Crosby (spotlit left) of Crosby, Stills and Nash. David turned around and gave him such a dirty look. Gene came running, sweating and scared, back out to Stanley and I, as we sat in the reception area. We almost died laughing.'

TRICKY WICKED

In 1974, Gene Simmons, Peter Criss, Ace Frehley, and Paul Stanley were duped by *Creem* into being shot by Charlie Auringer without their makeup. 'They said, "We just spoke to your management and they said we could take pictures of the band without your make-up,"' recalled Stanley. 'Being green, we said, "Really?" And they said, "Yes, really." And we said, "Okay!"'

LAST LAUGH

The artwork intended for Wicked Lester's album was eventually used for the self-titled debut album by new wave band The Laughing Dogs, released by CBS in 1979. The Kiss connection (band member Carter Cathcart also co-wrote a song on Ace Frehley's 1989 solo album *Trouble Walkin'*) is the band's sole claim to fame.

vocal booth going, 'Gee, does anybody have a tape head cleaner or something?' He was really concerned about catching a disease.'

Ron Johnsen was more concerned about Wicked Lester's material. 'The producer was screaming that we didn't have any singles,' said Simmons, 'and suggested that we find another song at a publishing house.' The result was 'We Wanna Shout It Out Loud,' written by Allan Clarke and Tony Sylvester of British pop group The Hollies. Johnsen's friend – and Phil Spector co-writer – Barry Mann weighed in with 'Sweet Ophelia' and 'Too Many Mondays', while other up and coming (albeit subsequently obscure) composers contributed '(What Happens) in the Darkness', 'Long Road', and 'When the Bell Rings'. Wicked Lester's own songs amounted to the McCartney-esque 'Molly', the country-rocking 'Keep Me Waiting', 'She', an old Simmons effort called 'Simple Type', and 'Love Her All I Can'. (Titles that hit the cutting room floor included future Kiss concert staple 'Firehouse'.)

MUSICAL SUICIDE

'Some of those songs were unbelievable,' Stanley marvelled to Ken Sharp of Johnsen's arrangements. 'There would be a horn part, then there's a slide guitar that comes in. And banjos. Some really weird stuff. . . . We were happy to be in the recording studio and we would do anything anybody told us.'

By the summer of 1972, however, he and Simmons were disenchanted. 'All we had to do was put the record out,' the latter reflected in 1996. 'But we decided to literally commit musical suicide by keeping true to our point of view, which is, "We don't believe in this music. We don't believe this is who we are."' As it turned out, Epic A&R director Don Ellis agreed. When manager Lew Linet delivered the album, '(Ellis) said, "I hate it. Not only do I hate it, I'm not even going to release the record. That's the end of the story."'

WHAT HAPPENED NEXT . . .

Now a trio featuring drummer Peter Criss (second from left), Wicked Lester showcased their new direction for their Epic nemesis Don Ellis. 'We played "Firehouse",' Simmons recalled, 'and, at the end of the song, we start ringing this bell, and Ellis thinks it's a real fire. So Paul runs over to the corner and grabs a red pail with the word "Fire" on it, and goes over and throws it at Don, who freaks as a bucketful of confetti goes all over the place. He gets up and starts to walk out, saying, "Okay, thank you, I'll call you." As he's heading out the door, he trips and falls. Then Peter's drunken brother, who was sitting behind Don, throws up on his foot. We never heard from him again.'

The trio enlisted guitarist Ace Frehley (far right) in 1972 and became Kiss – whose mid-1970s success inspired Epic to salvage the album from the archives. Neil Bogart, founder of Kiss's label Casablanca, bought the rights to it, solely to keep it from being released – rights that were subsequently sold to the similarly reluctant band.

Intent on a new, glam-rocking direction, Simmons and Stanley rehearsed with guitarist John Segall, later to find fame as Jay Jay French in Twisted Sister. When that didn't work out, they tried to convince Leejack, Ostrander, and Zarrella to adopt theatrical identities. But, said Stanley, 'The guys just didn't see the same vision we did. So we fired them.' For his part, Leejack maintains that the pair asked *him* to fire Ostrander and Zarazella, and that he quit in protest. Either way, the band was down to a duo by September 1972.

Evidently not quite prepared to give up on their months of work, the pair took the Wicked Lester material to a New Jersey radio station. 'The disc jockey started taking calls to "talk to this new band,"' Stanley recalled in the band's *Kisstory* autobiography, 'and, of course, no one called. During the commercial break, we called all our friends and asked them to phone in. One girl who called was asked by the DJ why she wanted to talk to this band. She said, 'Because they called me up and asked me to." **BM**

WILL IT EVER HAPPEN?

1/10 'Nobody's heard a quality version of it,' Stanley observed. 'I've played all the bootlegs and they're horrible. They're either sped up or they're missing parts.' Remarkably, however, Kiss's money-making schemes have never extended to making the Wicked Lester album available, although they allowed its versions of 'Keep Me Waiting', 'She', and 'Love Her All I Can' onto a Kiss box set in 2001 (while 'Simple Type' evolved into 'Charisma' on 1979's *Dynasty*). 'From a Kiss fan's point of view,' Simmons admitted, 'it's, "Oh, it's obscure and vintage." But it didn't hold up.' The party line is toed by Paul Stanley too: 'There is some pretty fun stuff on that record,' he confessed. '(But) you had to be there to really appreciate it.'

'AMERICAN TOUR '72'

Artist The Rolling Stones **Year** 1972 **Country** UK/US **Genre** Rock **Label** Rolling Stones Records
What Stevie and the Stones come unstuck

JOHN PASCHE
The beautiful albeit deceptively serene
poster for the tour was designed by John
Pasche, best known for creating the
Stones' iconic tongue logo. This and other
works for the band are available as prints
from rollingstonesposters.co.uk.

Of 1972's 'Stones Touring Party', writer Stanley Booth recalled: 'Fettucine on flocked velvet, hot urine pooling on deep carpets, and tidal waves of spewing sex organs.' Not to mention 'a travelling physician, hordes of dealers and groupies, (and) big sex-and-dope scenes.' Much of that was captured in Robert Frank's *Cocksucker Blues,* a movie so debauched that the Stones themselves withheld its release. Amid it all, however, was rock 'n' roll's greatest band, touring arguably their greatest album, supported by the decade's greatest soul star. You'd have to be nuts not to capture *that* on vinyl, right?

HORRIBLE DEATH

'Eventually there'll be a live album,' predicted Mick Jagger, three months before the tour got underway in June. He had every reason to be optimistic: the band's previous US outing, in 1969, had yielded the acclaimed live set *Get Your Ya-Yas Out!*. Now they had two more gem-packed sets – both issued on their own Atlantic imprint, Rolling Stones Records – to showcase: 1971's *Sticky Fingers* and the soon-to-be chart-topping *Exile On Main St.*

Half the tour's repertoire came from those freshly minted classics: 'Brown Sugar', 'Bitch', 'Rocks Off', 'Happy', 'Tumbling Dice', 'Sweet Virginia', 'Loving Cup', 'All Down the Line', and 'Rip This Joint'. The rest were from their 1968-69 axis of evil, *Beggars Banquet* and *Let It Bleed:* 'Gimme Shelter', 'Love in Vain', 'You Can't Always Get What You Want', 'Midnight Rambler', and 'Street Fighting Man'. Rounding things off were Chuck Berry's 'Bye Bye Johnny', and a trio of 1960s hits: 'Jumpin' Jack Flash', 'Honky Tonk Women', and 'Satisfaction' – the latter performed with Stevie Wonder in a medley with his 'Uptight (Everything's Alright)'. And it was those hits that, when a live album of the tour was compiled, proved problematic for a record company and manager who had represented the Stones in the 1960s.

'Decca Records and Allen Klein stopped it because it included three old songs they have the rights to,' Jagger explained to *NME.* 'They wanted to release their own repackaged album in time for the Christmas rush and they didn't want competition. They thought they could make more money by stopping us. We offered them a substantial amount, which they refused.'

Cover: Akiko Stehrenberger

WHAT HAPPENED NEXT . . .
Several 1960s songs were included in the movie *Ladies & Gentlemen: The Rolling Stones,* released in 1974 but filmed on the 1972 tour. Meanwhile, following March 1972's *Milestones,* Decca released two further compilations: *Rock'n'Rolling Stones* in October and *More Hot Rocks (Big Hits & Fazed Cookies)* in December. They also issued – as they had done since the Stones decamped to the Atlantic label – 1960s fillers (in 1972, 'Carol' and 'Route 66') as 45s. 'I don't really mind them packaging old stuff if they use a little bit of imagination,' conceded Richards, 'but putting out old flipsides as singles is shit.'

(*Necrophilia* – a rarities set compiled by bassist Bill Wyman, and intended to follow the hits collection *Hot Rocks* – also fell victim to Klein's intervention, when he demanded the album include more Jagger/Richards songs. It was ultimately scrapped in favour of *More Hot Rocks* [see What Happened Next].)

'We just can't put the motherfucker out . . .' fumed Keith Richards, 'because recordings of those songs belong to them until nineteen-seventy-whatever. Decca are supposed to be making records but they might just as easily be making baked beans. . . . They're the biggest bunch of shits in the world.'

'We would not be in business very long if we were to wash our hands of a product that is rightfully ours,' Decca retorted primly. 'We have been very easy with the Stones in the past, some of us feel too easy . . . they owed (*Sticky Fingers*) to us. But the time had come when we felt we should have a bit of a fight back.' *NME* gave the last word to a Stones spokesperson: 'I'm afraid the album, brilliant though it is, seems doomed to die a horrible death.' **BM**

WILL IT EVER HAPPEN?

8/10 Songs from both the Decca and Atlantic eras graced live Stones sets from 1977's *Love You Live* onwards. And the band's Promotone BV label has begun issuing shows best known as bootlegs, so the omens are good.

A KICK IN THE HEAD IS WORTH EIGHT IN THE PANTS

Artist Bee Gees **Year** 1973 **Country** UK **Genre** Pop **Label** RSO **What** A misstep that paved the road to recovery

ROBIN GIBB
The story of the Bee Gees 'is a story of missed opportunities,' opined the *NME Book of Rock* in 1973. 'At one point their commercial success looked as if it would carry them to the very top.' 'We were in a real dead zone,' confirmed Robin Gibb.

After eighteen months of solo projects and legal bickering (see page 38), the Bee Gees were, by 1972, firmly in the groove again. The second half of the year found them particularly active, recording two separate albums for release in 1973 as they strove to recapture their niche in the public's heart. It wouldn't be easy. Sales had declined, with the brothers struggling to find a sound that would suit them in a new decade, their traditional balladeering having frayed around the edges. There were still personal problems to tackle as well, with Maurice Gibb fighting alcoholism and facing up to separation from his wife Lulu. It's a wonder they were so prolific.

UNFATHOMABLE PATHOS
Their work ethic could partly be traced to loyalty. Manager Robert Stigwood was looking to get his RSO label off the ground, and a hit would be just the boost it needed. The first of the two albums laid down was *Life in a Tin Can,* released in January 1973 but crippled from the start when its lead single 'Saw a New Morning' barely scraped the *Billboard* Hot 100. The stakes for *A Kick in the Head Is Worth Eight in the Pants* were raised to unattainable levels.

Like *Life in a Tin Can,* the songs that made up its still-unconfirmed track listing were recorded in Los Angeles, with work completed on ten numbers in November 1972. Another four, captured when the band decamped to London in the New Year for an overdue return to the British stage (at the Festival Hall, with the London Symphony Orchestra), were probably pencilled in as B-sides.

The notional running order actually begins with a B-side, 'Elisa': the flip to the first single, 'Wouldn't I Be Someone'. Both songs stay true to the Bee Gees' sense of drama, augmented by orchestral arrangements from Jimmie Haskell. 'Elisa' holds a place in Gibb folklore for being the first song in which all three brothers take a lead vocal, but Robin steals the show, investing lines like 'All I need is just a sheet of paper / Say a few lines . . . so she can read it later' with unfathomable pathos. 'Wouldn't I Be Someone' is equally lovelorn, but its twangy guitar solo is typical of the warm tone of the rest of the album, which serves up a touch of country on 'It Doesn't Matter Much To Me' and 'Home Again Rivers', and Allman Brothers-style bluesy boogie on 'Rocky L.A'.

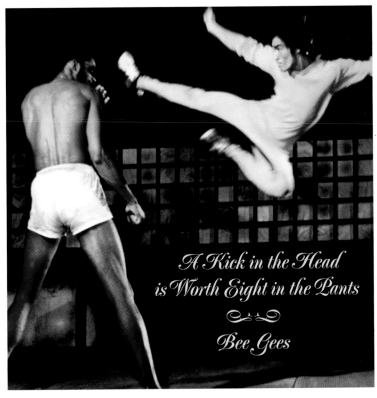

A Kick in the Head
is Worth Eight in the Pants

Bee Gees

Cover: Tom Howey

WHAT HAPPENED NEXT . . .

'We got into pills – Dexedrine – and liquor too,' recalled Barry. Despite these dire straits, Atlantic had enough faith in the brothers' talents to come up with a new idea. Label boss Ahmet Ertegun suggested they work with R&B producer Arif Mardin and the rest is – genuinely – history. Mardin teased out the Gibbs' soulful side and although their first collaboration, 1974's *Mr. Natural*, wasn't a commercial hit, it was an artistic triumph. They built on it with 1975's *Main Course*, conjuring 'Jive Talkin'', 'Nights on Broadway', and 'Fanny (Be Tender with My Love)'. The happy ending wrote itself.

So, some great stuff – but, according to a decision-maker, the songs were not up to scratch. Whether that was the Gibbs themselves or their record company is moot – either way, RSO would not release the album. 'No one wanted to hear us,' Robin later told *Q*. 'The record company wasn't interested.' RSO's hand may have been forced by the poor performance of the single 'Wouldn't I Be Someone', which fell short of the US Top 100, crawled to No. 52 in Australia, and didn't chart at all in Britain. ('It's a shame,' Lulu sympathised in *Melody Maker*. 'You always like to be successful in your own country.') Maurice suggested Stigwood's burgeoning involvement in movies and musicals had distracted him from the job. Whatever the facts, *A Kick in the Head* . . . turned out to be a pivot in Bee Gees history. **MH**

3/10 **WILL IT EVER HAPPEN?**

Ask Barry Gibb. Now the sole keeper of the Bee Gees legacy, it comes down to his appetite for revisiting the past. There's nothing in *A Kick in the Head Is Worth Eight in the Pants* to shame his brothers' memories – indeed, the album is unlucky to gather dust while the inferior *Life in a Tin Can* had its moment. Considering the lingering demand for bootleg versions, *A Kick in the Head* . . . would be a welcome release.

HUMAN HIGHWAY

CROSBY, STILLS, NASH & YOUNG

Cover: Isabel Eeles

HUMAN HIGHWAY

Artist Crosby, Stills, Nash & Young **Year** 1973 **Country** US **Genre** Rock **Label** Atlantic **What** Ditch of despair

C rosby, Stills & Nash had been together barely a year before the honeymoon period wore off. 'It started off as a really beautiful idea,' Stephen Stills reflected to *Disc and Music Echo* in early 1970. 'We were full of enthusiasm and ideals. Now a lot of that feeling has gone . . . Maybe that feeling of us all liking each other a lot will return and we'll go on working together.' That feeling *did* return – and, during a four-month reunion, *Déjà vu,* their first album with Neil Young, topped the US chart. But by September 1970, the group had splintered once more. Nearly three years after *that,* the quartet reunited in Hawaii to create what could have been, in David Crosby's optimistic view, 'the best album we ever made.'

GLORIOUS MESS
By early 1973, Stephen Stills' project Manassas had begun to run its course, Crosby had experienced a less than scintillating reunion with The Byrds, and Crosby and Graham Nash had answered Young's call to help out the Canadian's patchy *Time Fades Away* tour. The clamouring from fans and the Atlantic label for a new album by CSN&Y – who had racked up a second US chart-topper with 1971's live *4-Way Street* – grew relentless. 'I found it personally frustrating that a group with so much talent should not be active or productive,' Atlantic supremo Ahmet Ertegun told *Uncut.* 'It's a terrible waste . . . when the genius is there but the product is not.'

Solo efforts suggested the four had more to deliver collectively, if they could tolerate each other's company long enough. 'They're all still good friends on some level or another,' observed David Geffen, who had once attempted to manage the quartet. 'Whether they could live together for any period of time is questionable.' But, in June 1973, it happened: they escaped to the village of Lahaina on the Hawaiian island Maui to vacation together and rehearse a new album. The motivation, Nash declared, was musical, not monetary: 'They couldn't make us do what we didn't want to do. . . . We were incredibly cocky fuckers and sure of ourselves. We thought we were hot shit. So what brought us together in 1973 came out of a giant fog of psychic and musical connections between the four of us – some unspoken, some spoken.'

STEPHEN STILLS
'Nobody could take criticism from their partners,' Stills observed of the *Human Highway* sessions. 'It was silly.' Neil Young's verdict on the mooted return of the quartet was even blunter: the album, he said, 'just turned into a piece of shit.'

HIGH IN HAWAII
Graham Nash (far right) shot the intended
Human Highway artwork. 'The cover of
the album was to be a Hawaiian sunset,'
David Crosby (second from right) told
Johnny Rogan. 'It was the last picture
on a roll of film – a stunner. . . . the best
picture anyone ever took of us.' Nash
grabbed Stills' Hasselblad camera and,
with pal Harry Harris, set up a shot that
Stills (far left) immediately designated
'the new CSN&Y album cover!' 'In the last
ten minutes of sunlight,' Nash told Dave
Zimmer, 'I got everyone together, focused
the camera, set the time exposure – with
no meter – placed the camera in the sand,
and ran into the picture.'

The location was perfect. Crosby's sailing boat and Young's beach house
amid the palm trees provided a relaxing break from the expectations faced by
the four millionaire hippies. According to Crosby, songs for the album – to be
called *Human Highway* – included his own 'Homeward Through The Haze'
and 'Time After Time', Young's title track and 'Pardon My Heart', and Nash's
'And So It Goes', 'Prison Song', 'Wind on the Water'. Other candidates included
Young's 'Through My Sails' and Stills' 'See the Changes' and 'As I Come of
Age'. 'We thought, "We've done *4-Way Street* – we're on this 'travelling through
the universe' mindset,"' Nash recalled to *The Huffington Post,* 'so *Human
Highway* sounded like an incredible album title, which I still think it is.'

NOTHING BUT DIFFICULTY
The Hawaiian vacation failed to create anything tangible, but the four
reconvened at Young's Broken Arrow ranch in California, with bassist Tim
Drummond and drummer Johnny Barbata. Young decided he wanted producer
and engineer Elliot Mazer's help on the project and tracked him down to
England. Despite Mazer's reluctance – 'I'd witnessed working with two or
three of them on (Young's) *Harvest* and the live stuff and I saw nothing but
difficulty,' he told writer Johnny Rogan – Young eventually persuaded him,
using at least one transatlantic phone call to play the new songs. But Mazer's
suspicions proved correct. One day the music stopped and CSN&Y downed
guitars, amid disputes about whether they should persevere with the recording
or work through their problems by touring. (A mooted tour for late 1973 fell
through when Young – wryly dubbed 'Mr Dependable' by Crosby – pulled out.)

> *'Stills was burnt out. I was burnt. Even Nash was
> less than his usual nice self.'*
> David Crosby

The increasingly faint possibility that the album would see the light of
day briefly burned brighter when CSN&Y shared a stage at San Francisco's
Winterland in October 1973. The unscheduled appearance occurred when
Crosby and Nash, then Young, ambled up to join Stills as Manassas cleared
the stage for an acoustic airing of potential *Human Highway* tracks: 'As I Come
of Age', 'New Mama', and 'Roll Another Number'. 'I could,' remarked Stills'
Manassas sidekick Chris Hillman, '*smell* another CSN&Y reunion.'

More songs might have found their way onto *Human Highway* had such a
reunion materialised in the studio: Young's 'Traces' and 'Hawaiian Sunrise',
Stills' 'First Things First', and Nash's 'Another Sleep Song' were all plausible
candidates. Instead, they elected to hit the road in July 1974. The two-month
tour was huge in every respect: it was among the first in rock to focus on
stadiums and the box-office takings were suitably mind-boggling.

Commercially and musically, it was a triumph. But different factions had
their own entourages – Young travelled separately to the other three – and
drugs were abundant. And, as Crosby told biographer Dave Zimmer, 'I didn't

dig playin' stadiums. That was Neil and Stephen's trip, especially Stephen's. He was into being bigger than the Stones. Bigger than everybody. But the music suffered, I feel. When we got into the electric set, Neil and Stephen started competing on guitar simply by turning up. We clocked 'em once and they got up to 135 decibels. So Nash and I were unable to sing harmony. It was a drag.' In his own defence, Stills declared, 'Crosby's Alembic 12-string was the loudest motherfucker you ever heard. Half the time, Neil and I would have to turn up to hear past the bastard, who was between us.' Crosby duly dubbed the trek, which concluded in September 1974, 'the doom tour'.

A HOPELESS CAUSE

In November, the retrospective *So Far* became their third US number one and, in December, they regrouped once more at Sausalito's Record Plant studio. Where *Déjà vu* had rarely featured all four recording together, these sessions saw full-on live takes, with limited overdubbing of harmonies. Stills and Young were in their guitar-duelling element, while Crosby and Nash took care of keyboards, supported by bassist Leland Sklar and drummer Russell Kunkel.

But it was, Crosby confessed to *Creem*, 'a hopeless cause. Stills was burnt out. I was burnt. Even Nash was less than his usual nice self.' ('It was insane,' Nash agreed. 'We ended up not talking to each other.') Young was under no illusions about the album's prospects. 'If they'd had new songs with the authority that their old songs had, we could've knocked off four and five of mine so that just the best two surfaced,' he told Nick Kent ('Pushed It Over The End', 'Traces', and 'Love-Art Blues' were among his songs premiered on the 1974 tour). 'That would have truly been CSN&Y. But it wasn't to be.' Indeed, having cut 'Wind on the Water', 'Human Highway', 'Through My Sails', and 'Homeward Through the Haze', they were at each other's throats.

Astonishingly, they tried yet again in January 1975, this time with Grateful Dead drummer Bill Kreutzmann. But when Stills and Nash rowed over a single harmony note, Young walked out. 'It wasn't anything more,' Crosby rued, 'than the practicality that we couldn't get along with each other any more.' **DR**

WILL IT EVER HAPPEN?

3/10 Nash and Young are such avid archivists, there must be a chance of the recordings being compiled for release. CSN&Y have had their differences but get along fine now – witness the 2006 *Freedom of Speech* tour. The positive vibes from the sun-kissed Hawaiian vacation were good back in 1973 and the urge to recycle is strong. *Human Highway: The Fiftieth Anniversary*, anyone?

WHAT HAPPENED NEXT . . .

In spring 1976, the previous years' spats were eclipsed by an almost terminal falling out. Crosby and Nash, then working on what would become their *Whistling Down The Wire* album, were invited to add harmonies to a Stills and Young project. When the duo then wiped Crosby and Nash's contribution to what became the Stills-Young album *Long May You Run*, the hurt and accusations ended any chance that the songs each of them had been stockpiling for a new group album would be recorded by CSN&Y.

Young eventually used the *Human Highway* title for an offbeat 1982 movie starring himself, Dennis Hopper, and Devo (left). And when CSN&Y finally got round to recording a second studio album, it was Young who called the shots. *American Dream* (1988) was a helping hand from him to Crosby, whose drug addiction and subsequent imprisonment had all but destroyed a once golden career. The album was not a great success and featured none of the tracks that might have made it onto *Human Highway*.

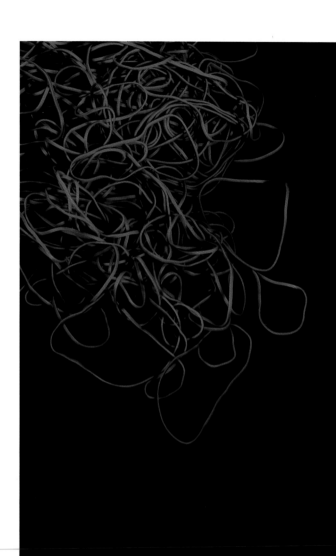

PINK
FLOYD
**Household
Objects**

Cover: Damian Jaques

HOUSEHOLD OBJECTS

Artist Pink Floyd **Year** 1974 **Country** UK **Genre** Prog rock **Label** Harvest
What An idea so nuts, it made an inflatable flying pig seem sensible

When 1973's *Dark Side of the Moon* proved Pink Floyd's mainstream breakthrough, it was, mourned bassist and de facto leader Roger Waters, 'the end of the road. We'd reached the point we'd all been aiming for ever since we were teenagers and there was really nothing more to do in terms of rock 'n' roll.' Faced with following up what would become one of rock's most successful albums, the genteel British quartet took the bewildering step of putting down their instruments . . . and picking up their Sellotape.

SOMETHING WEIRD, FAR OUT
Dark Side of the Moon, conceived in late 1971, consumed the Floyd for a year and a half. They previewed it in concert in January 1972, tinkered with it onstage and on tape over the ensuing months, released it in March 1973, and finished touring it in June that year. But then the band – never the most prolific of writers – found their well of inspiration had run dry. 'I occasionally pick up a guitar and strum a few chords, or jot a few words down,' remarked Waters towards the end of the tour. 'But when I say occasionally, I mean occasionally.'

When they returned to the studio in October, the enormity of following an international smash weighed heavily upon them. 'That was the hardest thing,' recalled keyboard player Rick Wright. '"What do we do after *this*?"' The answer, according to guitarist David Gilmour – tongue lodged firmly in cheek – was 'something weird, far out, that nobody could possibly understand.'

Defying musical convention was hardly new territory for the Floyd. Their early psychedelia was summarised by drummer Nick Mason as the band performing 'rather nasty operations' on Chuck Berry material. In the ensuing years, novelty numbers like 'Several Species of Small Furry Animals Gathered Together in a Cave and Grooving with a Pict' (*Ummagumma*, 1968) and 'Alan's Psychedelic Breakfast' (*Atom Heart Mother*, 1970) found them messing around with tape loops and *musique concrète* – doubtless influenced by British radio comedy troupe The Goons and, latterly, by Ron Geesin, who orchestrated *Atom Heart Mother* and collaborated with Waters on the same year's defiantly non-musical soundtrack, *Music from The Body*. Now they took the next step: trying to make an album with no musical instruments at all.

ROGER WATERS
'The name "Pink Floyd" . . .' observed their cynical leader, 'is probably worth one million sales of an album – any album we put out. Even if we just coughed, a million people will have ordered it simply because of the name.'

DARK SIDE OF THE DUNE

A group who played a burning gong on 'Set the Controls for the Heart of the Sun' (right). A psychedelic director. A sci-fi epic. A marriage made in heaven, thought director Alejandro Jodorowsky, who had created one of Waters' favourite movies (*El Topo*) and wanted the Floyd to soundtrack his mid-1970s adaptation of Frank Herbert's *Dune*. However, his recollection of visiting Abbey Road during the *Wish You Were Here* sessions, only to storm out when the band insisted on finishing their steak and chips before talking to him, is refuted by Nick Mason: 'We wouldn't have treated someone we admired in such a cavalier fashion.' The Floyd did no work on the soundtrack and the film collapsed, unfinished and fatally over budget, in 1976.

PINK TANGERINE

Getting one of Pink Floyd to mix Tangerine Dream's *Stratosfear* (1976) seemed a marriage made in prog rock nirvana – but was not one destined to last. Nick Mason, said the Dream's main man Edgar Froese, 'was a very nice guy and pleasant to work with. He liked our stuff a lot.' But . . . ? 'We finalized the mix on our own.'

'I've always felt that the differentiation between a sound effect and music is all a load of shit,' Waters maintained to *ZigZag*. 'Whether you make a sound on a guitar or a water tap is irrelevant, because it doesn't make any difference.' For what became known as *Household Objects,* he explained, 'We don't use any recognisable musical instruments at all – bottles, knives, anything at all, felling axes and stuff like that. . . . It's turning into a really nice piece.'

'Most of the ideas we've tried seem to work really well...' Mason agreed in *Sounds*. 'It's in very random form at the moment, not in pieces. There are things like sixteen tracks of glasses tuned to a scale across the 16-track (tape recorder). It can be played across the faders, but what it really needs is each one going through a VCS3 (an analogue synthesiser used on *Dark Side's* 'On the Run') or something, and then coming in to a keyboard. I suppose, really, it's a very, very, very, very crude Mellotron. There's a whole load of things we've done – some of them just down as sounds that work, others as bass-lines . . .'

'If you tap a wine bottle across the top of the neck,' added Gilmour, 'you get a tabla-like sound close up. Or you can fill it partly with water and do the same thing, and just tap it in the conventional way. We used rubber bands: we actually built a long, stretched rubber band thing, about two feet. There was a G-clamp at one end, fixing it to a table, and another G-clamp at the other end, fixing it to a table. There was a cigarette lighter under one end for a bridge and a set of matchsticks taped down the other end. You stretch it and you can get a really good bass sound. Oh, and we used aerosol sprays and pulling rolls of Sellotape out to different lengths – the further away it gets, the note changes.'

DIFFICULT AND POINTLESS

After weeks of intermittent sessions, the lunacy of this endeavour began to dawn on them. 'We'd spend days getting a pencil and a rubber band till it sounded like a bass . . .' Wright marvelled in the fine 2007 BBC documentary *Which One's Pink?*. 'Nick would find old saucepans and stuff, and then deaden them to try and make them sound exactly like a snare drum. I remember sitting down with Roger and saying, "Roger, this is insane!"'

Engineer Alan Parsons – creator of sound effects on *Dark Side of the Moon* (notably the introductory clocks on 'Time') – recalled, with some exasperation, 'We spent something like four weeks in the studio on it and came away with no more than one and a half minutes of music.' In fact, the final tally was more like five minutes: a rubber bass-driven piece, dubbed 'The Hard Way' when it appeared on a *Dark Side* reissue in 2011, and what became the entrancing opening drone on 1975's 'Shine On You Crazy Diamond' (given the self-explanatory title 'Wine Glasses' when it was included as a stand-alone track on 2012's *Wish You Were Here* reissue).

> ## *'I remember sitting down with Roger and saying, "Roger, this is insane!"'*
>
> Rick Wright

'It's a dead easy thing to do today with samplers,' Gilmour told writer Jim DeRogatis decades later, 'but, (back) then, we abandoned it. . . . It just got too difficult – and pointless. . . . After you've spent weeks trying to make cardboard boxes sound like bass drums and snare drums, you think, "Well, why the fuck don't I use a bass drum and snare drum?"'

Only the most dogged of fans rue the demise of this wacky wheeze, although Floyd biographer Nick Schaffner pondered how it would have been received at the US record company who poached the band from the Capitol label after *Dark Side*'s success: 'One does almost regret the abandonment of *Household Objects* – if only for the expressions that might have crossed the faces of the CBS execs upon contemplating the first fruits of their seven-figure investment.'

'It seemed like a good idea at the time,' was Waters' final verdict, 'but it didn't come together. Probably because we needed to stop for a bit.' **BM**

WILL IT EVER HAPPEN?

0/10

'Almost everything we've ever recorded . . . has been extracted by someone at some point and subsequently bootlegged,' wrote Mason in his memoir *Inside Out: A Personal History of Pink Floyd*. 'However, no such recordings exist of the *Household Objects* tapes for the simple reason that we never managed to produce any actual music.' The release of 'The Hard Way' and 'Wine Glasses' (see left) suggest otherwise, but don't hold your breath for more.

WHAT HAPPENED NEXT . . .

The Floyd toiled on a triumvirate of new songs – 'Shine On You Crazy Diamond', 'You Gotta Be Crazy', and 'Raving and Drooling' – and road-tested them on a French tour. These would 'almost definitely be part of whatever we do next,' predicted Mason in a 1974 interview, during which he also suggested that *Household Objects* had been merely set aside rather than abandoned altogether. Had Gilmour won an ensuing power struggle, Mason's prediction would have been correct: the guitarist favoured banging the three lengthy pieces down and issuing them as an album. Waters, however, insisted on a new cycle of songs, relating to the band's angst-ridden creative inertia. The result was 1975's *Wish You Were Here* (left). 'You Gotta Be Crazy' and 'Raving and Drooling' were retooled as 'Dogs' and 'Sheep' for 1977's furious *Animals*.

dusty *longing* springfield

Cover: Isabel Eeles

LONGING

Artist Dusty Springfield Year 1974 Country US Genre Pop Label Dunhill What Done and dusted

The Atlantic years were good to Dusty Springfield, to a point. She had signed to the label in 1968 in a canny bid to arrest artistic and popular decline – not because things were desperate, but to avoid a slip into irrelevance. And the first results were great. Working with destined-to-be-legendary producers Jerry Wexler, Tom Dowd, and Arif Mardin, Springfield struck back with 1969's *Dusty in Memphis:* from start to finish a convincing slab of blue-eyed soul. A fan of Aretha Franklin, Springfield had challenged the Queen of Soul at her own game, using many of the same tools. 'I always wanted to be Aretha,' she admitted. Granted, *Dusty in Memphis* was not a huge commercial hit but as a calling card – as a demonstration of what she had always promised – it would remain unmatched for the rest of her career. Her endorsement of her former session man John Paul Jones also helped his band Led Zeppelin secure a deal with Atlantic. What could possibly go wrong?

CRAZIEST THINGS
During this period, Springfield had largely uprooted to the States, despite telling *NME* in 1968, '(Just) because I leap off to work there occasionally does not mean I'm going to stay there.' New direction and new opportunities changed her tune and further albums followed: *A Brand New Me* in 1970 and *Faithful* in 1971. Except *Faithful* didn't appear at all. The failure of a couple of singles punctured Atlantic's confidence and precipitated her exit from the label. 'Dusty Springfield is a hundred times better singer than Janis (Joplin),' Ike Turner lamented to *Blues & Soul,* 'but she doesn't have the same amount of success.'

Springfield retreated to LA, issuing *See All Her Faces* in Europe but not in the US in 1972. Nonetheless, that year she signed to New York label ABC Dunhill Records and set about writing her next chapter. The first fruits came in 1973 with *Cameo,* a solid collection of smooth soul that met a tepid reaction and barely existent sales. Her reputation as a singer was being swamped by gossip about her sexual proclivities and unreliability. 'I've given up on this business about 'gay reputation' . . .' she sighed to *Rolling Stone*'s Ben Fong-Torres. 'I was once accused of raping a thirteen-year-old black boy in the corridors of (British TV show) *Ready Steady Go!,* so I really don't know where

DUSTY SPRINGFIELD
'America was the place I'd always dreamed of as a girl,' Springfield told the *New York Times.* 'The vastness of it. It was where the music came from.' Sadly, this initially mutually fruitful relationship was to have an inconclusive end.

LOSING FAITH

What would have been Springfield's third album for Atlantic – *Faithful* (its title derived from the track 'I'll Be Faithful') – fell foul of her diminishing status with record-buyers and label executives. Its predecessor, *A Brand New Me,* had set alarm bells ringing in 1970, failing to match the critical acclaim of 1969's *Dusty in Memphis* and falling short even of that album's lowly chart peak. When the singles 'I Believe in You' and 'Haunted' did nothing on the *Billboard* charts, cold feet turned to outright refusal. Springfield's once creatively fruitful relationship with Atlantic was over. However, 'Someone Who Cares' and 'Nothing Is Forever' (the respective B-sides of the singles) made it onto 1972's *See All Her Faces* (above), and the remaining tracks turned up on a 1999 deluxe reissue of *Dusty in Memphis.*

I'm at . . . One of the reasons I'm very insecure is that I have many reputations, and many things that are totally unfounded. Being unreliable. Not turning up for a show. Never finishing an engagement. Doing the craziest things.' The writing was on the wall for her next outing *Elements* – later to become *Longing* – almost before it was completed.

The album was recorded in New York in the summer of 1974 with producer Brooks Arthur. Featuring songs by Barry Manilow ('I Am Your Child', from his self-titled 1973 debut), Holland Dozier Holland, Mann & Weil, Carole Bayer Sager, and Colin Blunstone, it's a surprisingly assured set under the circumstances. The players are accomplished, too, including former Aretha Franklin guitarist Cornell Dupree, future Steely Dan cohort Hugh McCracken, and members of the legendary Muscle Shoals band: a heavyweight cast for an album that would end up on the scrapheap.

TURBULENT PSYCHE

Opening with a caress of electric piano, the soulful 'Exclusively for Me' is the first of many songs utterly inhabited by Springfield. 'This is a song written exclusively for me,' she sings. 'Something to warm me on a lonely winter night.' From the outset, *Longing* taps into Springfield's turbulent psyche. 'Beautiful Soul' begins with rolling piano reminiscent of her appearance on Elton John's *Tumbleweed Connection* (1970), and there's a brush of Elton's spirit, too, on 'Make the Man Love Me', in which lush piano gives way to a swell of gospel voices before Springfield breaks into a kind of Laura Nyro vaudeville groove. (Sadly, Elton's plans to sign her to his Rocket label came to nothing.) Whatever anxiety brewed beneath, *Longing*'s surface flows calmly.

There was a sense, however, of Springfield moving from Atlantic soul into the singer-songwriter arena of the early 1970s. It wasn't a question of penning the

> *'You can hang from a chandelier and set fire to yourself . . . but they still won't promote you.'*
> Dusty Springfield

songs herself – she didn't – but of Laurel Canyon country-rock butting against her R&B stylings. Accordingly, 'Home to Myself' boasts piano reminiscent of Carole King's *Tapestry* and a bittersweet lyric ('I know I've come a long way'), while a cover of Janis Ian's 'In the Winter' is delicately reflective until it bursts from dramatic string undercurrents to a barnstorming chorus. This graceful but strident evolution from ballad to anthem sounds like The Carpenters, and there are hints of that duo's poppy immaculacy throughout. Other paths to possible futures came in the proto-disco strings of 'Angels' and light funk flurries of the closing 'Turn Me Around' and 'A Love Like Yours (Don't Come Knocking Everyday)'. 'Angels' moves from tinkles of eerie, autumnal piano to a chorus – 'Let your soul take you higher' – that blends horns and gospel backing to go somewhere almost spiritual: whether the church or the dancefloor.

BLONDES HAVE MORE FUN
Like Dusty (left), Rod Stewart (right) would earn more respect for soulful vocals in the US than in his native UK. *Unlike* Dusty, Stewart's deployment of the Muscle Shoals musicians revitalised his fortunes: *Atlantic Crossing* (1975) turned him into a superstar at around the same time as his fellow singer slipped off the radar.

Springfield evidently invested faith in the final two tracks, as both reappeared on 1978's *It Begins Again.* She even performed one – the Martha Reeves & the Vandellas cover 'A Love Like Yours . . .' – on BBC TV's *Top of the Pops* to little commercial effect. 'Turn Me Around', meanwhile, opened *It Begins Again* in buffed-up form, Springfield gossamer-light over its parping country-soul.

The rest of *Longing* survives only in bits and bobs and anthologies. But the album *nearly* made it. It was assigned a catalogue number and a cover, and advertisements were prepared. The explanation of its fate is murky: a suggestion that its material was below par is hard to swallow, because *Longing* more than holds its own in her truncated run of early 1970s albums. More plausible is that Springfield's reclusiveness, substance abuse, and catastrophic lack of self-esteem hindered her viability as a marketable pop star, and possibly her ability to finish the record. 'I was directionless and I was tired and record companies treated me as a tax write-off,' she told *Q* in 1989. 'And when record companies do that, there's nothing you can do. You can dance up and down and hang from a chandelier and set fire to yourself and they'll say, "Hey, that's beautiful," but they still won't promote you.' **MH**

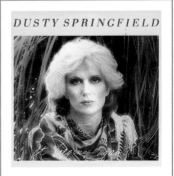

DUSTY SPRINGFIELD

WHAT HAPPENED NEXT . . .
Springfield withdrew. Substance issues had made her a shadow of that blue-eyed soul diva, and the issue of her sexuality continued to excite more comment than her music. She would eventually come out in an interview with the *Evening Standard* in 1975 – but, as far as the wider world was concerned, she was now a recluse. After a brief re-emergence in 1978 with *It Begins Again* (above), her output would remain sporadic and under the radar until the Pet Shop Boys shoved her back to centre stage in 1987.

WILL IT EVER HAPPEN?

2/10 As a fully annotated, pristine package? Probably not. In a piecemeal way, *Longing* has had its day in the sun. First there were those hangovers on *It Begins Again.* Then, in 2001, all the completed tracks from the original sessions turned up on *Beautiful Soul: The ABC Dunhill Collection.* There would be a second lease of life, however, for the aspirational pop of 'Corner of the Sky': Springfield's 1960s contemporary Petula Clark dusted it down and added her own vocal for her *Duets* album in 2007.

THE GOUSTER

Artist David Bowie **Year** 1975 **Country** US **Genre** Blue-eyed soul **Label** RCA **What** *Young Americans* minus Beatles

DAVID BOWIE
'That period in my life is none too clear,' Bowie told *Musician*. 'A lot of it is really blurry.' Preserved with clarity, however, is an appearance on *The Dick Cavett Show,* during which the scarily stoned star, as biographer Paul Trynka notes, 'manages to impersonate a normal human being, but mostly . . . revels in his fractured condition.'

A 'very strange experience', recalled producer Tony Visconti of the album that ultimately evolved into one of Bowie's biggest sellers of the 1970s. 'David said, "I've got the most fantastic band lined up . . . and I'm really into black music." This was by transatlantic phone call, and I said, "Great, who have you got?" and he said, "Willie Weeks on bass, Andy Newmark on drums, and this new guy from New York called Carlos Alomar." I said, "Say no more, I'll be on the next plane."' The band toiled on the music to near-completion, before Visconti mixed and finished it. But then Bowie called to say that he had a fresh incarnation of the album in mind – thanks to John Lennon.

VERY STRANGE

The evolutionary process had begun in earnest in June 1974. The two-year-old *Ziggy Stardust* had just gone gold in the US, and fans arrived for that summer's tour expecting the carrot-topped spaceman of *Ziggy* and *Aladdin Sane.* Instead, they were presented with the *Diamond Dogs* show, which transformed the recently released album of that name into a theatrical event. So, by night, Bowie peddled a bizarre – albeit brilliant – blend of proto-punk and cabaret. By day, however, as the flight-phobic star crossed the States by car, his soundtrack of choice was not the glam rock with which he was popularly associated, but R&B – especially the 'Philly Soul' sound that, thanks to producers like Kenny Gamble and Leon Huff, and artists like The O'Jays, filled American airwaves. This increasingly fed into the band's live sound, hence the version of Eddie Floyd's soul standard 'Knock On Wood' that found its way onto *David Live,* recorded just before the tour paused in late July.

David Live was taped over a six-night residency in Philadelphia, during which Bowie visited the city's Sigma Sound Studios: the birthplace of Gamble and Huff's 'Philly Soul' productions. His restless imagination already thinking beyond the *Diamond Dogs* tour, the star despatched his assistant to purchase contemporary soul albums. And – having failed to enlist Sigma Sound house band MFSB (who reportedly had no desire to lend their sound to this peculiar white boy) – he recruited new musicians to augment or replace his in-concert cohorts. Saxophonist David Sanborn, pianist Mike Garson, and percussionist

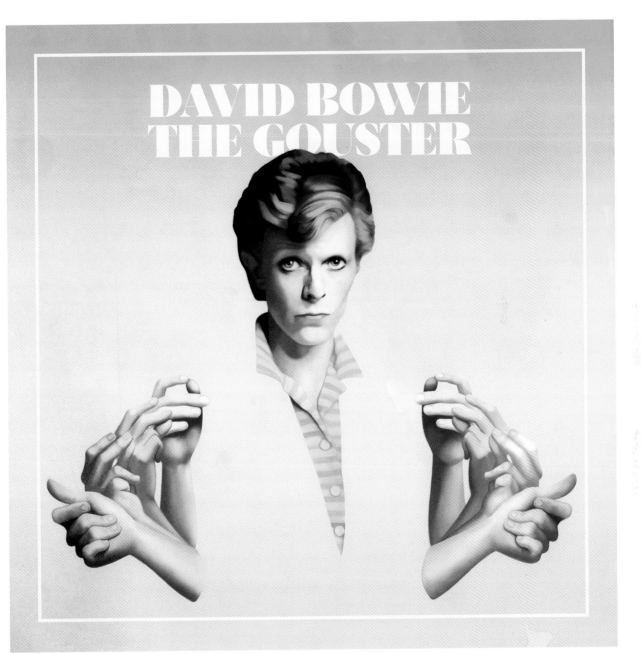

Cover: Akiko Stehrenberger

DIAMOND DOGS

MINISTRY OF SOUND

The Gouster wasn't the only abandoned genesis for a Bowie classic. A year earlier, he had begun contemplating a musical production of George Orwell's *Nineteen Eighty-Four*. 'I shall look very different in it and there's lots of good music . . .' he told *Rolling Stone.* 'Some of it is as much as three years old. I kept a lot of songs back because I knew I wanted them for some kind of show.' Unfortunately, as co-writer (and Warhol associate) Tony Ingrassia said in October 1973, 'We have not fully acquired the rights to the book yet and it's still possible we will have to call it *1983* or something like that!' Just weeks later, Orwell's widow extinguished any hope that permission might be forthcoming, judging the request 'bizarre'. Undaunted, Bowie transformed the songs into *Diamond Dogs,* with only song titles like '1984' and 'Big Brother' hinting at its origins.

Pablo Rosario were joined by the trio whose involvement Bowie had reported to Visconti: Willie Weeks, best known for his work with Donny Hathaway; Andy Newmark, fresh from Sly and the Family Stone; and Carlos Alomar, formerly of the Harlem Apollo's house band. Equally important, however, was a twenty-three-year-old friend of Alomar: singer Luther Vandross. Invited to hang out at Sigma, Vandross began improvising backing vocals to pass the time. One chorus – 'Young Americans, young Americans, we are the young Americans, all right!' – caught Bowie's ear and, within 24 hours of the jetlagged Visconti's arrival, he found himself recording the song that would become a classic.

However, as the producer told the BBC, 'That album did get very strange because we didn't know what we were doing. . . . Although all the songs were written, they were being heavily rearranged as time went on. But nothing was organised and it turned out to be one enormous jam session.'

Songs cut included a funky reworking of the post-*Ziggy* single 'John, I'm Only Dancing', the sweeping 'Who Can I Be Now?' and 'It's Gonna Be Me', and the never released 'Shilling the Rubes' and 'I Am a Laser' (the latter a revisiting of a song cut in 1973 by Bowie's protégés the Astronettes).

THIS WEIRD GUY

Two other songs eventually surfaced on 1989's *Sound + Vision* box set: the disco-flecked 'After Today' and a cover of then cult artist Bruce Springsteen's 'It's Hard to Be a Saint in the City'. At Visconti's request, a DJ at Philadelphia radio station WMMR station invited Springsteen – then a year away from hitting the big time with *Born to Run* – to the studio. The soon-to-be Boss duly made his way by public transport from his Asbury Park stomping ground to Philly. 'That ride had a real cast of characters . . .' he told *The Drummer.* 'Every bus has a serviceman, an old lady in a brown coat with one of these little black things on her head, and the drunk who falls out next to you.' Those characters, however, were no match for the increasingly skeletal coke vampire who swanned into the studio after dark. 'I was out of my wig,' Bowie confessed to *Musician* in 1987. 'I just couldn't relate to him at all. It was a bad time for us to have met. I could see what he was thinking: "Who is this weird guy?" And I was thinking, "What do I say to normal people?" There was a real impasse.'

Visconti took the Sigma Sound tapes back to England – where he customarily worked with Bowie's one-time rival Marc Bolan – and compiled them into an album dubbed *The Gouster.* Its title, the producer recalled, 'was a black word which meant a cool guy, a hip guy who walks down the street snapping his fingers.' The track listing, at that point, read thusly:

Side 1: John, I'm Only Dancing (Again) · Somebody Up There Likes Me · It's Gonna Be Me
Side 2: Who Can I Be Now? · Can You Hear Me · Young Americans · Right

In September, Bowie returned to the road, but *Diamond Dogs* had given way to 'Philly Dogs'. Bored by the theatrical trappings of the summer, he turned his new band – including Vandross – into a soul revue whose repertoire included

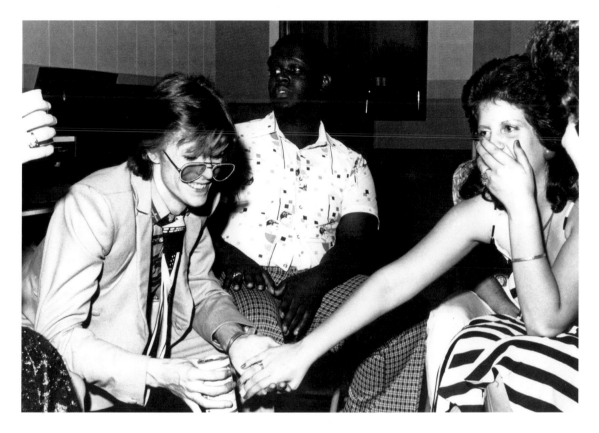

The Flares' 'Foot Stomping pt 1', a proto-R&B cut from 1961. 'I "glit" from one thing to another a lot,' he told chat show host Dick Cavett in a legendarily odd interview. 'It's like "flip" but it's the seventies version. . . . Now that I'm working just with the band and singing – which is something I haven't done for years: just stand there and sing my songs – I'm finding a new kind of fulfilment.'

ONE DAMN SONG
Bowie gave reporter Robert Hilburn a preview of the album, then tentatively titled *One Damn Song* (a quote from 'Young Americans'). 'We cut it in a week in Philadelphia and it can tell you more about where I am now than anything I could say . . . ' he explained. 'I think it is the closest thing I've ever done on record to being very, very me . . . On most albums I was acting. It was a role, generally. And this one is the nearest to actually meeting me since that very first *Space Oddity* album, which was quite personal. I'm really excited about it.'

But Bowie could not resist tinkering further. When the 'Philly Dogs' tour wrapped in December, he and Visconti entered New York's Record Plant studio to cut 'Win' and 'Fascination' – the latter making Vandross one of the few people, at that point, to earn a co-writing credit on a Bowie album. '"Fascination" was a song (of mine) called "Funky Music" . . .' the singer told *Q*. 'He wanted to record it but he had to change the title. He said, "I'm doing an

SIGMA KIDS
Bowie, future superstar Luther Vandross, and fan Marla Kanevsky at the Sigma sessions, shot by photographer Dagmar. Kanevsky was one of the 'Sigma Kids': fans who hung out at the studio and were invited to hear the work in progress. When she boldly asked Bowie to marry her, 'He said something like, "You'll have to speak to my wife about that, love."'

R&B album but I don't want to be so presumptuous as to call anything "Funky Music". He changed it to a song about this girl called Fascination. At that time, I had six dollars in the bank. I said, "Fine – please, whatever, help yourself!"'

Disc magazine duly announced the album was to be titled *Fascination,* with 'Win' and 'Fascination' displacing 'Who Can I Be Now' and 'Somebody Up There Likes Me'. However, the road to release was to yield yet another twist.

SPUR OF THE MOMENT

'About two weeks after I'd mixed the album,' explained Visconti, 'David phoned to say that he and John Lennon had got together one night and recorded this song called "Fame".' The pair had met at a party in Beverly Hills in September. Lennon, then enjoying his 'Lost Weekend' (a trial separation from Yoko Ono) with mistress May Pang, was introduced to Bowie by Elizabeth Taylor. 'David was odd,' Pang told writer Paul Trynka. 'He seemed stand-offish.' When Bowie excused himself after just seconds to retreat to another room with Taylor, Pang recalled, 'John didn't know what to think. Me, him, and Elton (John) were looking at each other: 'What was *that* about?''

Nonetheless, Bowie called Lennon to arrange a meeting when, after the end of the Dogs tour in December 1974, he visited New York. Visconti, invited along to ease his charge's nerves, recalled to the *Daily Telegraph*: 'We stayed

TOO COOL TO FOOL
Of his time with John Lennon (below, with Bowie and Yoko Ono at the Grammys in February 1975), Bowie recalled, 'We spent endless hours talking about fame, and what it's like not having a life of your own any more. How much you want to be known before you are, and then, when you are, how much you want the reverse.'

up with John Lennon until 10.30 a.m. We did a mountain of cocaine – it looked like the Matterhorn, obscenely big – and four open bottles of cognac.' (Visconti evidently also hit it off with May Pang, whom he married in 1989. In the meantime, she appeared in the video for Bowie's 1980 hit 'Fashion'.)

At a subsequent rendezvous in mid-January 1975, where Lennon and Pang were joined by Paul and Linda McCartney, Bowie endlessly played mixes from his still unreleased album. With both Beatles' patience tested, Lennon asked – to Bowie's mortification – 'Is there anything else we can listen to?'

> ## *'We did a mountain of cocaine – it looked like the Matterhorn, obscenely big.'*
> Tony Visconti

Just days later, with ruffled feathers smoothed, Bowie invited Lennon to the recording of 'Across the Universe', a 1969 Beatles song that he intended to cover. While they were at New York's Electric Lady studio, Lennon fooled around with an acoustic guitar, singing disco act Shirley & Company's freshly minted classic 'Shame Shame Shame'. Mishearing 'shame' as 'fame', Bowie conjured a vicious lyrical concept that he married to a funky riff Alomar had adapted from The Rascals' 'Jungle Walk' to bolster the live set's 'Foot Stomping'. (This adaptation can be heard in a performance of the latter from the *Dick Cavett Show* appearance, available on 1995's *Rarest One Bowie*.)

'I hope you don't mind, Tony,' Bowie told Visconti. 'It was so spontaneous and spur of the moment. And we also did "Across the Universe" and took out a few words and added a few, and we got on great.' 'He was very apologetic and nice about it,' recalled the producer, who was aggrieved only to have missed the opportunity to record Lennon himself. 'He said he hoped I wouldn't mind if we took a few tracks off, and included these, and I said that was all right.'

The Gouster was long dead and Bowie, living on milk and cocaine, arguably should have been. (*David Live,* he conceded, should have been called *David Bowie Is Alive and Well and Living Only In Theory.*) Instead, with an album that had gestated longer than *Ziggy Stardust* and *Aladdin Sane* combined, he was about to enter a whole new chapter of superstardom. **BM**

WHAT HAPPENED NEXT . . .
Bolstered by the US chart-topping success of 'Fame', *Young Americans* – issued less than a year after *Diamond Dogs* – followed its predecessor into the British, American, and Australian top tens. Described by Bowie as 'relentless plastic soul', the album withstood the weediness of its 'Across the Universe' cover, the choice of which baffled even its composer. 'I like it a lot,' Bowie insisted to *NME,* 'and I think I sing very well at the end of it. People say I used John Lennon on the track – but let me tell you, no one *uses* John Lennon. John just came and played on it. He was lovely.'

WILL IT EVER HAPPEN?
3/10 Cuts dismissed from *The Gouster* would, as Tony Visconti predicted in the early 1980s, 'be released at some point in the future' (namely 'Who Can I Be Now' and 'It's Gonna Be Me', on Rykodisc's 1991 reissue of *Young Americans*). However, while fans would be delighted to have the songs cut at the Sigma sessions released in full, Bowie has not taken an active interest in the repackaging of his old albums since the excellent but sadly curtailed Rykodisc campaign kickstarted by *Sound + Vision.* And – bar an excellent *Station to Station* set in 2010 – his corporate paymasters seem obsessed with endless reissues of *Ziggy Stardust* and *Aladdin Sane.*

BLOOD ON THE TRACKS

Artist Bob Dylan **Year** 1975 **Country** US **Genre** Folk rock **Label** Columbia
What His defining 1970s masterpiece . . . ditched

BOB DYLAN
Dylan, said *Blood on the Tracks* engineer Phil Ramone, 'is truly spontaneous in all ways of life.' While this is most evident on stage – live collaborator Tom Petty tells tales of starting songs with no idea how they were supposed to sound – it also informed his last-minute decision to junk half of what became his best-loved album.

Settling down at A&R Recording in New York to cut his first fully-fledged solo album since 1970, Bob Dylan was looking to do justice to songs he had written since his marriage to Sara Lowndes hit the rocks. The intervening years had seen a self-titled collection of off-cuts, a soundtrack, and a brace of albums with The Band. After an over-subscribed tour with the latter at the start of 1974, Dylan was emerging from a six-month hiatus, his position in the rock pantheon not yet as solid as it is today. Hiring session musicians – at least one of whom (bassist Tony Brown) he had never met – Dylan quickly cut fifteen tracks, beginning on 16 September 1974, and finishing just four days later. His plan was to recapture the swift working practices that had defined his early, pre-electric career. But the musicians – including banjo player Eric Weissberg, who had topped the US chart with an album featuring his *Deliverance* classic 'Dueling Banjos' – had trouble keeping up with the pace, with songs they hadn't heard, and with keys that were entirely unfamiliar.

LETTING HIS SOUL BLEED
'*Blood on the Tracks* was the result of a year of letting his soul bleed into the songs again . . .' wrote Dylan chronicler Clinton Heylin. 'The process, though, of getting an album out of the fifteen songs he scribbled into his notebook that summer (proved) the most tortuous since (1966's) *Blonde on Blonde.*' As engineer Phil Ramone observed to *Billboard*'s Craig Rosen, the session men – though 'all natural players who could shift with the wind' – were often baffled by an artist who 'doesn't telegraph what chords he is going to play. . . . He will change his mind about how many bars there should be between a verse, or eliminate a verse, or add a chorus when you don't expect it.' 'It was weird,' Weissberg agreed. 'You couldn't really watch his fingers 'cos he was playing in a tuning arrangement I had never seen before. It put us at a real disadvantage.'

The tunes Dylan laid down were sparse, harking back to the more simple, one-man-and-his-guitar approach that had propelled him into the public consciousness over a decade previously. 'Buckets of Rain' feels like a grown-up, world-weary take on his *Freewheelin'* (1963) period, while the original cut of 'Tangled Up In Blue' has the loping sound of an early strum-along.

Cover: Isabel Eeles

WHAT HAPPENED NEXT . . .

David Zimmerman set up a session for Dylan at Sound 80 Studios in Minneapolis, employing relatively unknown musicians to re-cut the songs with which his brother was unhappy. 'Tangled Up in Blue', 'Lily, Rosemary and the Jack of Hearts', 'Idiot Wind', 'If You See Her, Say Hello', and 'You're a Big Girl Now' were reworked, ditching the sixties vibe for a band-focused approach.

The album emerged a month later than planned, on 20 January 1975. As it rose to the US No.1, the original acetate became an in-demand bootleg. Pete Hammill's liner notes earned a Grammy, despite being based on the acetate and therefore citing lyrics and musicians absent from the final album.

Whittled down to ten songs ('Up to Me' and 'Call Letter Blues' hit the cutting room floor), the results were presented to Columbia – to whom Dylan had recently re-signed after a flirtation with Asylum that yielded the two albums with The Band. The label duly pressed an acetate of the LP and sent it out to reviewers ahead of a planned Christmas release. This first version, opined *Village Voice* writer Robert Christgau, 'struck me as a sellout to the memory of Dylan's pre-electric period.' The artist apparently felt the same. He took the pressing back home to Minnesota and played it to his brother, David Zimmerman, who suggested it lacked commercial appeal. Dylan's mind was made up. He binned half of the record, despite it being due to hit shelves in a matter of days. 'I thought the songs could have sounded differently – better,' he said, years later. 'So I went in and re-recorded them.' **JM**

9/10

WILL IT EVER HAPPEN?

Only one track from the acetate has been officially released: 'You're a Big Girl Now,' on the box set *Biograph* (1985). However, alternate takes appeared on *The Bootleg Series Volumes 1–3* (1991). A complete set of the original recordings is expected as part of *The Bootleg Series 11,* reported to focus on the sessions for *Blood on the Tracks* and mooted for release in 2014.

HOMEGROWN

Artist Neil Young **Year** 1975 **Country** US **Genre** Country rock **Label** Reprise
What A break-up album that could have been the next *Harvest*

NEIL YOUNG
'You gotta keep changing . . .' Young told *Rolling Stone* in 1975 about his habit for reinvention. 'I'd rather keep changing and lose a lot of people along the way. If that's the price, I'll pay it. I don't give a shit if my audience is 100 or 100 million. It doesn't make any difference to me.'

Neil Young's world fell apart in March 1974. The singer-songwriter had landed in Hawaii, hoping to reunite with actress Carrie Snodgress – his estranged wife and the subject of songs including 'A Man Needs a Maid' and 'Motion Pictures'. He soon discovered that Snodgress – the mother of his first son, Zeke – wasn't waiting for him. She was out on a boat trip with another man. 'I kinda had a major bummer, which resulted in drinking a lot of tequila,' he told biographer Jimmy McDonough. 'And then I went out and played my guitar in God knows where, for God knows who.' In the months that followed, the songs would stream from him like tears.

GOING THROUGH HELL
Young's state of mind hardly improved on the mammoth 'doom tour' with Crosby, Stills & Nash (see page 62). That summer's *On the Beach* was duly hailed by *Rolling Stone* as one of the 'most despairing albums of the decade'. In November, he headed to Quadrafonic – the Nashville studio where he had laid down the bulk of his breakthrough 1972 album *Harvest* – to begin sessions for a sixth solo LP, *Homegrown*. The desolate title of one of the first songs attempted, 'Frozen Man', set the tone for much of what was to come. 'The theme of that album was basically the demise of his relationship with Carrie,' said producer Elliot Mazer. 'It was intense, like trying to make a record in the middle of 42nd Street or Vietnam. . . . Here's a guy going through hell, and this is like a fuckin' catharsis for him – a chance to get these songs out. It was a great relief.' Young detailed his crumbling marriage in painful detail on the bluesy 'Separate Ways'. With The Band's drummer Levon Helm laying down a soulful beat, and longtime collaborator Ben Keith picking out a stark pedal steel solo, Young sang, 'As we go our separate ways / Lookin' for better days / Sharin' our little boy / Who grew from joy back then.'

Throughout December 1974 and January 1975, Young recorded both in Nashville and at his Broken Arrow ranch in California. Among the tracks were sparse solo acoustic performances, like 'Homefires' and 'Love-Art Blues', in which Young accepted some of the blame for the collapse of his marriage, admitting he had prioritised music over love. Others were recorded

Cover: Damian Jaques

NOT FADE AWAY

Everything was going Young's way in early 1973. His most recent album, *Harvest,* had topped the US chart. 'Heart of Gold' was a radio hit. He was about to embark on an arena tour. But painful back problems and the loss of Crazy Horse guitarist Danny Whitten – who had fatally overdosed in November 1972 – turned the tour into a miserable slog.

'Neil was sort of dribbling out of the side of his mouth,' manager Elliot Roberts told writer Barney Hoskyns. 'He was getting booed off the stage on that tour, the mood was so down. He wasn't playing one hit, one song from *Gold Rush* or *Harvest* that you came to lay down your good poundage for.' 'The audiences,' confirmed second guitarist Nils Lofgren, 'were freaking out.' Young vented his anger by blasting unreleased material that would end up on 1973's live *Time Fades Away.* Tracks like 'Yonder Stands the Sinner' and 'Last Dance' were ragged, electric masterpieces, and the album went gold in a month, but Young subsequently dismissed it as 'the worst record I ever made' and refused to release it on CD.

with a band: 'Homegrown', a stomping, sloppy tribute to marijuana, and 'Old Homestead', an oblique, hallucinatory tale of a 'naked rider' chasing his muse. The album's one bright note was 'Try' – a gentle piano ballad, featuring background vocals from Emmylou Harris, that could have been pulled from 1970's *After The Gold Rush* – in which Young called out to his love, 'We've got lots of time / To get together if we try.'

To finish *Homegrown,* Young and Ben Keith relocated to the Village Recorders studio in Los Angeles. 'Neil left the ranch, had to get away,' said his friend, *Zuma* cover artist James Mazzeo. 'Too many ghosts.' The resulting tracks were short, fragmentary, and dream-like. On the solo number 'Mexico', Young imagined fleeing south of the border, 'to live beyond the fears.' 'Florida',

CORN IN THE USA.
The leafy connotations of the *Homegrown* title were subverted by an innocuous central image of a farmer on the album's original artwork. The cover was by Tom Wilkes, who had created Young's *Harvest* sleeve and whose later credits included the star's compilation *Decade.*

'It was intense, like trying to make a record in the middle of 42nd Street or Vietnam.'

Elliot Mazer

meanwhile, was a surreal spoken word experiment, accompanied by the high-pitched drone of a wet finger drawn around the rim of a glass.

After final mixing, Mazer headed to Britain, where he played a tape of the album to a friend: Chris Wright, then head of the Chrysalis label. Impressed, Wright assured Mo Ostin, then president of Warner Bros/Reprise, that the US label had another multi-million seller on their hands. A cover was duly designed for the album, depicting a barefoot farmer chomping on a corncob.

PRETTY FUCKED UP

Meanwhile, Young gathered friends at Los Angeles' Chateau Marmont hotel – including pianist Richard Manuel and bassist Rick Danko of The Band, Louisiana singer-songwriter Bobby Charles, and drummer Ralph Molina and bassist Billy Talbot of Young's sometime backing band, Crazy Horse – to get their opinion of the finished work. 'It was late at night,' Young told McDonough. 'We were all pretty fucked up, listenin' to tapes, on the edge.'

When *Homegrown* had played through, a recording of Young's abrasive and, at the time, unreleased 1973 set *Tonight's the Night* came on. The album was a tribute to deceased Crazy Horse guitarist Danny Whitten and CSNY roadie Bruce Berry. 'What we were doing was playing those guys on their way . . .' Young told *NME*. 'I'm not a junkie and I won't even try it out to check out what it's like. But we'd get really high . . . drink a lot of tequila, get right out on the edge, where we were so screwed up that we could easily just fall on our faces, and not be able to handle it as musicians. But we were wide open also . . . So we'd just wait until the middle of the night, until the vibe hit us, and just do it.'

On hearing *Tonight's the Night,* '(Rick) Danko freaked,' reported Molina. 'He said, "If you guys don't release this fuckin' album, you're crazy."' Undeterred by Reprise's verdict – 'If you put this album out, it could be the end of your career' – Young released *Tonight's The Night* instead of *Homegrown* in June 1975. (Mazer chortled when he recalled Chris Wright's endorsement of the new album to Mo Ostin. 'They gave Mo *Tonight's the Night* instead,' he told Young biographer Johnny Rogan. 'Mo must have wondered, Is Chris crazy?')

TOO RAW, TOO HONEST

Young himself hadn't required much persuading to shelve *Homegrown,* having suspected for some time that the album was too raw and emotionally honest. 'That record might be more what people would rather hear from me now, but it was just a very down album,' he confessed to *Rolling Stone* in 1975. 'A lot of the songs had to do with me breaking up with my old lady. It was a little too personal . . . it scared me. Plus I had just released *On The Beach,* probably one of the most depressing records I've ever made. I don't want to get down to the point where I can't even get up.' (Somewhat ironically, when Snodgress and Young first got together, the actress said she 'fell in love with Neil's pain'.)

About a third of the cuts from the *Homegrown* sessions would appear within years: 'Star of Bethlehem' on *American Stars 'n Bars* (1977), 'Deep Forbidden Lake' and 'Love Is a Rose' on the compilation *Decade* (1977), 'Little Wing' and 'Old Homestead' on 1980's *Hawks & Doves* (1980). Others – including 'Separate Ways', 'Mexico', and 'Love-Art Blues' – have only been performed on stage and hence can be found on bootlegs. 'But to hear *Homegrown* in its entirety,' suggests Jimmy McDonough, 'is to hear Neil Young at his best.' **TB**

WHAT HAPPENED NEXT . . .
Young separated from Snodgress and finally kicked the blues. Rejuvenated, he reunited with his backing band Crazy Horse, with whom his last full album was 1969's *Everybody Knows This Is Nowhere*. The group settled in a six-bedroom house in Malibu across the street from Goldie Hawn's mansion, partied with beautiful California girls, and laid down an album of crude and catchy hard rock. The resultant *Zuma* was released in November 1975, just five months after *Tonight's The Night*. 'Neil was the happiest I've ever known him during *Zuma*,' producer David Briggs told Jimmy McDonough. 'The recording was just an extension of our everyday life.'

WILL IT EVER HAPPEN?

8/10

After almost two decades of broken promises, delays, and disappointments, Young finally gave fans access to his vast vault of unreleased recordings. In 2009, he put out *Archives Vol. 1* – a long-anticipated box set chronicling the first decade of his career and boasting forty-seven never-before-heard tracks. At the time, Young's management promised that *Vol. 2* would hit stores within three years, and would feature four 'lost' albums from the 1970s, including a remastered version of *Homegrown*. Fans are still waiting for that fabled box set to appear and, judging by the star's history of missed deadlines, could be left hanging for a long time yet.

HOODOO

Artist John Fogerty **Year** 1976 **Country** US **Genre** Swamp rock **Label** Asylum **What** When the chooglin' stops

JOHN FOGERTY
'Could I wear eye shadow and get away with it?' the star asked *Phonograph Record* as he readied *Hoodoo,* wondering how to fit in with a decade that had left him behind. 'I'm trying to make this album a more accurate representation of what I feel,' he continued. 'I don't know – you'll have to hear it, really.' As it turned out, however, only determined pursuers of bootlegs would be able to make the call.

With classics like 'Proud Mary', 'Bad Moon Rising', and 'Who'll Stop the Rain', singer and guitarist John Fogerty defined US roots rock, as hungover hippies adjusted to the advent of the 1970s. His band Creedence Clearwater Revival scored two chart-topping albums – and etched in the grooves of *Green River* and *Cosmo's Factory* were influences on future stars from Bruce Springsteen to Pavement's Stephen Malkmus. But Creedence's explosive success preceded a sharp decline. Amid grumbles from Fogerty's bandmates about his domination of the group, his brother and rhythm guitarist Tom quit after 1970's *Pendulum,* while bassist Stu Cook and drummer Doug 'Cosmo' Clifford insisted on co-producing 1972's *Mardi Gras.* The result, according to *Rolling Stone* reviewer – and future Springsteen manager – Jon Landau, was 'the worst album I have ever heard from a major band' (although both it and *Pendulum* quickly went gold). Riven by dissent, the band split in October 1972. And, for Fogerty, things went from bad to worse.

A LOT OF DAMAGE

His first solo album, issued in 1973 under the name Blue Ridge Rangers, crept into the US top fifty. But while Creedence's legacy was milked by their label Fantasy, Fogerty's self-titled 1975 album stalled at number seventy-eight, despite its hit 'Rockin' All Over the World' (subsequently adopted by Status Quo). The relationship between Fogerty and Fantasy grew increasingly litigious, affecting the star's world-view and bank balance. 'It did a lot of damage . . .' he told *Billboard* writer Craig Rosen. 'There were times in those years when I was scared to go in and buy a pair of socks in a department store.'

Under the circumstances, it was unsurprising that *Hoodoo* did not find Fogerty at his finest. ('It stunk,' he subsequently conceded to *Q.*) Barely half an hour long, the album echoed former glories only on 'Hoodoo Man'. The rest – including a funky cover of Ray Charles's 'Leave My Woman Alone' – was hardly disgraceful, but nor was it likely to challenge Springsteen or Bob Seger, who had inherited his blue-collar fanbase. The album's chances were fatally torpedoed by its opening song: the disco-flecked 'You Got the Magic' ('A kind of love song,' he observed, 'but not, you know, strings or any of that crap').

Cover: John Pasche

WHAT HAPPENED NEXT . . .
Thoroughly disillusioned, Fogerty
retreated to a farm in Oregon and
effectively disappeared until 1985.
His comeback proved spectacularly
successful: *Centerfield* made him
one of the select few to score US
chart-toppers in the 1960s, 1970s,
and 1980s. But there was a sting in
the tale: Fantasy chief Saul Zaentz
threatened to sue unless its barely
veiled 'Zanz Kant Danz' was re-titled
on subsequent pressings. Then he
did sue, alleging that *Centerfield*'s
hit 'The Old Man Down the Road'
sounded too similar to Creedence's
classic 'Run Through the Jungle',
the copyright to which Fantasy held.
Happily, Fogerty won the case.

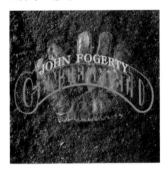

Issued as a single, it charted at a deservedly unremarkable No. 87. And though
Hoodoo had both a cover and a catalogue number ready to go, Fogerty and his
label Asylum agreed the album was best shelved.

'This was not a humiliation,' he told *BAM* magazine. 'This was constructive,
really, because the company was willing to back me up all the way. . . . I felt
pressured myself: that I owed product to Asylum. The first album I gave them
wasn't very good . . . This one was obviously worse than that, and (label boss)
Joe Smith was saying, "John, you don't have to make another record right
now. We'd like it when it's ready, but we're not standing here with a rock over
your head demanding a record." He said it seemed like I was having some
problems, and why didn't I go work those out, whatever they were? That was
the greatest thing that ever happened.' **BM**

WILL IT EVER HAPPEN?

2/10 Fogerty asked for the master tapes to be destroyed, but it's not
inconceivable that *Hoodoo* might find its way into a box set. 'I
understand it's a lukewarm bootleg album,' he remarked. 'It's only interesting
if you're a die-hard fan and you want to hear an outtake or something.' A
straightforward reissue of the original, therefore, is extremely unlikely.

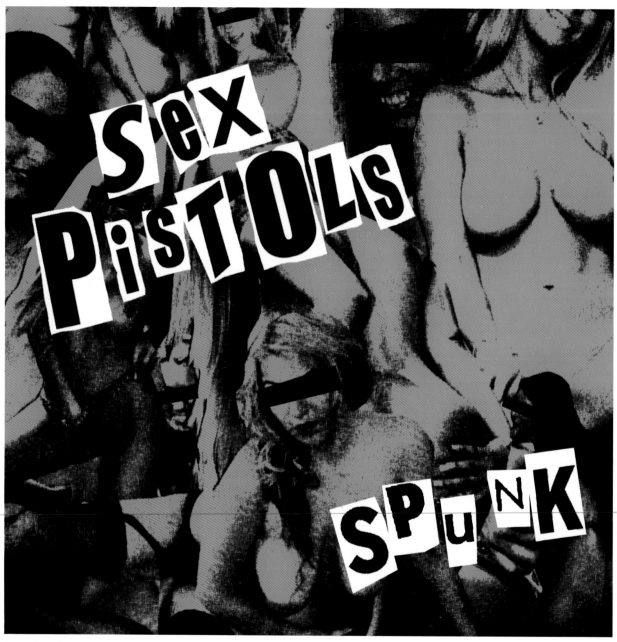

Cover: Tom Howey

SPUNK

Artist Sex Pistols **Year** 1977 **Country** UK **Genre** Punk **Label** Virgin **What** A tale of two albums

For a long time during 1976, it appeared a safe bet that Dave Goodman – soul bassist turned producer – would helm the Sex Pistols' debut album. Even during the band's ultimately doomed courtship with their first label EMI, Goodman claims that manager Malcolm McLaren told him: 'Your tapes done the trick – play your cards right and your name could be on the records of the biggest musical phenomenon since Gene Vincent.' Little did Goodman know what the immediate future would hold . . .

DEFINITIVE ROCK MADNESS
Late 1977: the standard-bearers of punk are not leading from the front. First albums by The Damned and The Clash have long been in the record racks. But the world is still waiting for the Sex Pistols, despite their forming the best part of a year before either of those rival bands made their live debuts. Suddenly, however, persistent patrons are offered two options. Just before *Never Mind the Bollocks Here's the Sex Pistols* lands, the mysterious *Spunk* surfaces, with no one stepping forward to take credit for its release.

Goodman, an important figure often airbrushed from Pistols lore, is thought to have played his mixes of tracks including 'Anarchy in the UK' to *NME* gunslinger Tony Parsons in March 1977. By October, knowing customers at an independent London record store were able to pick up a twelve-track album in a plain, white sleeve with a bare minimum of information, but with the following track listing (later titles are in square brackets):

Lazy Sod [Seventeen] · Satelite [Satellite] · Feelings [No Feelings] · Just Me [I Wanna Be Me] · Submission · Nookie [Anarchy in the UK] · No Future [God Save the Queen] · Problems · Lots of Fun [Pretty Vacant] · Liar · Who Was It [EMI] · New York (Looking for a Kiss) [New York]

'Stunningly inventive . . .' marvelled *Sounds'* Chas de Whalley. 'Real, definitive rock madness.' *Spunk* was on its way to becoming, as Clinton Heylin declared in *Bootleg: The Rise & Fall of the Secret Recording Industry,* 'undoubtedly the 1970s' most legendary bootleg.'

JOHNNY ROTTEN
'They're the best we've had so far,' said the Pistols front man of Virgin, the band's third record label. (They had signed to, and been booted off, both A&M and EMI within six months.) 'At least they don't overwhelm us with political bullshit. . . . *No one* tries to tell us what to bring out.'

UH OH ZONE

In a 1977 interview, John Lydon swore retribution against the unnamed party behind *Spunk*. Later, he engaged in another feud, this time with Public Image Ltd co-founder Keith Levene (left, with the singer in more harmonious times). *Commercial Zone* (1984) was made up of tapes that the guitarist – who left in 1983 – took to America. Copies of this US-only release found their way to Britain, where they trod on the toes of PiL's *This Is What You Want . . .* (1984). 'It's not supposed to be sold or released anywhere,' complained drummer Martin Atkins, but *Melody Maker* claimed the album was 'not such a bitter PiL to swallow.'

COMMERCiAL ZONE

PiL

LiMiTED EDiTiON

ROTTEN RECORDING

'If you played any of the demos, you would recognise they were by the Sex Pistols, not least because Johnny's (above, with Goodman, left) voice is so distinctive,' *Never Mind the Bollocks* co-producer Bill Price told *Sound on Sound*. 'They might have had slightly different tempos and slightly different arrangements, but there was nothing too drastic . . . There weren't harps or violas!'

FOCUS THE BLITZKRIEG

Singer Johnny Rotten, guitarist Steve Jones, drummer Paul Cook, and bassist Glen Matlock had laid down tracks in May 1976, but the major moves were made under Goodman. A self-confessed hippie, Goodman was nevertheless quick to be swept up in the teeth of the gale after working on the sound at a Pistols gig in April that year. On hearing the demos, as he said in *My Amazing Adventures with the Sex Pistols,* 'I knew immediately I could do better.'

The first stop – in July 1976 – was a space on London's Denmark Street that was also a makeshift home for Jones. Matlock judged it 'squalid' in *I Was a Teenage Sex Pistol,* but – with a little producer's feng shui, such as angling a flight case a certain distance from the amp to focus the blitzkrieg – it served its purpose. Jones's guitar sounded, said Goodman, like it was 'being played at ten million watts.' To what Goodman called 'seven happening backing tracks,' Rotten added vocals in less than four hours at Riverside Studios in London.

'Pretty Vacant' was the prime contender for the first single, before it was supplanted by 'Anarchy in the U.K.' However, doing justice to what became punk's call to arms was not easy at London's Lansdowne Studios in October 1976. Acts aimed at creating an incendiary atmosphere – setting fires and smashing bottles – failed. Goodman tried the diversionary tactic of having the band run through covers before returning to 'Anarchy in the U.K.' at Wessex Studios. The result, he declared, was 'a great, pounding take.'

A third burst of activity with Goodman took place in January 1977. By the middle of the month, Matlock had played his last live Pistols gig (in Amsterdam), but remained for studio purposes. (Jones would later take over bass duties on Pistols recordings, Matlock's replacement Sid Vicious being unable to play even after lessons from Lemmy of Motörhead.) At Gooseberry Studios in London, six tracks were laid down, including 'God Save the Queen'.

However, the waters were beginning to get murky: producer Chris Thomas – who had worked with The Beatles and Pink Floyd – had been engaged to work on 'Anarchy in the U.K.' 'I later played both versions back to back and still couldn't see why mine hadn't been released,' said Goodman, but his track record could not compare to Thomas's résumé. 'I was never given the chance to finish the record I'd started,' he complained. Those who had not heard the bootleg could gauge his work from B-sides – 'I Wanna Be Me' on 'Anarchy in the U.K.' and 'No Fun' on 'Pretty Vacant' – but it is *Spunk* that is his legacy.

As for who unleashed that beast, Goodman denied any culpability: 'I didn't do it – honest.' Fingers pointed at Malcolm McLaren, especially as EMI A&R man Nick Mobbs said the manager 'retained the full rights to everything the band ever did.' But even for a self-styled master manipulator, to have upstaged his own cause célèbre with a scene-stealing album just before the Virgin release of *Never Mind the Bollocks* seems a provocation too far. And with both Goodman and McLaren now deceased (in 2005 and 2010, respectively), the main suspects have departed the scene.

> *'I was never given the chance to finish the record I'd started.'*
>
> Dave Goodman

BRUTAL SNAPSHOT

Both *Spunk* and *Never Mind the Bollocks* have supporters. The latter feels more like a finished product, but many contend that Thomas and co-producer Bill Price's buffing of the music to the point of being muscle-bound missed one of punk's points. *Spunk,* in contrast, was made up of – as Clinton Heylin put it – 'gut-wrenching, taut performances captured in all their rough 'n' ready earthiness.' And while Matlock's melodic bass diverts some attention from Jones's monolithic leads, it also makes for a more complete sound. Punk chronicler Jon Savage states that McLaren, perversely, preferred *Spunk.*

At the close of an obscenity trial in Nottingham in late November 1977, a weary-sounding chairman had to declare that *Never Mind the Bollocks* was not an affront to British society. 'We must reluctantly find you not guilty,' he said. Had the provocatively titled *Spunk* been more on the radar than under the counter, it too may have prompted another examination of the acceptable limits of the English language. As it is, the album is the best, most brutal studio snapshot of the original Sex Pistols, before caricature set in. As Clinton Heylin put it, this was young men 'cutting loose the cobwebs of the 1970s.' **CB**

WHAT HAPPENED NEXT . . .

Spunk did not noticeably affect sales of *Never Mind the Bollocks Here's the Sex Pistols,* which topped the UK album chart in December 1977. Richard Branson's Virgin label still had cause for complaint over its existence and, especially, its timing, but investigations into unmasking the culprit were evidently not exhaustive and no prosecutions were launched. Two further Goodman productions did see the light, though neither are likely to have been enthusiastically sanctioned by him or the band. Ramshackle versions of 'Johnny B Goode' and 'Roadrunner', from the October 1976 'Anarchy' sessions, were immortalised on the soundtrack of *The Great Rock 'n' Roll Swindle.*

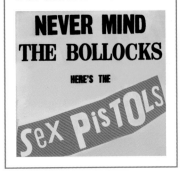

WILL IT EVER HAPPEN?

10/10 The lure of an album that has been tagged the Pistols' alternative debut proved too much to resist. The bootleg was itself bootlegged very quickly, 'the sound quality deteriorating with every repressing,' bemoaned Goodman. One of the better efforts was *No Future U.K?,* which supercharged the content with three extra tracks from Goodman's 1976 sessions, including the quartet's heart-stopping assault on the Stooges' 'No Fun'. Virgin, having worked through their initial ire, released a slightly abbreviated *Spunk* as part of a package entitled *Spunk/Cut the Crap* in 1996.

CHROME DREAMS

Artist Neil Young **Year** 1976 **Country** US **Genre** Country rock **Label** Reprise **What** Just a dream

NEIL YOUNG
The maverick's abrupt changes of mind bewildered not only fans and critics, but even his own band. 'No one ever mentioned we were doin' an album *ever,*' Crazy Horse guitarist Frank Sampedro told biographer Jimmy McDonough. 'We just played and recorded. Every once in a while Neil would say – and I remember it shocking us – "Hey man, I sent in a record." I said, "Oh yeah? What was on it?"'

Biographers have tried and failed to pin him down, but this much we do know about Neil Young: there are lots of them. And that's before we take parallel dimensions into account. In another universe, Neil never met Stephen Stills and Richie Furay in an LA traffic jam. Never played Woodstock with Crosby, Stills & Nash. Came from nowhere to build a following with whiny confessionals like *Homegrown,* later jumping on the grunge bandwagon with *Times Square.* Among his obsessive fans, legends abound of scrapped masterpieces like *Everybody Knows This Is Nowhere* and stabs at mainstream success, like the country-tinged *Harvest* and punk-inspired *Rust Never Sleeps.* Young promises to issue them all as part of his *Archives* series, a retrospective that will only be released when someone invents the MP3 – the low bitrate holy grail for which he's been striving since his only brush with the mainstream: *Chrome Dreams,* one of *the* unheralded classics of the 1970s.

TOO GOOD TO BE TRUE
In *this* dimension, the album is one of many Young has delayed, disowned, or abandoned on his long, eccentric journey. It may even have never existed. 'What *Chrome Dreams* really was,' its creator told Jimmy McDonough, 'was a sketch that (producer David) Briggs drew of a grille and front of a '55 Chrysler – and, if you turned it on its end, it was this beautiful chick.'

More an idea than an album, *Chrome Dreams* nonetheless captures perfectly the whirlwind of Young's personal and musical associations between 1974 and 1977. It includes classics – often in superior form to their official versions – and obscurities that would still be finding their way onto albums in the early 1990s. The idea was implanted in a 1976 issue of *Rolling Stone,* which announced a tour with Crazy Horse, 'scheduled for November, just about when he'll release his next LP, planned as *Chrome Dreams.*' Also scheduled for that November was *Decade,* a retrospective Young had been compiling for months. *Decade* would be delayed for almost a year, but *Chrome Dreams* vanished as *American Stars 'n Bars* (1977) and *Comes A Time* (1978) emerged in its place.

Was *Chrome Dreams* just an early title for *Stars 'n Bars?* If so, why had that not appeared in 1976? Was it a lost album like 1975's *Homegrown* (see

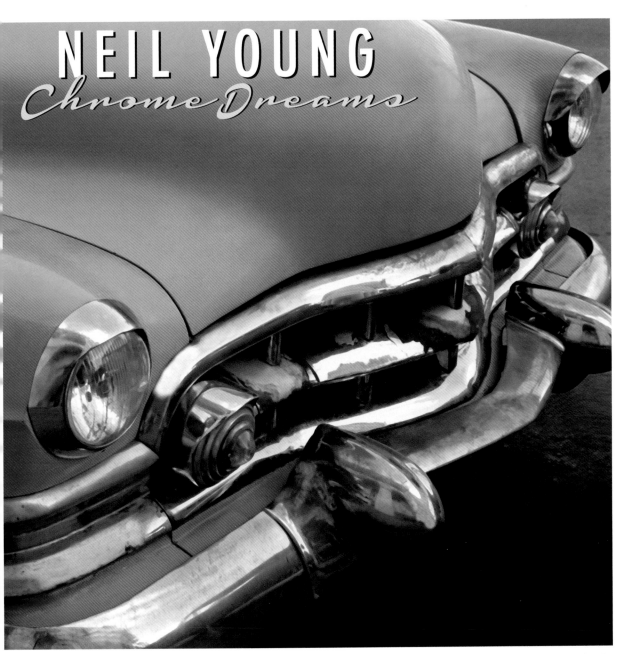

NEIL YOUNG
Chrome Dreams

Cover: John Pasche

RUSTED STUFF

As the internet took off, Young's 'Rustie' fan community augmented *Chrome Dreams* with six tracks from the period, creating the *Rust Edition*.

'River of Pride' was first attempted as a duet with The Band's Robbie Robertson in England, just before the final CSNY show in 1974. The *Rust Edition* version, cut in November 1975 with Crazy Horse, would never win an official release, but the song was re-recorded as 'White Line' for the quartet's 1990 reunion *Ragged Glory*. The desperately sad 'Campaigner' – which sounds a tender note of empathy for disgraced president Richard Nixon – ended up on *Decade*. The *Rust Edition* version, cut at Broken Arrow in 1976, includes an extra verse.

The 1976 Crazy Horse tour yielded the unreleased 'Give Me Strength', future *Comes a Time* cut 'Peace of Mind', (both from Chicago in November), and 'No One Seems to Know', a.k.a. 'Don't Say You Lose, Don't Say You Win' (from Tokyo in March). 'Human Highway' – cut with Crosby, Stills, and Nash in April 1976, at the *Long May You Run* sessions – was the last gasp of a project that had occupied them on-and-off for three years and about which you can read on page 60 . . .

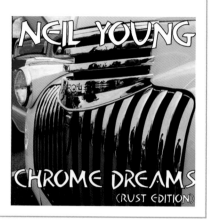

BARS 'N BRICKBATS

American Stars 'n Bars – boasting *Chrome Dreams* cuts 'Like a Hurricane', 'Star of Bethlehem', 'Hold Back the Tears', 'Will to Love', and 'Homegrown' – emerged in 1977. Young, grumbled *NME*'s Nick Kent, 'could have . . . thrown a great album together from unreleased gems already in the can. The fact that he hasn't and that the overall effect of *Bars* is uneven and unsatisfactory just isn't good enough.'

page 80)? With no explanation from Young, it seemed destined to languish in limbo, its existence to be proved or disproved by the promised *Archives* project. Then, in 1992, a test pressing was reported to exist. Dated 16 March 1977 – around three months before the release of *Stars 'n Bars* – it was accompanied by details of the tracks, personnel, and recording dates:

> Side 1: Pocahontas (September 1975) · Will to Love (May 1976) · Star of Bethlehem (November 1974) · Like a Hurricane (November 1975) · Too Far Gone (November 1976)
>
> Side 2: Hold Back the Tears (November 1976) · Homegrown (November 1975) · Captain Kennedy (September 1975) · Stringman (live, March 1976) · Sedan Delivery (November 1976) · Powderfinger (September 1975) · Look Out for My Love (November 1976)

Bootleg CDs of the set – each, confusingly, featuring different versions of the same tracks – promptly emerged. The revelation was that not only did several of the test pressing's songs appear on *American Stars 'n Bars, Comes A Time,* and 1979's *Rust Never Sleeps,* but a few had received belated official release on more recent albums, notably 1989's return to form, *Freedom.*

It seemed too good to be true, because it probably was. But while super-fan and collector Joel Bernstein declared the test pressing and accompanying document fakes, he did concede the veracity and detail of the information itself.

REALLY HIGH, FUCKED UP

The period the album captured was Young's passage from what he called 'the ditch' – the fallout from the commercial explosion of 1972's *Harvest*. The fatal heroin overdoses of Crazy Horse guitarist Danny Whitten and CSNY roadie Bruce Berry, Young's estrangement from girlfriend Carrie Snodgress and their young son Zeke, and his own drug and booze intake became recurring themes on *Time Fades Away* (1973), *On the Beach* (1974), and *Tonight's the*

Night (1974). Writer's block, however, wasn't one of his problems. With few constants in his life other than manager Elliot Roberts, producer Briggs, and cocaine, the songs on *Chrome Dreams* trace Young's chaotic path.

As far as his colleagues Crosby, Stills, and Nash went, that path was in the opposite direction. They barely figure on *Chrome Dreams,* save for 'Human Highway', which features their distinctive harmonies and Stills' slide guitar. The countrified 'Star of Bethlehem' (with Emmylou Harris on vocals), meanwhile, dates from after the group's 1974 'Doom Tour' (see page 62), when Young fled to Nashville to make *Homegrown.*

Having canned the deeply personal *Homegrown* in favour of *Tonight's the Night,* some of Young's most affecting solo songs of the period are on *Chrome Dreams,* cut at full-moon sessions at Malibu's Indigo studios in 1975 and 1976. Among them were future classics 'Pochahontas' and 'Powderfinger': 'Long instrumental guitar things – progressive, *progresso supremo* – about the Incas and the Aztecs . . .' he promised *NME.* 'It's like being in another civilisation. It's a lost sort of form, sort of a soul-form that switches from history scene to history scene, trying to find itself, man in a maze.' The *Chrome* 'Pocahontas' lacks only the overdubs of the *Rust Never Sleeps* version, but 'Powderfinger' is a stark solo acoustic reading, radically different from the finished Crazy Horse version. Yet it's no less powerful, while making just as little lyrical sense. Young shelved it until 1977 when he gave it to Lynyrd Skynyrd; their devastating plane crash that year meant they never recorded it.

The aching 'Will to Love' began on a cassette recorder at the composer's Broken Arrow ranch (you can hear a fire crackling in the background). Young ran the tape through his Magnatone amplifier and overdubbed vibes and drums at Indigo. Sung from the perspective of a migrating fish, it's reminiscent of sprawling dreamscapes like 'The Last Trip to Tulsa' on 1968's *Neil Young.*

ON BROADWAY
Among other unrealised and faintly insane Young projects of the era was a Broadway play, which made it to script stage, based on *Tonight's the Night.* 'The plot was about a roadie who made it and then OD'd on drugs,' he told *Mojo.* '*From Roadie to Riches* was the name of it (laughs). For Broadway in 1974 it was a little ahead of its time, as you can imagine.'

> ## *'Long instrumental guitar things – progressive, progresso supremo.'*
>
> Neil Young

In 1975, Young was reunited with Crazy Horse, rejuvenated with guitarist Frank 'Poncho' Sampedro replacing Danny Whitten. Together they cut the triumphant *Zuma* – Young's second release of the year after *Tonight's the Night* – and toured Californian bars as a warm-up for a tour the following year. In rehearsals at Broken Arrow, the Horse nailed the clomping 'Homegrown' and classic 'Like A Hurricane'. Written in the back of a friend's sedan while Young recovered from vocal cord surgery, unable to speak, the latter's evocation of romantic longing became a staple of almost every Crazy Horse show and the battleground for some of Young's wildest solos. 'We were all really high, fucked up,' he explained to *Uncut* of its inspiration. 'Been out partying.' Bar subtle mix differences, the *Chrome Dreams* and *Stars 'n Bars* 'Hurricane's are the same first take, with Sampedro lumbering through the chords on a string synthesiser.

'Sometimes it does sound as if we're really playing fast, but we're not,' Young said. 'It's just everything starts swimming around in circles.'

EGOS AND COCAINE

The 1976 tour saw Crazy Horse's debuts in continental Europe and Japan. Shows in Tokyo and London were recorded for a live album – unreleased,

> *'The rock 'n' roll craziness on Stephen's tour upset him too much . . . He just said, "Fuck it all!"'*
>
> Nils Lofgren

naturally. The band's druggy, boozy wobbliness didn't put off DJ John Peel, who wrote: 'Not since Little Feat at the Rainbow have I been so exhilarated.' The Tokyo and London shows yielded 'No One Seems to Know' (a.k.a. 'Don't Say You Lose, Don't Say You Win') and 'Stringman', a tribute to erstwhile friend and arranger Jack Nitzsche. Both recordings remain officially unreleased.

The tour had seen Young at his most dynamic and audience-accommodating in years. It had to end. With eighty US stadium shows looming, he changed direction, recording 1976's half-good – guess whose half – *Long May You Run* with old sparring partner Stephen Stills. Young had popped up at Stills shows in 1975 and it transpired the pair had secretly been recording in Miami.

With egos and cocaine consumption in overdrive, it seemed logical to turn the project into a CSNY album. Crosby and Nash halted work on their own album and joined the sessions until Young abruptly bailed on this latest attempt at a reunion. However, he had already agreed to a Stills/Young tour, forcing him to complete *Long May You Run* (Crosby and Nash's contributions were wiped, sparking years of acrimony). The outing lasted eighteen dates before Young turned his tour bus in the opposite direction, advising Stills by telegram, 'Funny how some things that start spontaneously end that way. Eat a peach, Neil.'

NUMBER ONE WITH A BULLET

Reprise pressed 200,000 copies of *Comes a Time*, featuring *Chrome*-era songs, only for Young to object that the records didn't properly reflect the frequencies he had committed to tape. Acknowledging that this was his fault, he bought the entire shipment for $200,000 – and, to ensure that no inferior pressings found their way into circulation, shot each box with a rifle.

MEET THE BEATLE

Young – with (front, left to right) Crazy Horse's Ralph Molina, Billy Talbot, and Frank Sampedro – backstage in Rotterdam in 1976 with Paul and Linda McCartney. The latter photographed Young in 1967 (a shot from the session adorns his 2008 album *Sugar Mountain – Live at Canterbury House*). 'I love Neil!' said her husband, whom Young inducted into the Rock and Roll Hall of Fame in 1999.

WHAT HAPPENED NEXT . . .

In original or re-recorded form, many *Chrome Dreams* songs graced *American Stars 'n Bars, Decade* (1977), *Comes a Time* (1978), *Rust Never Sleeps* (1979), and *Hawks and Doves* (1980). 'Too Far Gone' ended up on the career-reviving *Freedom* (1989) and a live version of the long-lost 'Stringman' graced *Unplugged* (1993).

Chrome Dreams was such a good idea that Young himself fell in love with it. On the release in 2007 of *Chrome Dreams II* (left) – that's right, a sequel to an album that never existed – he told the *New York Times, Chrome Dreams* 'just passed me by. I did it, I got to a certain place, and then something would happen and distract me, and I would get into something else and forget what I was doing before. That's happened a lot.'

Like its predecessor, *Chrome Dreams II* mixed new songs with unused material that might have bolstered albums including *Old Ways* (1985), *Freedom,* and the unreleased *Times Square* (1989). It was arguably his best album of the decade.

('The rock 'n' roll craziness on Stephen's tour upset him too much,' Nils Lofgren explained to *Creem,* 'to the point where he just said, "Fuck it all!"')

ULTIMATE FANTASY

As *Decade's* scheduled release date came and went, Young and Crazy Horse reconvened in November 1976 for a run at small theatres, intended to make up for the truncated Stills/Young tour. During rehearsals at Broken Arrow, he cut a solo acoustic version of 'Hold Back the Tears' – superior to the countrified version on *Stars 'n Bars* – and a desolate 'Too Far Gone' with Poncho on mandolin. 'Sedan Delivery' – a full-tilt rocker on *Rust Never Sleeps* – is slower on *Chrome Dreams* (on which it contains an extra verse) and wouldn't have seemed out of place on *Zuma.* The tender 'Look Out for My Love', later issued on *Comes a Time,* represents the first sighting of an all-acoustic Crazy Horse.

By the end of 1977 – with *Stars 'n Bars* and *Decade* in shops and *Give to the Wind,* the album eventually known as *Comes a Time,* in the can – *Chrome Dreams* was already a footnote. Decades later, it has become Young's ultimate unrealised album – a gem he was moving too fast to realise he was holding. If he had, might it have included 'Traces', from the *Tonight's the Night* sessions? 'Goodbye Dick', a kiss-off to disgraced president Richard Nixon from CSN&Y's 1974 tour? The *Homegrown/Human Highway*-era 'Hawaiian Sunrise', 'Love-Art Blues', and 'Homefires'? 'Born to Run' from the *Zuma* sessions? 'Evening Coconut' from the Stills/Young tour? 'Sad Movies' from the 1976 Crazy Horse tour? The nakedly autobiographical 'Hitchhiker' from August 1976, a song that wouldn't make it onto a record until 2010's *Le Noise?* All in all, *Chrome Dreams* may not have ever existed, but it *was* a damn good idea. **MB**

WILL IT EVER HAPPEN?

5/10 It's possible. Likely, even. All the tracks exist in their original form.
If Young gets a move on and releases the second volume of *Archives* (Volume 1 emerged roughly *two decades* late in 2009), there's no reason why we couldn't be enjoying a remastered *Chrome Dreams* by Christmas 2045.

LÄTHER

Artist Frank Zappa **Year** 1977 **Country** US **Genre** Rock, jazz, orchestral **Label** Warner Bros
What Zappa bites, and Warner Bros get more than they can chew

FRANK ZAPPA
Warner Bros, Zappa complained to *Record Review,* 'ain't doing me no favours . . . They have me pegged as a catalogue artist. Just release it and leave it in the rack and, after fifteen years, it'll still sell. And if they spend extra money on advertising, they figure it's not really gonna do any good because who cares about Zappa stuff? Just stick it in the racks and those twenty-five freaks out there who like that shit will go out and buy it, no matter what it's packaged in.'

A s he took to the airwaves on Los Angeles's KROQ in December 1977 to play all eight sides of a proposed new album, Frank Zappa advised his fans: 'My future as a recording artist is dangling in mid-air pending court procedures, which in California for civil cases can take anywhere from three to five years just to get a day (to) have your case heard. Since I don't think that anybody wants to wait three to five years to hear my wonderful music, I have taken it upon myself to come down here and advise anybody interested in the stuff that I do to get a cassette machine and tape this album. You can have it for free: just take it right off the radio . . . Don't buy it, tape it!'

DONE DIDDLY-SHIT
When Warner Bros refused to issue the *Zappa in New York* live album in the format that he had delivered it, Zappa claimed breach of contract and sued them. But to fulfil his contractual obligations, he sent the label the masters – minus artwork and liner notes – for three further albums: *Studio Tan, Hot Rats III* (later rechristened *Sleep Dirt*), and *Orchestral Favorites.* Unmoved by this seemingly conciliatory gesture, Warners refused to release them.

Believing he was now a free agent, Zappa filleted material from all four albums (including the disputed track excised from *Zappa In New York,* of which more later), and added more songs and segues of dialogue, sped-up percussion, and so on (the sort of thing popularised by The Beatles on 'The White Album'). The resulting four-disc box set – *Läther* (pronounced 'leather') – was shopped to other labels. EMI passed but a deal with Mercury led to test pressings being produced. When Warners got wind of this, they counter-sued Zappa, and Mercury swiftly backed off. Concerned that his recording career could be on hold for years, Zappa took the unusual step of giving his music away by airing the Mercury test pressing on KROQ – but the tale of this great lost album had actually begun a year earlier.

On the road promoting *Zoot Allures* towards the end of 1976, Zappa began to openly bad-mouth Warners. 'They say I owe them four more albums,' he told *Gig's* Susin Shapiro. 'I'm trying to decide whether I'll hand them all four when I get home from this tour, 'cause I got 'em. And they know that. They're sitting

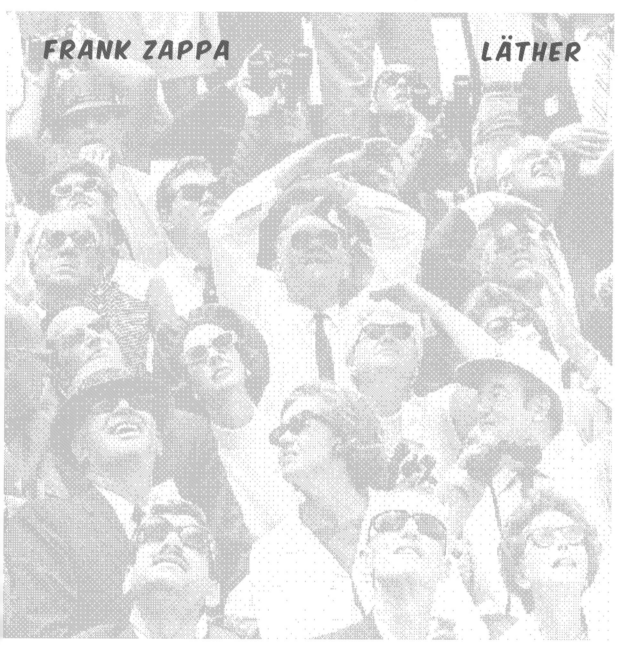

FRANK ZAPPA   LÄTHER

Cover: Ivan Markovic

in California waiting to come out. If Warners keeps fucking around like this, they're gonna get a little present when I get home. . . . I am giving Warners a fair chance this time. I'm saying, "Perform on this record." This is my first release for Warners, not DiscReet (the record label established by Zappa and his manager in 1973). It's not a subsidiary, it's not a little independent company . . . It's, "Hey, here I am on your mainline label – now what are ya gonna do about it?" So far they've done diddly-shit.'

This was before the New York shows that spawned the disputed live set, so Zappa had four separate albums ready to roll. The orchestral one aside, their exact contents may never be identified. Throughout his career, the maestro tinkered with recordings he stockpiled, compiling them into albums that might be re-edited, re-titled, and never released in their original configuration. (The 1976 double set *Night of the Iron Sausage,* for example, was whittled down into *Zoot Allures,* its leftovers finding homes on *Läther* and *Sleep Dirt.*)

GIVE ME YOUR LIPS
The man recorded as many of his live shows as possible, as well as – sometimes surreptitiously – rehearsals, band members' conversations, and other on-the-road shenanigans. All could – and many would – be edited, overdubbed, and, in inventive and entertaining ways, added to the 'official discography'.

Zappa in New York was recorded during the final week of 1976, at shows at the now demolished Palladium. His band was augmented by percussionist Ruth Underwood (described by bandmate Ed Mann as 'Frank's eternal soul sister') and a horn section that comprised the Brecker brothers and members of the house band from TV's *Saturday Night Live* – two of whom would appear as part of the Blues Brothers band in the 1980 movie (look out for Tom 'Bones' Malone and 'Blue Lou' Marini). The centrepiece of these concerts was a new, 'statistically dense' composition called 'The Black Page', split into 'The Black Page Drum Solo', 'Black Page #1' ('The hard version'), and 'The Black Page #2' ('The easy teen-age New York version'). 'He was always hearing the studio musicians in LA talking about the fear of going into sessions some morning and being faced with 'the black page', drummer Terry Bozzio told Zappa chronicler Andrew Greenaway. 'So he decided to write *his* 'Black Page.'

PUNK'S NOT DEAD
'I thought it was cool,' Angel guitarist Punky Meadows told *Washington City Paper* of the song that fanned the flames between Zappa and Warner Bros. 'Frank is very satirical, so you can't have a thin skin. . . . Around the time he wrote the song, he was playing in LA. He asked if I'd be willing to come onstage in my Angel costume and play with him on the song. I went to the concert, the curtain goes up, and there's this giant publicity photograph of me doing this pucker kind of thing. It was like Dean Martin's roast or something. Afterwards, Frank asked me to his place to drink some beer and play some tunes.'

Having declined an invitation to join Kiss after Angel's demise, Meadows opened a tanning salon in Oakton, Virginia.

> *'This is my first release for Warners. . . . So far they've done diddly-shit.'*
> Frank Zappa

But it was another piece showcasing Bozzio that would rupture his relationship with Warners. The twelve-minute 'Punky's Whips' describes the drummer's fascination with a publicity photo of Punky Meadows, the guitarist in glam rock band Angel. 'Punky, give me your lips to die on . . .' Bozzio sings, 'I promise not to come in your mouth.' This was a step too far for Warners. 'They took it out because they didn't have permission from Punky Meadows to use it,' Zappa marvelled. 'Then they have the audacity to go ahead and release the album with twelve minutes missing. There was something in one of the papers complaining about how short the album was. It wasn't my fault. I didn't have any control over it.' It later transpired that Meadows 'found it kind of flattering', but the damage was done. (Copies of *Zappa In New York* featuring both 'Punky's Whips' and a further namecheck for the guitarist on 'Titties & Beer' *did* slip out in the UK before Warners intervened.)

'I've been associated with Warners for five years and . . . it's time to go some place else,' Zappa told *NME*. That 'some place' was CBS, then EMI, with both of whom he also fell out. In the end, he set up his own Barking Pumpkin label.

UNUSUAL GESTATION

Läther is arguably the best one-stop shop for an overview of Zappa's oeuvre, combining studio and live versions of his idiosyncratic guitar soloing, orchestral compositions (more palatable in this context than on his actual orchestral sets), rock songs, and complex, almost-jazzy instrumentals. 'If that *Läther* album would have come out with all four records on it, it wouldn't have been like a summing up – it would have just been business as usual,' he told *Record Review*. 'I wish that I could release something like that a couple of times a year because there's that much stuff going on. But it's difficult.' Perhaps because of *Läther*'s unusual gestation, it's an often neglected gem – but hardcore fans rank it near the pinnacle of Zappa's prodigious discography. **AG**

WILL IT EVER HAPPEN?

0/10 The four-record set was posthumously released in 1996 as a three-CD set, with bonus tracks and new artwork. Then, in 2012, the Zappa Family Trust issued *Läther* in what is arguably – cover artwork and format aside – the closest approximation of the composer's intent. However, the CD booklet provides evidence that Zappa was tinkering with the track listing when he was shopping the original box set around different labels in 1977, so the 'true' *Läther* can, by definition, never be compiled.

WHAT HAPPENED NEXT . . .

Zappa filleted *Läther* and other material into four albums, issued by Warners in 1978 and 1979. 'If I insist that (fans) bootleg these things, Warner Bros will come after me . . .' he remarked. 'If I tell them to go and buy the records, then I'm sticking money in Warner Bros' pocket, which they in turn use to finance lawyers to fight me. How about, "Just let your conscience be your guide?"'

A common misconception holds that he simply split the set into *Zappa in New York, Studio Tan, Sleep Dirt,* and *Orchestral Favorites.* In fact, *Läther* featured material not on those albums, and vice versa. Warners, he grumbled, were 'so stupid about it. They should have released it all at once. It would have sold more units – it would have been a really exciting package. But no.'

Nonetheless, when Zappa gained full control of the bulk of his output in the late 1980s, he chose to reissue the albums as released by Warners, albeit restored and expanded in the case of *In New York,* and with drum overdubs and new vocal tracks on three songs that had originally been instrumentals on *Sleep Dirt.* 'Stores are reluctant to stock anything that I do,' he told *Society Pages* of the decision not to issue *Läther* instead, 'but they're even more reluctant to stock a box.'

12 OF THE BEST

Artist AC/DC Year 1978 Country Australia Genre High voltage rock 'n' roll Label Albert Productions
What AC/DC, short-circuited

BON SCOTT
The roguish singer was AC/DC's front man during the period that the proposed *12 of the Best* commemorated. 'I like to put my feet up – not to mention other parts of my body,' he told *Sounds*. 'They say to me, "Are you AC or DC?" and I say, "Neither, I'm the lightnin' flash in the middle."'

With a stealth few would associate with such louts, AC/DC's 1980 classic *Back in Black* has become one of rock's most successful albums. As of its most recent multi-platinum award, in 2007, it had shifted an astonishing twenty-two million copies in the US alone – equivalent to the combined certifications of *Led Zeppelin I* and *II*. Much of this tally must be attributed to the fact that if you wanted to purchase a set featuring the rock radio staples 'You Shook Me All Night Long' and 'Back in Black' itself, you needed their parent album. The group – founded and led by notoriously strong-minded rhythm guitarist Malcolm Young – stubbornly refused to sanction a 'greatest hits' collection and, before late 2012, would not allow their music to be sold on iTunes. However, the story of the quintet's arms-length relationship with compilations began two years before *Back in Black* was even released.

INJECTIONS OF CASH
In mid-1978, AC/DC were not the commercial juggernaut they are today. Worryingly, they seemed to be going backwards: that spring's *Powerage* (later cited as their best by Keith Richards) was the first of the band's five albums not to crack the top twenty in their native Australia. In America, it was the third to fall short of the top 100. Nonetheless, they were touring tirelessly, which required injections of cash from their Sydney-based label Albert Productions. Head honcho Ted Albert (who had produced Malcolm Young's brother George's band The Easybeats) duly decided to make the most of the existing catalogue by repackaging cuts from *High Voltage, T.N.T.* (both 1975), *Dirty Deeds Done Dirt Cheap* (1976), and *Let There Be Rock* (1977) as *12 of the Best*:

> Side 1: It's a Long Way to the Top . . . · High Voltage · Problem Child ·
> T.N.T. · Whole Lotta Rosie · Let There Be Rock
> Side 2: Jailbreak · Dirty Deeds Done Dirt Cheap · The Jack · Dog Eat Dog ·
> She's Got Balls · Baby, Please Don't Go

Rudimentary cover artwork was prepared, featuring Malcolm Young's brother Angus – the band's lead guitarist and, thanks to his schoolboy attire, most

12 of the best

Cover: Herita MacDonald

Atlantic persevered with its plan for a live album and, less than five months after *Powerage,* issued *If You Want Blood You've Got It.* Although far from the hoped-for blockbuster, it became the band's highest-charting album in Britain, took them within tantalizing distance of the US Top 100, and has subsequently been acclaimed as one of hard rock's finest in-concert sets. (And, like every AC/DC album issued in the US from 1976 to 2008, it has earned a platinum certification.)

Meanwhile, although they have endured forty years without issuing an album entitled *Greatest Hits* or *The Best Of,* AC/DC have sanctioned classic-packed sets in the form of movie soundtracks *Who Made Who* (1985) and *Iron Man 2* (2010).

recognisable member – and a catalogue number was assigned. However, AC/DC's US label Atlantic was far from convinced, its enthusiasm for an album that required no recording investment outweighed by its reservations about a 'best of' from a group whose Stateside sales were nothing to write home about. Doubtless influenced by the career-transforming success of sets like Kiss's *Alive!,* Atlantic instead set its sights on an in-concert collection (for which the groundwork was laid by *Live from the Atlantic Studios,* a promo LP recorded in December 1977, distributed for radio airplay, and relentlessly bootlegged until its belated official release as part of 1997's *Bonfire* box set).

The band – then engaged in a four-month American tour – were equally unenthusiastic about a competitor to the newly released *Powerage.* Even when Albert scaled down his ideas and proposed to restrict the album to Australia, the word from the band camp, reinforced by Atlantic, was a firm negative. **BM**

WILL IT EVER HAPPEN?

0/10 Although acdccollector.com has valued proofs of the artwork and a cassette edition of the album (the only non-bootleg pressing) at over $1,500 each, there is no commercial or musical incentive to release it even as part of an archive collection: all the songs are readily available elsewhere.

Cover: Paul Palmer-Edwards

LOVE MAN

Artist Marvin Gaye Year 1979 Country US Genre Soul Label Tamla What Drugs, despondency, and disco

By the late 1970s, Marvin Gaye's star was fading fast. His 1978 double album *Here, My Dear* – an intimate, bitter account of his divorce from Anna Gordy Gaye, sister of Motown founder Berry Gordy – had alienated fans and critics, who were now listening to a new generation of smooth crooners. Struggling with a crippling cocaine problem and a rapidly shrinking bank balance, he vowed that his next album, *Love Man,* would be a commercial success. 'I'm tired of watching Teddy (Pendergrass) and Peabo (Bryson) and Michael Henderson get all the glory,' the singer told biographer David Ritz in 1979. 'All these boys are romancing my fans and I don't like it. I'm getting my fans back. I'm doing a straight-ahead make-out party album.'

THE TOOT AND THE SMOKE

What Gaye laid down, though, was anything but party music – because more powerful than his desire for commercial rebirth was his obsession with his second wife, Janis Hunter. The daughter of jazz legend Slim Gaillard, she was a talented singer in her own right. Gaye met her during the recording of *Let's Get It On* in 1973, when he was thirty-three and she had just turned seventeen. 'In my mind I was older and in his mind he was younger,' she told broadcaster Tavis Smiley, 'and we met somewhere in the middle.' The pair married in 1977, and Gaye controlled almost every aspect of his spouse's life. He refused to let her pursue a music career and ordered her to have affairs with other men. 'I'm the last of the great chauvinists,' he told Ritz. 'I like to see women serve me. . . . In Jan's case, serving me meant feeding my fantasies – my evil fantasies.' Unable to cope with Gaye's bizarre behavior, Hunter retreated to the arms of Teddy Pendergrass in early 1979, taking their children Frankie and Nona with her. 'It was,' Gaye said wryly, 'quite a blow to my ego.'

The first songs he wrote for *Love Man* saw him plead for his wife's return. On 'Come Back, Baby', he argued that if God could forgive him, so could Hunter. On 'Life's a Game of Give and Take', Gaye admitted his mistakes and declared his inability to go on living without her. Yet on 'Life Is Now in Session', that desire for reunion is paired with a confession that he would never stop fantasizing about Hunter sleeping with other men.

MARVIN GAYE
'I'm unmanageable,' the star confessed to *Melody Maker* in 1979. 'I'm my own worst enemy. I refuse to be manageable, and it sometimes gets me in trouble.' That trouble tended to revolve around drugs and sex. However, he told *NME,* 'Anything I do is done out of my lust for life – my curiosity and my dedication as an artist. I should live to the depths of depravity and I shall rise to the heights of spirituality.'

TOO VULNERABLE
In 1967, Gaye began work on ballads that he would fuss over for nearly a decade, taking the multi-layered vocals that had distinguished his pop hits and using them in a jazz context. Reworking standards and personal favourites, he squeezed fresh hurt from classics like 'I Wish I Didn't Love You So'. But, frustrated by the underwhelming sales of his later albums, Gaye shelved the recordings in 1979. They remained locked away until 1997, when Motown released seven tracks – along with three compelling alternate takes – as *Vulnerable* (above).

Even the one upbeat song, 'Ego Tripping Out', was something of a downer. Over squelching synths and a mid-tempo disco beat, he parodied his hyper-sexualized image: rapping, 'I got the baddest cool / Could never be the fool / The ladies wait to get down with me.' Later in the song, he admits to using drugs to conquer his self-doubt, singing, 'Turn the fear into energy / 'cause the toot and the smoke won't fulfil the need.' Issued as a single in September 1979, 'Ego Tripping Out' failed to achieve the success Gaye craved: it peaked at No. 17 on the US R&B chart, and fell short of the *Billboard* Hot 100.

WANTED TO KILL HER
Halfway through the recording process, US authorities hit Gaye with a $4.5 million tax bill, forcing him to put *Love Man* on hold. He headed out on a world tour, but his heart wasn't in the cash-raising enterprise. 'I do enough drugs in

'I'd given up. I just wanted to be left alone to blow my brains away with high-octane toot.'

Marvin Gaye

my normal life,' he complained, 'but on the road the quantity triples.' Gaye quit following mediocre shows in Japan and Hawaii, and was sued for thousands of dollars by backing musicians and concert promoters.

The singer retreated to his Los Angeles studio, Marvin's Room, and tried to finish *Love Man*. He may have been losing his mind, but Gaye remained in control at the mixing desk. Ritz witnessed how the singer 'executed all his vocals at the console, modulating his voice with extreme subtlety, singing effortlessly.' Gaye would sing a phrase, play it back and then edit out all but a tiny section. 'Every grunt and groan, which sound so natural to the listener, is selected scrupulously, like a painter mixing colours,' the writer reported.

THE HUNTER AND THE HAUNTED
While Gaye tried to finish *Love Man* at his LA studio, he remained fixated on his estranged wife (right, with the star). 'This letter is to your heart,' he whispered on one track. 'Jan, I'm going to be loving you as long as there's breath in my body.'

Financial reality would again intrude on the recording process. With debts piling up fast, Gaye filed for bankruptcy, shuttered his studio, and fled to Hawaii for what he would later call 'one long nervous breakdown'. He begged for money from friends and family, but they refused, fearing the money would be spent on drugs. They were right. At one point during his Hawaiian interlude, Gaye snorted an ounce of cocaine in an hour and called his mother to say goodbye, certain he would die of an overdose. 'I'd given up,' he told Ritz. 'I just wanted to be left alone to blow my brains away with high-octane toot.' Hunter flew to Honolulu to try to help Gaye, but their reunion was short-lived. He pulled a knife on his wife, holding it close to her heart. 'I wanted to kill her,' he said. 'I almost did. I wanted to kill myself, but I didn't have the guts.'

MOANIN' AND BITCHIN'

Realising how low he had sunk, Gaye attempted to regain control of his life. He sent for some of his musicians in late 1979, but not to finish *Love Man*. 'No matter how much money Motown would give me to release *Love Man,* I couldn't do it,' he told Ritz. 'I needed to get my mind off Janis and all the agony we were putting each other through.' Gaye realised the album had become *Here, My Dear Part Two*. 'Who needed another record moanin' and bitchin' 'bout some woman?' he told Ritz. 'Why did I have to regain my throne as the sex king? Who cared about competing with Michael Jackson and Prince? Look what was happening in the world. I had a message to spread.'

Over the next year, Gaye reshaped the tracks from *Love Man* into something startlingly different. The album was no longer about his obsession with Hunter, but instead examined humanity's self-destructive nature. The funk song 'I Offer You Nothing But Love' became 'In Our Lifetime', which hinted at a coming nuclear apocalypse. Meanwhile, the bluesy 'Just Because You're So Pretty' grew into 'Love Me Now or Love Me Later', a conversation between the 'good lord' and 'evil lord' that Gaye thought existed in every human. At London's Odyssey studios in 1980, Pete Townshend encountered Gaye, 'who took over Studio 2 for a few weeks. . . . Marvin was in terrible shape (and) I struggled to process the music he was making: he played all the keyboard parts himself over drum machine rhythms. . . . I didn't understand what I was hearing.' For their part, Motown were frustrated by these endless revisions and, in January 1981, the label released *In Our Lifetime* while Gaye was still mixing it. It was the final indignity – but not, sadly, the final unhappy ending. **TB**

WHAT HAPPENED NEXT . . .
'I was humiliated,' Gaye told Ritz of Motown's decision to take *In Our Lifetime* out of his hands. '(They) added guitar licks and bass lines. How dare they second-guess my artistic decisions? Can you imagine saying to an artist, say, Picasso, "Okay, Pablo, you've been fooling with this picture long enough. We'll take your unfinished canvas and add a leg here, an arm there?"' The relationship was beyond salvaging, and in 1982 Gaye left the label – his home since 1961 – for CBS.

WILL IT EVER HAPPEN?

0/10
We will never know how Gaye might have finished *Love Man*. On 1 April 1984 – on the eve of his forty-fifth birthday – he was shot dead by his abusive father, Marvin Gay, Sr. It has been speculated that the singer deliberately provoked his parent in order to commit suicide by proxy.

Those curious to hear how the album might have sounded should check out the extended version of *In Our Lifetime* released in 2007 by Hip-O Records, which includes six raw tracks culled from its ill-fated antecedent's sessions.

THE TIES THAT BIND

Artist Bruce Springsteen **Year** 1979 **Country** US **Genre** Rock **Label** Columbia **What** The stream that led to *The River*

BRUCE SPRINGSTEEN
'I was trying to find a fundamental purpose for my own existence,' The Boss told writer Neil Strauss. 'Basically trying to enter people's lives in that fashion and hopefully maintain that relationship over a lifetime, or at least as long as I felt I had something useful to say. That was why we took so long between records. We made a lot of music. There are albums and albums' worth of stuff sitting in the can. But I just didn't feel they were that useful.'

Steven Van Zandt had had enough. 'I can't,' the guitarist complained, 'do this again.' He'd witnessed, as a friend, the agonising conception of *Born to Run*. He'd endured, as a band member, albums' worth of songs being recorded for *Darkness on the Edge of Town* – not to mention the hits 'Fire' and 'Because the Night' being given away to the Pointer Sisters and Patti Smith. Now his patience was being tested once more at endless sessions for Springsteen's fifth album. 'I quit,' he told The Boss. Springsteen assured him it would be different this time. 'But,' Van Zandt told biographer Peter Ames Carlin, 'contemplating the whole fucking *years* it was gonna take to make a record, I couldn't do it. Didn't have the patience.' With the guitarist promoted to co-producer as a peacekeeping measure, they made a concise, tune-packed album that reflected Van Zandt's radio-oriented inclinations. But what they *released,* over a year later, was a set that was twice the size and half the fun.

BURNING UP, MAN

The year 1979 began in grand style for Springsteen: onstage in Cleveland, Ohio, wrapping up the triumphant, seven-month *Darkness on the Edge of Town* tour with a three-and-a-half hour show that was his longest to date. Some performers return from the road with the creative well run dry, but when he returned to duty in March, it was with the barnstorming 'Roulette', that swung in a style quite distinct from the dour *Darkness* material. 'A great song,' drummer Max Weinberg enthused to Springsteen chronicler Charles R. Cross. 'That was the very first thing we recorded when we went into the studio.' Said studio was New York's Power Station, where Weinberg (with fellow E Streeters Garry Tallent on bass and Roy Bittan on keyboards) had worked on Ian Hunter's *You're Never Alone with a Schizophrenic*.

Also cut early on were 'The Ties That Bind', honed in the final weeks of the *Darkness* tour, and 'Hungry Heart', which Springsteen had to be talked out of donating to the Ramones. 'He owes us something . . .' quipped Joey Ramone. 'He wrote the song, inspired by us, and then he takes the money and runs!' Perhaps it was karma that in April, while fooling around with his girlfriend and comedian Robin Williams, Springsteen injured his leg in a motorcycle accident.

Cover: Sarah Holland

'BRUCE WAS A JERK . . .'

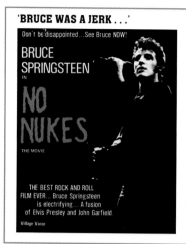

Don't be disappointed...See Bruce NOW!

BRUCE SPRINGSTEEN IN

NO NUKES

THE MOVIE

THE BEST ROCK AND ROLL FILM EVER... Bruce Springsteen is electrifying... A fusion of Elvis Presley and John Garfield.

Village Voice

Springsteen's misgivings about *The Ties That Bind* may have been compounded by the pair of 'No Nukes' shows that he headlined at New York's Madison Square Garden in September 1979. Were his new songs weighty enough to be played at a protest against nuclear energy? In fact, they were: the inexplicably abandoned 'Roulette' had been inspired by the partial meltdown at the Three Mile Island reactor earlier that year.

However, the only new cuts Springsteen chose to play in his eleven-song sets were 'The River' and 'Sherry Darling'. (Other performers included Jackson Browne, James Taylor, Bonnie Raitt, and Chaka Khan, the last of whom was particularly unnerved by 'Broooce!' – the traditional baying of Springsteen crowds that can sound like 'Booo!' to the uninitiated. 'Too bad his name wasn't Melvin,' quipped Raitt.)

Adding to his anxiety, The Boss was to turn thirty the day after the second show. 'I'm officially over the fucking hill,' he joked to the audience, masking his actual misgivings. This might partly explain his uncharacteristically shameful treatment of photographer and former lover Lynn Goldsmith, whom he dragged onstage, introduced as 'my ex-girlfriend', then had escorted out of the building. The more chivalrous Meat Loaf, Goldsmith wrote later, 'went to Bruce's dressing room and told him he was a jerk.'

bruce springsteen tougher than the rest

SPECIAL 4 TRACK 12" MAXI SINGLE 33⅓ RPM

TOUGH LUCK

When *Backstreets* fanzine editor Charles R. Cross learned that 'Roulette' would finally be released as a B-side in 1988 – with a live take of *The Ties That Bind*'s 'Be True', on a UK version of the 'Tougher Than the Rest' single – 'there was more screaming in our office than you'd hear if the actual (Three Mile Island incident) was happening right across the street.'

The resultant hiatus proved brief and the group returned to work. 'Five days a week . . .' Weinberg told *Billboard*'s Craig Rosen, 'I drove into New York. The sessions started at 7 or 8 p.m. and went to 4 or 5 a.m. I saw the sun come up almost every day.' By May, sufficient songs had been recorded for leaked tapes to turn into a bootleg – unamused, Springsteen and his label sued the pirates for $1.75 million. In a rare respite, the E Street Band played at the wedding of Springsteen's lighting man and travel agent. The set included another rambunctious number premiered on the *Darkness* tour, 'Sherry Darling'.

As work dragged on, Springsteen missed the stage. However, as he laughed to *Creem,* 'I'm going as fast as I can. I was burning up, man.... We didn't do a whole lot of takes of each song. I don't think there's a song on there that went any more than ten takes, and most of them were done under five. The only overdubbing is vocal overdubbing, and that's not on everything. Most of the stuff we recorded very fast.' Weinberg agreed: 'Bruce would be in the studio writing and we would be in the lounge waiting for him to finish. . . . He would call us in and we would record the song he just wrote there and then.'

SURE-FIRE SMASH

By September 1979, an album had been completed to the point that a Christmas release was scheduled and its artwork was planned (the front a shot of Springsteen with a barn behind him, the back his face covered by a screen door). While Springsteen would recall a year later that he 'had an album of thirteen songs finished,' ten tracks were – as Power Station log sheets confirm – dubbed to master tapes and labelled sides one and two:

Side 1: The Ties That Bind · Cindy · Hungry Heart · Stolen Car · Be True
Side 2: The River · You Can Look (But You Better Not Touch) · The Price You Pay · I Wanna Marry You · Loose Ends

The Ties That Bind was a lovely blend of the urgent title track and 'Be True', the country-flecked 'Cindy' and 'I Wanna Marry You', the rockabilly 'You Can Look (But You Better Not Touch)', and the swaying 'The Price You Pay' and 'Loose Ends'. The piano-led 'Stolen Car' and mini-epic 'The River' – the latter inspired by Springsteen's sister Virginia – added a depth that the album could otherwise have been accused of lacking, while the sure-fire smash 'Hungry Heart' meant it could hardly have failed. There was only one problem: the man who wrote it all 'didn't feel it was big enough'.

CONFLICTING EMOTIONS

'I wanted to live with particularly conflicting emotions,' Springsteen explained to Creem. 'Because I always personally, in a funny kind of way, lean towards the Darkness kind of material. When I didn't put the album out in '79, it was because I didn't feel that that was there.'

In October 1979, the band returned to the studio. 'I wanted to capture the themes I had been writing about on Darkness,' Springsteen recalled. 'I wanted to keep those characters with me and, at the same time, add music that made our live shows so much fun and joy for our audience.' Consequently, he told Creem, 'We wrote and recorded about forty-eight songs. . . . What I wanted to do, and what I hoped was working out, was those little four-song albums they tried to put out for a while.' These ten-inch EPs were 'Nu Disks' – issued by his record company Columbia's sister label Epic – of which the best-known is The Clash's Black Market Clash (1980). 'I wanted to, from time to time, release those with all the stuff that's in the can and all the stuff that for one reason

WHAT HAPPENED NEXT . . .
The River's atrocious sound may have confirmed Steven Van Zandt's suspicions that the production team – manager/producer Jon Landau, and engineers Jimmy Iovine and Chuck Plotkin – 'didn't have a fucking idea about what they're doing.' Nonetheless, the album became Springsteen's first chart-topper, and many of its twenty songs – all of which, admittedly, sound much better onstage – remain live favourites to this day.

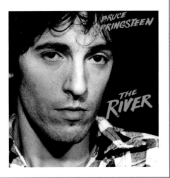

'Contemplating the whole fucking years it was gonna take to make a record, I couldn't do it.'

Steven Van Zandt

or another didn't make it on.' However, the format never caught on and was abandoned – meaning gems would go unreleased for years.

In the end, the actual result – issued in May 1981, over two years after the sessions began – was The River, which, as Weinberg observed, 'was both light and dark in tone.' Unfortunately, that meant a wearying double set packed with hollow attempts to sound spontaneous, inferior reworkings of 'Stolen Car' and 'You Can Look (But You Better Not Touch)', and other songs sandbagged by a lumpy mix that was far from the sprightly sound of The Ties That Bind (engineer extraordinaire Bob Clearmountain, who worked on the latter, was unfortunately not available to complete The River). Of all the wasted opportunities in Springsteen's history, this is definitely the biggest. **BM**

2/10 **WILL IT EVER HAPPEN?**
Darkness-era outtakes were exhumed to form The Promise (2010), so a resurrection of The Ties That Bind isn't impossible. However, much of the material has already appeared on the 1998 box set Tracks.

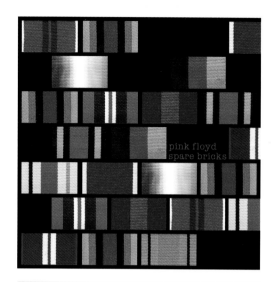

Chapter 3

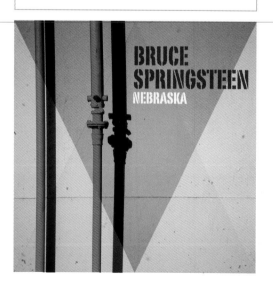

The Eighties

Cover: Simon Halfon

COLD CUTS

Artist Paul McCartney Year 1981 Country UK Genre Pop-rock Label Parlophone What The best of the rest that never was

PAUL McCARTNEY
'I have no problem with bootlegs,' the star told the *New York Times*, 'although, every time I say that, my lawyer says, "Oh yes you do."' Bootlegs, however, have picked up the slack where the star's official discography has fallen short, allowing fans to hear otherwise unreleased oddities of the sort that fills *Cold Cuts*.

An unusually prolific superstar, Paul McCartney averaged an album a year from 1970 to 1980 – not counting the live *Wings Over America* or *Thrillington,* the orchestral version of *Ram.* Equally remarkably, eleven of his singles in the same period – notably 'Mull of Kintyre' – stood alone from albums. By 1980, not a year had gone by since 1962 without new McCartney music. But the new decade brought one event after another that shook the confidence of this most assured of stars: his imprisonment in Tokyo for marijuana possession, the collapse of his band Wings, and – worst of all – the assassination of John Lennon. So, to fill an uncharacteristically barren release schedule, he resurrected a six-year-old project, now known as *Cold Cuts.*

GOOD STUFF

By late 1974, McCartney's stock was at its highest since the dissolution of The Beatles. That year's *Band on the Run* was his third album with Wings but his first to score a hat trick of chart-topping positions in Britain, the US, and Australia. It was also the first to score near-unanimous favourable reviews, even from as harsh a critic as John Lennon. '*Band on the Run* is a great album . . .' he told *Rolling Stone.* 'It doesn't matter who's playing. You can call them Wings, but it's Paul McCartney music. And it's good stuff.'

To capitalise on this success, a budget-price collection called *Hot Hitz & Kold Kutz* was proposed, doubtless to appear just in time for Christmas. There was an abundance of material from which to choose: the stand-alone hits 'Another Day', 'Give Ireland Back to the Irish', 'Mary Had a Little Lamb', 'Hi, Hi, Hi', 'Live and Let Die', and 'Junior's Farm' – and their B-sides; choice album cuts like 'Maybe I'm Amazed'; 'Helen Wheels', which appeared only on the US version of *Band on the Run;* 'Walking in the Park with Eloise', a song written by McCartney's father and issued by Wings under the alias The Country Hams; and outtakes that – to judge from the ones later appended to deluxe reissues – could have included 'Suicide', 'A Love for You', and 'Mama's Little Girl'.

As it turned out, however, there was no need for a stop-gap collection to bolster EMI's year-end figures: *Band on the Run* remained on transatlantic charts for over two years, and became the best-charting album of 1974 in

SPEED BUMPS

To give his fellow Wings an opportunity to shine, 1973's *Red Rose Speedway* was conceived as a double album. 'He was confused,' said engineer Glyn Johns. 'He didn't know if he wanted to be the bass player in the band or Paul McCartney.'

Side 1: Big Barn Bed · My Love · When the Night · Single Pigeon
Side 2: Tragedy · Mama's Little Girl · Loup · I Would Only Smile
Side 3: Country Dreamer · Night Out · One More Kiss · Jazz Street
Side 4: I Lie Around · Little Lamb Dragonfly · Get on the Right Thing · 1882
    (live) · The Mess I'm In (live)

Confirming Johns' judgment that 'the band itself was not very good,' the set was a mess, although guitarist Denny Laine's 'I Would Only Smile' was excellent, and 'Tragedy' and 'Mama's Little Girl' were considered worthy of *Cold Cuts*. A second pass at a track listing edged the album closer to its final incarnation:

Side 1: Night Out · Get on the Right Thing · Country Dreamer · Big Barn
    Red · My Love
Side 2: Single Pigeon · When the Night · Seaside Woman · I Lie Around
Side 3: Best Friend (live) · Loup · Medley: Hold Me Tight / Lazy Dynamite /
    Hands of Love · Power Cut
Side 4: Mama's Little Girl · I Would Only Smile · One More Kiss · Tragedy ·
    Little Lamb Dragonfly

Even trimmed to a single album, *Red Rose Speedway* remained frustratingly inconsistent. Nonetheless, it followed The Beatles' *1967–1970* to the top of the US chart, only to be displaced by George Harrison's *Living in the Material World*.

Australia and Canada. And by mid-1975, its successor, *Venus and Mars,* had followed it into the upper echelons of charts around the world. McCartney tinkered with the 'extras' concept throughout the decade, but gaps in his output were instead filled by, in 1976, *Wings Over America,* and, in 1978, *Wings Greatest.* His stand-alone singles continued, too, including 1977's 'Mull of Kintyre', and 1979's 'Goodnight Tonight' and 'Wonderful Christmastime'.

WRITING ON THE WALL

Wings ground to a halt in 1980. Their leader's *McCartney II* – created solely by him in mid-1979, and bolstered by the hits 'Coming Up' and 'Waterfalls' – confirmed he had outgrown the need to submerge himself in a collective identity. 'I got bored with the whole idea,' he confessed to *Music Express,* 'and I thought, "Christ! I'm coming up to forty now. I don't really have to stay in a group. There's no rule anywhere that says I have to do it that way."' In October 1980, he reunited with producer George Martin for the first time since 'Live and Let Die' to cut 'We All Stand Together' (eventually released with 1984's animated *Rupert and the Frog Song*) – an experience that went well enough for the pair to embark on what would ultimately become 1982's *Tug of War.*

'The writing was clearly on the wall,' latter-day Wings guitarist Laurence Juber told daytrippin.com. 'I didn't want to hang around when I knew there was other work to be done. Paul called in November and he was very nice and said, "Listen, I'm doing this album and George Martin doesn't want it be a Wings record, but we're still going to be working as a band in January."'

That January 1981 session turned out to be a stab at overdubbing on what was now known as *Cold Cuts*. Trimmed of instrumentals (such as a reggae version of *Wild Life*'s 'Tomorrow') and cuts sung by Linda McCartney and Denny Laine that had reportedly featured in previous permutations, it boasted twelve tracks: the *Ram* outtake 'A Love For You', 'My Carnival' (from the *Venus and Mars* sessions), 'Waterspout' (from the 1977 recording of *London Town*), 'Night Out', 'Tragedy', and 'Mama's Little Girl' (casualties of the *Red Rose*

> *'You can call them Wings, but it's Paul McCartney music. And it's good stuff.'*
>
> John Lennon

Speedway cull [see left]), 'Robbers' Ball' (demoed for *McCartney II*), 'Cage' (a leftover from *Back to the Egg*), 'Did We Meet Somewhere Before?' (cut during *Back to the Egg* but intended for the soundtrack of the 1978 movie *Heaven Can Wait*), 'Hey Diddle' (initiated during *Ram* sessions and re-worked in Nashville in 1974), 'Best Friend' (a bluesy rocker taped on a 1972 Wings tour), and 'Same Time, Next Year' (written for Robert Mulligan's 1978 movie of the same name, but rejected because it gave away too much of the plot).

CUSTOMARY CLUNKERS

It contained customary clunkers – 'Robbers' Ball' is mock-theatrical Eurodisco – but *Cold Cuts* boasted, as fansite thatwouldbesomething.com observed, 'at least a half dozen tracks that were equal to or better than the best of McCartney's legitimate output.' It even acquired artwork, whose declaration 'No baloney!' distinguished this incarnation of *Cold Cuts* from others issued as bootlegs. But it was shelved again, most likely due to McCartney's uneasiness in the wake of Lennon's murder and the end of Wings, who officially disbanded in April 1981. 'There was no real reason for there to be another Wings record,' Laurence Juber admitted to daytrippin.com, 'and why wait around if there was no tour to do? It was also coincidental with John Lennon's death, but the process was already underway. When John died, it reinforced the insecurity of being a former Beatle and being out in public at that point.' **BM**

WHAT HAPPENED NEXT . . .

The 'No baloney!' version was immortalized on a bootleg in the wake of McCartney's 1986 album *Press to Play,* providing a golden opportunity for critics who heard both to seize on the latter's weaknesses. With producer Chris Thomas and engineer Bill Price – both protégés of George Martin – McCartney took another stab at *Cold Cuts* in 1987. This yielded 'Blue Sway' (first mooted for *McCartney II* and now available, in its orchestrated 1980s incarnation, on that album's expanded reissue), and versions of 'Mama's Little Girl' and 'Same Time, Next Year' that wound up on 1990's 'Put It There' single. However, EMI opted for the hits set *All the Best!* and the star gave up on the project. Although he subsequently suggested there was no point revisiting it because much of the material has been bootlegged, rumours persist of an expanded version.

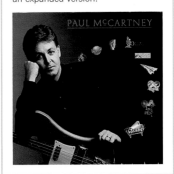

WILL IT EVER HAPPEN?

4/10 McCartney's output has remained prodigious, with the twenty-first century alone yielding (as of early 2014) five solo albums, three live sets, the *Wingspan* hits collection, three classical albums, three collaborative experiments (*Liverpool Sound Collage, Twin Freaks,* and *Electric Arguments*), and expanded versions of 1970s albums, the latter including a wealth of outtakes. So, while *Cold Cuts* could conceivably be resurrected, there's been no gap-plugging commercial motive to do so. And as McCartney has added over one hundred songs to his archive of unreleased material in the intervening three decades, a box set of all of them would make more sense.

RAT PATROL FROM FORT BRAGG

Artist The Clash **Year** 1982 **Country** UK **Genre** Punk funk **Label** CBS **What** Combative rock

MICK JONES
In a 2013 interview with *Rolling Stone*, the Clash guitarist cast his mind back to the difficult days of three decades earlier. 'We were just all fed up with each other,' he said. 'The bigger it got, the more difficult it became. We battled through constant issues. Then we started to get into whatever we were into individually – and that became an issue.'

The Clash was a name well chosen. Music as conflict – inflammatory rallying cries, an us-and-screw-them attitude of band and crowd conjoined against the world outside. Frontman Joe Strummer, guitarist Mick Jones, bassist Paul Simonon, and drummer Topper Headon were certainly on a war footing in the early 1980s, but this abrasiveness was beginning to turn destructively in on itself. Against this backdrop, *Rat Patrol from Fort Bragg* became *Combat Rock* and The Clash disintegrated amid their greatest success.

URBAN GHETTOLOGY

The immortal *London Calling* (1979) was a double album. *Sandinista!* (1980) trumped that with six sides of music. 'There was no stopping us,' recalled Mick Jones in Chris Salewicz's biography of Strummer. Jones was enjoying the opposite of songwriter's block, with the floodgates fully open. 'We'd write thirty songs and then put thirty-one out,' he cracked to *Rolling Stone.* 'We wanted to give value for money,' explained Topper Headon, 'and release as much material as we could, as often as we could.'

In two bursts of activity in London in 1981, tracks including 'Sean Flynn', 'Know Your Rights', and 'Should I Stay or Should I Go?' had been laid down. Jones, positioning himself as the producer, wanted to finish the album at the end of the year in New York, where he was absorbing intoxicating musical influences. 'The city's sounds of urban ghettology . . .' wrote Salewicz, 'inspired him.' (The inspiration flowed both ways: New York clubs were spinning the 'Magnificent Seven' remix 'The Magnificent Dance', giving The Clash a much more diverse audience than most of their punk contemporaries.)

However, the artistic visions of Strummer and Jones were moving further apart. Past and soon-to-be drummer again Terry Chimes said that the former 'didn't like Mick making lots of weird noises. . . . He wanted to sound more like Chuck Berry.' In Pat Gilbert's *Passion Is a Fashion: The Real Story of The Clash,* roadie Digby recalled that: 'Mick knew exactly what he wanted.' Which included synths. With positions becoming more entrenched, there were rows in the studio in which neither side would concede ground, even when Jones and Simonon – as observer Tymon Dogg recalled – looked like 'death warmed

THE CLASH
RAT PATROL FROM FORT BRAGG

Cover: Bill Smith

PIGS ON THE WING

The supplanting of *Rat Patrol from Fort Bragg* with *Combat Rock* was a difficult time for Mick Jones, but Joe Strummer had his disappointments, too. *When Pigs Fly* was a 1993 soundtrack album for a film by Sara Driver – whose partner, Jim Jarmusch, had directed Strummer in 1989's *Mystery Train* (right, with Rick Aviles). 'He was like an archaeologist with music,' said Driver. 'He had such a love of different kinds of music.'

After just four days, Strummer presented Driver with nine hours of music: 'It was the accumulation of all those years of not being in the studio. He was writing furiously.' Unfortunately, the film did not enjoy a wide release, which hamstrung prospects for the soundtrack. 'It's a lost body of my work, if I may use such a phrase,' said Strummer in 1999.

HIT OUT OF HELL

While his bandmates bickered, bassist Paul Simonon visited Jamaica to work with reggae star Mikey Dread – who contributed to *Sandinista!* and supported The Clash on tour. 'Stiff Records put up the money,' Simonon told *Creem,* adding, a tad undiplomatically, ''cause CBS fuck everything up.' The result was 1982's *Pave the Way* (above), whose 'Hit Shot' boasts a keyboard line reminiscent of the violin on *Rat Patrol's* 'Straight to Hell'.

up' after an all-night argument over the right tone for a bass part. It didn't help that a January 1982 deadline for the album came and went, obliging the group to combine gigs with studio mixing. 'At first, it was just us knocking it out in Electric Ladyland, trying to mix it, and it sucked,' Jones told *Uncut.* 'We toured Australia and, each night after the show in Sydney, we'd go down and mix the album. But, of course, that sucked as well.'

A wider power struggle divided the band into unequal camps: Strummer and Simonon against Jones, with Headon more concerned with feeding his drug habit. ('The great thing about The Clash is we haven't broken up yet,' Simonon cracked to *Creem.* 'It's a miracle. Maybe we'll do that next.') Even at the earliest sessions for the album – its title possibly inspired by late 1960s US TV drama *The Rat Patrol* – 'the last gang in town' was starting to splinter. 'There wasn't any energy,' observed former road manager Johnny Green. 'It looked like everyone was waiting for an excuse to go home.' Jones particularly objected to the re-hiring of punk-era mastermind Bernie Rhodes as manager in 1981. On a shoot, long-time photographer Pennie Smith witnessed the group dynamic fracturing: 'Suddenly, they weren't there as a unit any more.'

SYNTHESISERS AND SQUIGGLES

In early 1982, Jones was working on a track listing that read:

The Beautiful People Are Ugly Too · Kill Time · Should I Stay or Should I Go · Rock the Casbah · Know Your Rights · Red Angel Dragnet · Ghetto Defendant · Sean Flynn · Car Jamming · Inoculated City · Death Is a Star · Walk Evil Talk · Atom Tan · Overpowered by Funk · First Night Back in London · Cool Confusion · Straight to Hell

The clock stops on estimated running times at almost eighty minutes; not the stripped-down single album that some, such as long-time confidante Kosmo Vinyl, were pushing for after the excesses of *Sandinista!*. Strummer had issues other than the length. 'Mick, I don't think you can produce,' he told Jones. With little common ground on which to build a platform of communication, the decision was taken to parachute in producer Glyn Johns (the same man brought in to salvage two other troubled projects in this book – *Get Back* by The Beatles [page 24] and The Who's *Lifehouse* [page 44]). Long term, this had seismic implications, but, more immediately, progress replaced corrosive stasis. With an outsider's ear, the veteran Johns appreciated what Jones had done as 'really, really clever,' but also that it was 'incredibly self indulgent.' ('*Rat Patrol from Fort Bragg* was the more contemporised mix for the time,' Jones told avclub.com decades later, 'leaning towards more of a Big Audio Dynamite *(his post-Clash act)* thing. But ultimately . . . no one really remembers those synthesisers and squiggle noises.')

BETRAYAL OF A VISION
Jones dealt with the situation by, initially, staying away from the studio – then, when he appeared, being less than cooperative. 'As far as he was concerned,

> *'They say record companies fashion shit, but in our case it was always a shambles waiting to happen.'*
>
> Mick Jones

he had finished the work and there is nothing more annoying than having it taken away from you like that,' conceded Johns, whose surgery – taking just three days – was decisive and, he admitted, 'fairly drastic.'

The axe fell on five tracks: the power poppy 'The Beautiful People Are Ugly Too' and overheated calypso 'Kill Time', the heavily vibed 'First Night Back in London', the reggae workout 'Cool Confusion', and 'Walk Evil Talk', which immerses itself in jazz and classical, and is a contender for the most way-out recording even for a band known for a sense of adventure. ('They say record companies fashion shit, but,' Jones admitted, 'in our case it was always a shambles waiting to happen.') Other songs were overhauled to greater or lesser degrees. The end result now checked in at a svelte forty-six minutes.

Though Jones was bereft at what he viewed as a betrayal of a vision, he was, given the passage of time, able to view what had happened with an objective eye. 'I realised how pointless was all the fuss and the pain that I went through with *Combat Rock*: no one really remembers now how high the hi-hat was or the cymbals,' he said. 'It turned out all right for everybody.' Indeed it did, when considered with a cool, commercial eye, but the aftershocks would ripple to the end of the group. **CB**

WHAT HAPPENED NEXT . . .
Combat Rock was greeted with across-the-board critical acclaim, which translated into sales of worldwide significance. *Rolling Stone* called it 'a snarling, enraged, yet still musically ambitious collection.' Almost exactly a year after its May 1982 release, though, Jones played his last Clash gig, in Los Angeles, before being asked to leave the band, which staggered on to negligible effect. Ironically, it was his remix of 'Rock the Casbah' that gave the band its highest US singles chart placing. Looking back at *Rat Patrol from Fort Bragg/Combat Rock*, Jones said: 'The original is very contemporary. But the real record is better, so lasting . . . I shouldn't have put myself through all that grief.'

WILL IT EVER HAPPEN?

3/10 Although Jones's mix is easily located online, the chances of an official unveiling of *Rat Patrol* spiked when the *Sound System* box set was announced in 2013. It turned out to be a case of almost, but not quite. 'Cool Confusion', 'First Night Back in London' – both issued as B-sides – and the previously unreleased 'Kill Time' (now 'Idle in Kangaroo Court') and 'The Beautiful People Are Ugly Too' are included. Yet there is no place for 'Walk Evil Talk'. Jones considers it unlikely that they will revisit the archives again.

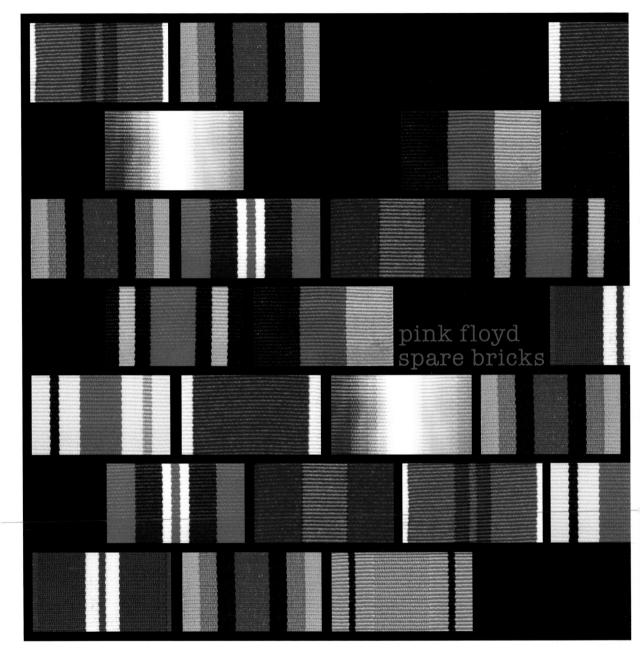

pink floyd
spare bricks

Cover: Herita MacDonald

SPARE BRICKS

Artist Pink Floyd **Year** 1982 **Country** UK **Genre** Rock **Label** Harvest **What** The movie soundtrack that finished the Floyd

Talking to US radio in 1981, Pink Floyd leader Roger Waters declared himself 'very iffy' about the idea of a soundtrack album for his then in-production movie *The Wall.* 'There was talk of it being a double album and I thought, "That's absurd,"' he clarified. 'If there's enough new material and stuff for it to be interesting for people to buy it, then it's worth putting out a single album. I think it will be. For Pink Floyd fans it will certainly be good stuff. I won't let it go out until it's really good. One does have one's reputation to consider.' Ultimately, however, that soundtrack – and the movie it was to accompany – would become two more bricks in the wall between himself and guitarist Dave Gilmour. Within two years, the incarnation of the group that shot into interstellar overdrive in the 1970s would plummet messily into the dirt.

TORTUROUS ASSEMBLY

'I went a little mad,' recalled producer Bob Ezrin of the album that spawned the movie, 'and really dreaded going in to face the tension.' *The Wall*'s conception was, indeed, riven with strife. The fractured band could hardly bear to be in the studio together – keyboardist Rick Wright was fired before the sessions were over – and there was, Ezrin told *Mojo,* 'even tension between the wives.' So frosty was the atmosphere that Waters' hoped-for guests the Beach Boys declining to sing about worms seemed like light comic relief.

The greatest problem, however, was that the Floyd's most ambitious project was subject to something that had rarely impinged on their working practices: a deadline. When their tax planning was sunk by a man later jailed for fraud, Waters told *Q,* the band 'lost a couple of million quid – nearly everything we'd made from *Dark Side of the Moon.* Then we discovered the Inland Revenue might come and ask us for eighty-three per cent of the money we had lost. Which we didn't have.' They eked out a record label advance of over £4 million on the condition that the album was in stores in time for Christmas.

Work began in late 1978 but, despite running two studios for much of 1979, they had yet to finish by August. With an October deadline looming, the increasingly unhelpful Wright was ousted in favour of session musicians, and the Floyd faced up to the problem of, as Gilmour explained, 'reducing it

BOB GELDOF
'Overblown and old hat,' was the verdict of *The Wall*'s star Bob Geldof (above) on the music of Pink Floyd. Creator Roger Waters' lyrics were, he wrote, 'social-conscience-stricken-millionaire leftism.' Nonetheless, he admired director Alan Parker and 'the money was good.'

RELEASE THE TIGERS

Having failed to make it onto *The Wall*
and the original version of *The Final
Cut,* 'When the Tigers Broke Free' finally
wound up on a 2004 reissue of the latter.
'(Co-producer) James Guthrie sent me
a compilation of the record when he'd
remastered it,' Waters told *Uncut*'s Carol
Clerk, 'and I was extremely confused for
a while because "Tigers" kept coming up
again and again. I said, "James, what the
fuck are you doing?" He said, "No, no, no,
dear boy . . . You have to choose which
place you think it works best." It's great
that it's found a little home on an album.'

down from a triple album to a double. Towards the end we were actually cutting
chunks out of songs to fit the time.' 'The Show Must Go On' lost a verse, although
too late to remove those lyrics from the sleeve. The same fate befell an entire song
earlier in the album. 'We discovered, when we were mastering the thing, that Side
Two was just too long,' Waters explained to DJ Jim Ladd. 'We had to get rid of
something – and 'Empty Spaces' and another cut that used to be on there called
'What Shall We Do Now?' were the same tune . . . so we just axed 'What Shall
We Do Now?' and left the lyrics because they helped to tell the story.'

Other songs were dropped long before the mastering stage. An improved
version of 'Sexual Revolution' became the highlight of Waters' solo *The Pros
and Cons of Hitch Hiking* (a concept first offered to the Floyd, who chose *The
Wall* instead). 'Death Disco' yielded elements of 'In the Flesh' and 'Young Lust',
while 'Teacher Teacher' became a sticking point over three years later.

The torturous assembly paid off. 'Another Brick in the Wall' and its parent
album topped charts around the world. That, however, was only Phase One.

UNPLEASANT, UNNERVING, AND UPSETTING

'From this album, there is going to be a film . . .' Rick Wright had blabbed
to Montreal Radio in late 1978. 'Not a film of the group, but a feature film
that will involve the group in it, musically.' 'As soon as the thing was down
on tape,' Waters confirmed, 'I knew that it should be made into a film . . . I'd
been trying, if you like, to work out a way of doing a show without having to
be there.' (This sprang from a 1975 US tour that Waters found so 'unpleasant,
unnerving, and upsetting' that he had fantasized about a black polystyrene wall
across the stage. His anguish was compounded on another US outing, two
years later, that concluded with him spitting at an over-enthusiastic fan.)

Waters and designer Gerald Scarfe devised 'a musical biography of a
character called Pink.' It was to be directed by Scarfe and cinematographer
Michael Seresin – the latter an associate of director Alan Parker, who was to

BEHIND THE WALL

Kevin McKeon (Young Pink) and Christine
Hargreaves (Pink's Mother) are pictured
on location – by stills photographer David
Appleby – with Pink Floyd main man, and
creator of *The Wall,* Roger Waters.

produce. 'I threw Michael the ball and expected him to run with it,' Parker recalled, 'but instead he just looked at the stitching and bitched about it.' With Scarfe equally unenamoured of Seresin, Parker reluctantly graduated to director.

His first move was to excise the Floyd themselves from the film. In this, he was aided by the poor quality of footage from *Wall* shows staged especially for the purpose in 1981 – which, Parker grumbled, 'looked like they'd been shot through soup.' Meanwhile, when Waters' screen tests proved he couldn't act, the role of Pink was awarded to Boomtown Rats singer Bob Geldof.

Shooting began in September 1981 and promptly degenerated into a power struggle between Waters and Scarfe on the one hand and Parker on the other. Geldof likened filming to a 'mine field . . . sown with exploding egos.' Gilmour characterised *his* role as 'begging the director to come back' whenever Parker

> *'There were no fisticuffs, but it was close on a couple of occasions. I may have had a little cry.'*
>
> Dave Gilmour

quit the set. He and Waters, meanwhile, oversaw the music for the film, including a delicate reinterpretation of 'Mother', and expanded versions of 'Bring the Boys Back Home' and 'Outside the Wall', the latter pair featuring the Pontarddulais Male Choir from Wales. The choir also graced 'When the Tigers Broke Free', a track about the death of Waters' father, which the Floyd had vetoed when he mooted it for *The Wall*. 'It was too personal to me,' he recalled. 'It's very specific about the time and place and so on, and therefore it would have made it clear that *The Wall* was about me.'

The soundtrack album might also have included an overture that Parker described as 'a quite remarkable piece of music which, sadly, didn't quite work with the rather unusual, quiet beginning of the *Wall* film' – and which therefore 'sadly had to be left out.' The Floyd's record companies would presumably also have wanted the hit 'Another Brick in the Wall, part two' – despite it having already reappeared on 1981's sardonically titled 'best of', *A Collection of Great Dance Songs* – perhaps in a medley with parts one and three, suffixed with the instrumental coda to the latter that appeared in the *Wall* shows.

NO PUSSYFOOTING

'It's mainly rearrangements,' Waters told Jim Ladd about the movie's music. 'For instance, "In the Flesh 2" has been rearranged for brass and chorus; no guitars, drums, or anything like that in it at all. Part one is exactly the same as it was, except Geldof sings it in the movie. He sings that and part two. Whether his vocal will appear on a soundtrack album depends on whether we can get him cheap enough. If we can't, I'll try and copy what he did.'

Geldof had, in fact, taken the role on the understanding that he would not have to sing. 'There was never any pussyfooting about what he thought about Pink Floyd or the music . . .' Waters remembered, "cos he was extremely scathing about the whole thing and I never tried to persuade him differently.

SPLIFF AND WHEN

Ten years after *The Final Cut,* with Waters long gone, Gilmour, Nick Mason, and the reinstated Rick Wright began work on *The Division Bell* by writing and jamming together for the first time since 1974. 'We put down over forty sketches in two weeks . . .' Mason told *Mojo.* 'Some of those initial ideas might actually end up on a satellite album.' However, as producer Bob Ezrin told *Q,* 'We started off great guns, then lost momentum. It was longer, more laboured.' The sessions were finally revived when Gilmour conjured 'High Hopes', the Floyd's finest post-Waters song. 'We eventually ended up with enough leftover material,' wrote Mason, 'that we considered releasing it as a second album, including a set we dubbed *The Big Spliff,* the kind of ambient mood music that we were bemused to find being adopted by bands like The Orb.'

(Drily) You know, these bog Irish: you can't tell them anything. They wouldn't understand. I'm not going to waste my time on Geldof, trying to explain *The Wall* to him. He understands; he just doesn't *realise* he understands.'

Summoned to Gilmour's studio to sing songs he despised, the erstwhile Boomtown Rat took his revenge. 'When it came to singing the six lines I had been allocated, I sang them in a highly accented Irish folk-singing manner,' he wrote in his autobiography. 'It was a delight to see the look of horror creep over the faces of Gilmour and James (Guthrie, co-producer).' After an 'even worse' second attempt, Gilmour objected that the vocal sounded 'very Irish'. 'I *am* Irish,' Geldof countered. 'Can't fucking help that.' The singer 'tormented them for as long as I could and then I sang it properly. At the end a voice came from the control room over the studio monitors: "You bastard!"'

WHICH ONE'S PINK?

Kevin McKeon and Bob Geldof played the young and old incarnations of the central character of *The Wall,* for which *Spare Bricks* was to have been the soundtrack. The movie proved as disastrous for their on-screen careers as it was for the future of the Floyd: between them, they earned only a handful of film credits in later years.

BORED WITH ALL THAT

'When the Tigers Broke Free' was issued as a single in July 1982 – backed with the reworked 'Bring the Boys Back Home' – and scraped into the British chart (then topped by Irene Cara's 'Fame', the title song of another Alan Parker movie). Its sleeve announced it was 'Taken from the album *The Final Cut'*. 'We were contracted to make a soundtrack album,' Waters explained to *Melody Maker*'s Karl Dallas before he left Britain for the film's US premiere. 'But there

really wasn't enough new material in the movie to make a record that I thought was interesting. The project then became called *Spare Bricks* and was meant to include some of the film music, like "When the Tigers Broke Free" and the much less ironic version of "Outside the Wall" which finishes the movie . . . plus some music written for the movie but left on the cutting-room floor.

'I decided not to include the new version of "Mother" . . . it really is film music and it doesn't stand up. It's a very long song and, besides, I'm bored with all that now. I've become more interested in the remembrance and requiem aspects of the thing, if that doesn't sound too pretentious. Anyway, it all seemed a bit bitty, when I came up with a new title for the album: *The Final Cut* . . . (and) I finally wrote the requiem I've been trying to write for so long – "Requiem for the Post-War Dream" – which became the sub-title of the album.

'We have got to the stage of a rough throw-together of all the work we've done so far. After about a week's work on the American launch, I'm going to take a holiday and, when we get back in September, we'll finish the album.'

THE FINAL STRAW

'Making *The Final Cut* was the final straw . . .' Waters told *Mojo*. 'Dave wanted me to wait until he had written some more material, but – given that he'd written maybe three songs in the whole of the previous five years – I couldn't see when that was going to happen.' Gilmour's specific objection, as he told Brisbane's FM104, was to previously rejected songs – such as 'Teacher Teacher', which became 'The Hero's Return' – being resurrected: 'I said things like, "Roger, this song isn't terribly good. We tried it on the *Wall* album and we decided it wasn't good enough then. Suddenly it got better?"'

'After we'd got into it a bit, he didn't come in very much,' recalled Waters, whose coping mechanism for sessions with his nemesis was playing *Donkey Kong* at the back of the studio. 'The big argument was whether he'd be getting a production credit and a point off the top for producing the record. He didn't produce it.' Even drummer Nick Mason, once Waters' strongest ally, sided with the guitarist. 'There were no fisticuffs,' Gilmour told *Mojo*. 'But it was close on a couple of occasions. I may have had a little cry at one point.' **BM**

1/10 **WILL IT EVER HAPPEN?**
The Floyd finally opened their archives for reissues of *Dark Side of the Moon, Wish You Were Here,* and *The Wall.* However, it seems unlikely that other albums will receive similar treatment – especially *The Final Cut,* whose making Waters recalls as 'absolute misery' and Gilmour as 'the most awful time of my life in terms of Pink Floyd.' They also remain divided about the material's merits, with Waters campaigning for six of its songs to be included on 2001's 'best of' *Echoes,* but Gilmour regarding 'The Gunner's Dream', 'The Fletcher Memorial Home', and 'The Final Cut' as the only good songs amid 'cheap filler'. *Spare Bricks,* it seems, will continue to gather dust.

WHAT HAPPENED NEXT . . .

pink
floyd
the
final
cut

'It just got to a point when I finally agreed to let him to do it because it was just too painful to do it any other way,' Gilmour explained of Waters' role in *The Final Cut.* 'It was just torture.' In an interview with *Guitar Player* intended to promote the album, released in March 1983, he complained: 'It's not personally how I would see a Pink Floyd record going. The sound quality is very good, it's very, very well recorded, and the string arrangements and orchestral stuff are very well done, but it's not me.'

'It sold three million copies, which wasn't a lot for the Pink Floyd,' Waters admitted to *Q.* 'And, as a consequence, Dave Gilmour went on record as saying, 'There you go: I knew he was doing it wrong all along.' But it's absolutely ridiculous to judge a record solely on sales. If you're going to use sales as the sole criterion, it makes *Grease* a better record than *Graceland.*'

'ELECTRIC NEBRASKA'

Artist Bruce Springsteen Year 1982 Country US Genre Folk Label Columbia What E Street exile

BRUCE SPRINGSTEEN
'They overruled the lyrics,' The Boss told *Uncut* of the E Street Band's versions of the *Nebraska* songs. 'It didn't work. Those two forms didn't fit. The band comes in and generally makes noise, and the lyrics wanted silence, y'know? They make arrangement, and the lyrics wanted less arrangement. The lyrics wanted to be at the centre and there was a minimal amount of music. The music was very necessary but it wanted to be minimal.'

By 1981, Bruce Springsteen had achieved the success he craved as a young singer-songwriter cutting his teeth in the New Jersey bar scene. With 1975's breakthrough *Born to Run,* 1978's *Darkness on the Edge of Town,* and 1980's *The River,* The Boss had established himself as a blue collar rock 'n' roll hero, his shows famed for lung-bursting passion. The last thing anyone – himself included – expected in 1982 was that he would release a bombast-free acoustic album recorded on a four-track in his rented house in Colts Neck, New Jersey. 'It was,' he told *Mojo,* 'not a mistake – an accident.'

AMERICAN ISOLATION

For all his arena-filling success, Springsteen lamented to *Rolling Stone,* by 1980, 'I had about twenty grand to my name. And this was after million-selling records and the cover of *Time* and *Newsweek.*' Back taxes, the cost of keeping the E Street Band together, and 'bad deals' that required heavy duty legal fees – a reference, presumably, to his battle to extricate himself from the grip of former manager Mike Appel – combined to create these financial woes.

However, when the touring cycle for *The River* came to a close in September 1981, Springsteen's bank balance had swelled considerably. But he wasn't about to fritter away his new-found fortune on another lengthy recording session. A two-month writing period over autumn and early winter had, by mid-December, yielded more than two dozen songs – but, rather than head straight for the studio, he despatched his guitar tech, Mike Batlan, to purchase a relatively new invention: the four-track recorder. 'I don't care what you get,' Springsteen told him. 'Just get me a little tape player I can sing some songs into and throw another track on, and I can tell if I have anything before I waste time and money in the studio with the band.'

On 3 January 1982, over a mammoth fifteen-hour recording session using just a Teac four-track, an acoustic guitar, and a couple of microphones, Springsteen and Batlan laid down fifteen songs in the singer's bedroom. Dubbing the results down onto cassette, Springsteen delivered it with a pages-long memo detailing the songs' themes to his manager Jon Landau. Inspired by his troubled childhood in Freehold, New Jersey, and sparked by

BRUCE SPRINGSTEEN
NEBRASKA

Cover: Isabel Eeles

COUNTRY MUSIC

Springsteen has habitually written and recorded more songs than he's seen fit to release. 2010's *The Promise* was a two-disc set of outtakes from *Darkness on the Edge of Town*; 1998's *Tracks* a sixty-six-song box set of unreleased material (including the 1982 version of 'Born in the USA'). Even in his seventh decade on this earth, little's changed. 'A while back,' Springsteen revealed to *NME* early in 2013, 'I recorded a country record and put it aside. I returned to it a couple of months ago and thought, "What am I going to do next?"' The answer was that the country album stayed on the shelf, and *High Hopes* came out instead.

Terrence Malick's movie *Badlands,* the stark, haunting songs veered from the autobiographical ('Used Cars', 'Mansion on the Hill') to bleak ruminations on criminals and cops ('Johnny 99', 'Highway Patrolman'), their DNA informed by bare-bones country and rockabilly.

'*Nebraska* was about . . . American isolation,' Springsteen told Kurt Loder in 1984. 'What happens to people when they're alienated from their friends and their community and their government and their job. Because those are the things that keep you sane; that give meaning to life in some fashion.'

SPOOKY INTIMACY

Jon Landau was convinced that the songs called for a different treatment to Springsteen's usual approach, and – according to biographer Peter Ames Carlin – 'proposed recording most of them with small, folk-like arrangements: acoustic guitars, stand-up bass, drums played with brushes.' But when the band entered New York's Power Station studios in February 1982, the initial burst of activity focused on Springsteen's more upbeat compositions, including 'Born in the U.S.A.', 'Glory Days', 'Cover Me', 'Darlington County', 'Working on the Highway', and 'Pink Cadillac' – most of which, it turned out, were bound for his 1984 smash, *Born in the U.S.A.*

> *'It was killing. It was all very hard-edged. As great as it was, it wasn't what Bruce wanted to release.'*
>
> Max Weinberg

After a short hiatus, the band returned to the studio and Springsteen produced his cassette tape of demos, upon which they spent a few days working out the arrangements. Full-band versions of songs such as 'Johnny 99', 'Mansion on the Hill', 'My Father's House', and 'Open All Night' were cut, but the spooky intimacy of the demos was lost in the pristine environment of the Power Station. 'The songs had a lot of detail, so that, when the band started to wail away into it, the characters got lost,' Springsteen told *Hot Press* in 1984. 'Like "Johnny 99" – I thought, "Oh, that'd be great if we could do a rock version." But when you did that, the song disappeared. A lot of its content

BOOTLEGGED IN THE U.S.A.

In *Bootleg: The Rise & Fall of the Secret Recording Industry,* Clinton Heylin ranks Springsteen alongside The Beatles, Dylan, Led Zeppelin, and the Stones as rock's most bootlegged acts. 'Electric Nebraska' in particular was regarded as a holy relic in the pre-internet era. Once indifferent to bootlegs, Springsteen's patience ran out in 1980 – when, as he told *Creem,* 'There were just so many that it was just big business, ya know? It was made by people who didn't care what the quality was.'

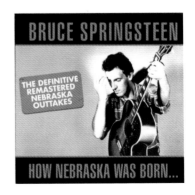

was in its style, in the treatment of it. It needed that really kinda austere, echoey sound: just one guitar – one guy telling his story.'

In April, an exasperated Springsteen threw the original demo to engineer Toby Scott and asked, 'Can we master a record off of this thing?' The answer was, ultimately, yes. 'It's amazing that it got there,' The Boss told *Rolling Stone,* ''cause I was carryin' that cassette around with me in my pocket without a case for a couple of weeks, just draggin' it around. Finally, we realised, "Uh-oh, that's the album." Technically, it was difficult to get it on a disc. The stuff was recorded so strangely, the needle would read a lot of distortion and wouldn't track in the wax. We almost had to release it as a cassette.'

In the event, *Nebraska* was released, on vinyl, on 20 September 1982. 'The title wasn't picked until the very last minute,' sleeve designer Andrea Klein told *Backstreets* magazine. 'There was another possibility: the other title was going to be *January 3, 1982* . . . I guess Jon Landau and Bruce thought it wasn't a good name for an album; it was too hard to say. (They) went through lyrics in the songs, looking for a title. They talked about *Open All Night* as a possibility (but) they thought *Nebraska* was more wide open.'

'IT WAS KILLING'
'The E Street Band actually did record all of *Nebraska,* and it was killing,' drummer Max Weinberg confirmed to *Rolling Stone* in 2010. 'It was all very hard-edged. As great as it was, it wasn't what Bruce wanted to release. . . . All those songs are in the can somewhere.'

In the ensuing years, Springsteen came to terms with how the songs of *Nebraska* could best be interpreted by his cohorts – indeed, several have emerged in full-band versions on official releases: 'Nebraska' and 'Johnny 99' on 1986's *Live 1975-85,* 'Atlantic City' on 1992's *MTV Plugged,* and 'Atlantic City' and 'Mansion on the Hill' on 2001's *Live in New York City.*

Live In Dublin (2007), with the Sessions Band, features a typically sombre rendition of 'Highway Patrolman', but 'Open All Night' is re-imagined as a Prohibition-era rave-up with fiddle, horn, bass, and drum solos, elaborate backing vocals and a party-hearty feel a million miles from the stark solitude of *Nebraska.* The other full-band renditions are more faithful to the original recordings, albeit with extra muscle. An insistent mandolin line and Weinberg's propulsive beat make 'Atlantic City' more anthemic, while 'Johnny 99' is realised as the rockabilly rave-up Springsteen attempted to capture in Studio A decades earlier. 'Mansion on the Hill' remains as mournful as it is on *Nebraska,* but with pedal steel guitar and Patti Scialfa's harmonies adding texture. To this day, many of the album's songs remain live favourites. **RY**

WHAT HAPPENED NEXT . . .
Nebraska was a surprisingly big hit, hitting the US top three and going gold in just two months. It also awakened a new fanbase. 'I didn't know there was music like that, that was as impactful and as heavy as *Nebraska* was,' Rage Against the Machine guitarist – and, of late, occasional E Street member – Tom Morello told Peter Ames Carlin. 'The alienation that I felt was for the first time expressed in music, and then I became a huge super-fan.' Other songs attempted in the 1982 band sessions became the bedrock of 1984's *Born in the U.S.A.,* a return to The Boss's rocking roots that sold an extraordinary fifteen million copies in his homeland alone.

WILL IT EVER HAPPEN?
5/10 The thirtieth anniversaries of *Born to Run* and *Darkness on the Edge of Town* yielded lavishly packaged reissues, but *Nebraska* received no such treatment. Perhaps Jon Landau's 2006 claim that the right version of the album had been released is the final word on the subject.

SESSIONS

Artist The Beatles **Year** 1985 **Country** UK **Genre** Pop-rock **Label** Parlophone **What** A proto-*Anthology*

GEORGE, PAUL, AND JOHN
'I hadn't heard anything of theirs that was any good, so they did "How Do You Do It?"' producer George Martin recalled. '(John Lennon) said, "Look, I think we can do better than this. If we write something better, can we do it?" I said, "Yes, but you're turning down a hit." They quickly came back with "Please Please Me".'

Sessions was slated for release in 1985, around eighteen months after Abbey Road's Studio 2 opened to the public and sharpened the appetite for intriguing Beatles rarities. The concept, however, was birthed much earlier. On the expiry of the Fab Four's original EMI contract at the start of 1976, the label acquired the right to reissue whatever it wished. It duly re-released every Beatles single and, on Sunday, 4 April, placed all twenty-two on the British chart simultaneously. 'Yesterday' – never before issued as a 45 in the UK – became the band's first top ten hit since 1970. Meanwhile, the rough and ready end of their back catalogue was repackaged as *Rock 'n' Roll Music:* a worldwide hit despite its inconsistent mixing and cover artwork so bad that John Lennon offered to design a replacement. Beneath this fresh wave of Beatlemania, however, was buried treasure: tracks lying dormant in the vaults.

BLISTERING
The cache of unheard material was little more than a rumour in the years following the band's split, piquing the interest of super-fans and conspiracy theorists who imagined there was a whole alternative Beatles history just out of reach. For its part, EMI systematically dug through dusty old tapes throughout the 1970s, hoping to salvage something worthwhile.

As bootlegs sprang up, EMI prepared an official release. A planned single comprised 'Leave My Kitten Alone' – a blistering Lennon performance that just missed a place on *Beatles For Sale* in 1964 – and a 1962 version of 'How Do You Do It?', a song they were happy to bequeath to Gerry and the Pacemakers (who took it to No. 1). Lennon's murder in 1980 wiped the single off the schedules, but EMI kept the compilation on the boil, whittling down tracks.

By the end of 1984 it had a selection it was happy with: 'How Do You Do It?' and 'Leave My Kitten Alone'; Paul McCartney's accomplished, fully solo demo of 'Come and Get It' (a hit for Badfinger around the time of The Beatles' demise); George Harrison's 'Not Guilty' (a 'White Album' reject that, its writer told *Rolling Stone*, 'would make a great tune for Peggy Lee'); an early, slow version of *Rubber Soul*'s 'I'm Looking Through You'; Lennon's deranged 'What's the New Mary Jane' (a track he proffered as a single after

Cover: Simon Halfon

WHAT HAPPENED NEXT . . .
The zeal for Beatles material never wavered. Repackaged versions of the original albums continued to chart, with *Sgt. Pepper* re-entering the UK top three on its twentieth birthday, and 1988's *Past Masters* rounding up rare mixes. Fans craving unheard tracks got a first boost with 1994's multi-platinum *Live at the BBC,* smoothing the path for the *Anthology* project the next year. With full Fabs endorsement, *Anthology* did everything that *Sessions* could not: packaging the story beautifully and delving into the recesses of the vaults. Now all we need is 'Carnival of Light' and the twenty-seven-minute version of 'Helter Skelter'.

'The White Album'); 'Bésame Mucho' (the Mexican ballad with which the band opened their audition for EMI in 1962); a 1963 version of Lennon's 'One After 909' (seven years before, with input from McCartney, it graced *Let It Be*); the *Help!* off-cuts 'If You've Got Trouble' (sung by Ringo) and 'That Means a Lot'; a version of 'While My Guitar Gently Weeps' created by Harrison alone; 'Mailman, Bring Me No More Blues' (popularised by Buddy Holly, and cut during sessions for *Get Back* [see page 24]); and 'Christmas Time (Is Here Again)' (made for the 1967 Christmas flexi-disc [see page 28]).

Sessions had a title, a cover, and a catalogue number – but not the backing of The Beatles, who exercised their veto. EMI made positive noises – 'We're now discussing the matter with the remaining Beatles . . . with an aim to releasing an album sometime' – but the power was back in the band's hands. **MH**

WILL IT EVER HAPPEN?

0/10

There's no need. All the songs ended up on the *Anthology* sets released in 1995 and 1996, bar 'Christmas Time (Is Here Again)', which appeared in truncated form on the 1995 single 'Free as a Bird'. And *Sessions* did make it to market one way or another anyway, with bootlegs feeding the desire for rare Beatles before *Anthology*'s mother lode.

TECHNO POP

Artist Kraftwerk **Year** 1983 **Country** Germany **Genre** Techno pop **Label** EMI **What** Hard werk

KRAFTWERK

'When the *Techno Pop* record was eventually finished,' percussionist Karl Bartos told *Sound on Sound,* 'Ralf (Hütter, founder) flew to New York and mixed it . . . The sleeve and everything was done, but Ralf felt insecure about it, and thought we should do the whole production again in New York and call it *Electric Café.* So we did. I think it was a mistake.'

There aren't many things that past and present members of Kraftwerk agree on, but one of them is the unreleased *Techno Pop.* It doesn't exist. 'I must say it very clearly,' former drummer Wolfgang Flür told author Dan LeRoy in 2005, 'There was never a *Techno Pop* album.' In an interview with *The Scotsman* – to promote Kraftwerk's first album of new material in seventeen years, 2003's *Tour De France Soundtracks* – founder Ralf Hütter clarified: 'We were working on an album concept called *Techno Pop,* but the composition was developed and we just changed the titles.' The album's name switching isn't really that mysterious, but its five-year gestation certainly is.

UNCERTAINTY BORDERING ON PARANOIA
In the late 1970s, Kraftwerk – once an oddball novelty – became synonymous with the future of pop. David Bowie was in their thrall, playing *Radio-Activity* (1975) as pre-show music during his *Station to Station* tour. Later, having moved to Berlin, he exhibited their influence on *Low, 'Heroes',* and Iggy Pop's *The Idiot* (all 1977). *'Heroes'* even contained 'V-2 Schneider', a dubious homage to Kraftwerk's enigmatic 'sound fetishist' Florian Schneider.

In 1981, the classic *Computer World* prompted the band's biggest tour. With their Kling Klang studio reincarnated as a mobile music-making machine, they roamed from Italy to India, via – remarkably for the time – East Germany and Poland. The shows were, by all accounts, amazing. Videos were synchronised to the music (straightforward now, teeth-grindingly tricky back then), the band's mechanical doppelgängers made their debut for 'The Robots', and hand-held instruments were given to front-row fans to play during 'Pocket Calculator'.

It seemed Kraftwerk and the world had agreed to meet halfway. Despite the snobbishness of German peers, the xenophobia of English-speaking critics, and the Luddite anti-synthesiser attitude of many rock fans, Hütter and Schneider's creation of a new German folk music, purged of American rock 'n' roll, had hit fruition. Kraftwerk were to become as pervasive an influence as The Beatles.

In the UK, with the advent of synthpop, a generation of teenage boys – always boys – wondered why their Casio keyboards sounded nothing like 'The Robots'. Americans were more direct in their appropriation. Grandmaster

KRAFTWERK

TECHNOPOP

Cover: Natalie Abadzis

EARLY WERK

Kraftwerk, biographer Pascal Bussy mourned to aktivitaet-fanzine.com, have often 'not been capable of completing their work. That goes from unreleased tapes to non-finished LPs . . . and even pure marketing nonsense (like) the fact that they refused to put their first three albums on CD.' To no fan's surprise, those first three albums – *Kraftwerk* (1970), *Kraftwerk 2* (1972), and *Ralf & Florian* (1973) – were omitted when the band played their catalogue in 2012 and 2013. Hütter suggested to *Dummy* magazine that they might one day be issued, remastered and with vintage artwork collected by Emil Schult, but that was in 2006 . . .

Flash invented hip-hop DJing by looping 'Metal on Metal', from 1977's *Trans-Europe Express,* between two turntables. Meanwhile, Afrika Bambaataa and Arthur Baker lifted the track's melody and paired it with drums from *Computer World*'s 'Numbers' to create 1982's seminal 'Planet Rock'. Later, in Michigan, Juan Atkins, Kevin Saunderson, and Derrick May fell in love with the German pioneers' hard electronics, and fused them with funk and R&B to birth techno.

Their influence was everywhere, but Kraftwerk vanished. What they were up to in the five years after the *Computer World* tour is still a matter of conjecture, but silence masked uncertainty that bordered on paranoia. Cut off from the world – the Kling Klang studio reputedly had no phone – they treated requests for collaboration from Bowie, Elton John, and Michael Jackson with disdain.

A BRIEF COMA

Maybe they were out on their bikes. The whole band took up cycling around the time of the *Computer World* tour, but Hütter became obsessive. 'Ralf got crazy about it, sometimes riding 200 kilometres a day,' percussionist Karl Bartos told biographer Pascal Bussy. 'Once I tried to keep up with him and I got exhausted. Florian was more lazy – he liked a glass of beer from time to time.' At one point, supposedly, a whole album based on cycling was planned. However, the only manifestation of Hütter's fixation would be 1983's 'Tour De France' EP, whose sampled breathing, bicycle pumps, and spinning gears were as beautifully evocative of cycling as 1975's 'Autobahn' was of motoring.

The pastime created a more definitive delay to new music. Hütter reportedly fractured his skull in a crash and spent a year convalescing. Emerging from a brief coma, his first words were said to be, 'How is my bike?' But the band were confident about material they had conjured between cycling trips. Initially called *Technicolor* but re-christened *Techno Pop* for trademark reasons, the album was scheduled for summer 1983, with press ads, a catalogue number, and artwork depicting the band on bicycles, like the 'Tour De France' EP. The release date was revised twice before both album and band vanished again.

'We spent three months in New York for the mixing,' Bartos told Bussy. 'But, when it was finished, nobody was really happy.' Bootlegs of *Techno Pop*'s title cut and 'Sex Object' provide a clue to the problem. Like 'Tour De France', both make heavy use of analogue synthesisers and effects the band had popularised in the 1970s. Kraftwerk had always pushed technology far beyond its intended capabilities. Where commercially available equipment was lacking, they made their own, like the electronic drums Flür and Bartos had played since the early 1970s. But now technology had out-paced them. Digital was the new thing: sampling, digital recording, and complicated machines like the Fairlight and Synclavier. *Techno Pop* sounded antiquated: Kraftwerk had to go digital. Hütter bought a Synclavier and more years were lost figuring out how to use it. 'I told him not to buy it – it was so terribly expensive!' Bartos told *Sound on Sound*.

Above all, though, the new material just wasn't funky enough, compared to the music they were hearing in clubs. As Flür told Dan LeRoy, 'We could consume it, but we weren't able to produce funk. It was, for example, one reason why we engaged co-producers and mixers for the first time.' One of those helpers was French producer François Kervorkian. Based in New York, he had alerted Hütter and Schneider to the influence Kraftwerk were having on dance music and had remixed 'Tour De France' for the soundtrack to early hip-hop exploitation movie *Breakin'*, making it a belated British hit in 1984.

BOING BOOM TSCHACK

Kervorkian's slick production characterised the album when it emerged, as *Electric Café,* in 1986. Little was left of the Kraftwerk fans knew and adored. The sleeve featured higher-resolution versions of the computer-rendered portraits of *Computer World,* courtesy of digital artist Rebecca Allen, who also made a futuristic video for the single 'Musique Non-Stop', a descendant of 'Techno Pop'. This itself had taken years to develop and been mothballed while the band completed the album. Typically, the sleeve bore precious little information, although Kervorkian is co-credited with Hütter for the mix.

Musically, it was mission accomplished. It was digital. It was funky. It just wasn't very good. Melody had been edged out by dancefloor-targeted workouts. The former 'Techno Pop' stretched over an entire side, with sampled vocals emulating drums ('Boing Boom Tschack') that linked minimalist pieces until 'Musique Non-Stop' provided a kind of culmination. It was tricky to tell where one track finished and the next began. A reworked, string-laden 'Sex Object' and Bartos's 'The Telephone Call' made concessions to traditional songwriting – the latter echoing *Computer World*'s sublime 'Computer Love' – but, by the closing 'Electric Café', it was evident that, in taking five years to construct thirty minutes of music, Kraftwerk had lost something vital: their humanity. Within months, house and techno would bring electronics to the masses, leaving Kraftwerk in the past. They had fought their way back to the forefront of technology, but their days as creative leaders were over. **MB**

WILL IT EVER HAPPEN?

1/10 In whatever form it existed before Kervorkian's involvement, no. When *Electric Café* was reissued in 2009, and performed in its entirety in New York in 2012 and London in 2013, it was re-christened *Techno Pop* – cementing the band's assertion that the two projects are the same.

WHAT HAPPENED NEXT . . .
Wolfgang Flür, who barely featured on *Electric Café,* was sidelined further as Hütter and Schneider digitised Kling Klang, feeding old master tapes into the Synclavier. He left in 1987 and published a lawsuit-attracting memoir, *I Was A Robot,* in 2000. Kraftwerk resurfaced with 1991's dire remix set *The Mix.* (By the time of its release, Bartos, too, had quit.) *The Mix* did however give an excuse to tour, which they did throughout the 1990s, with newbies Fritz Hilpert and Henning Schmitz. There were also promises of a new album and tantalising glimpses of its contents at shows in 1997 and 1998. Finally, 2003 brought *Tour De France Soundtracks,* a full-length exposition of the decades-old single.

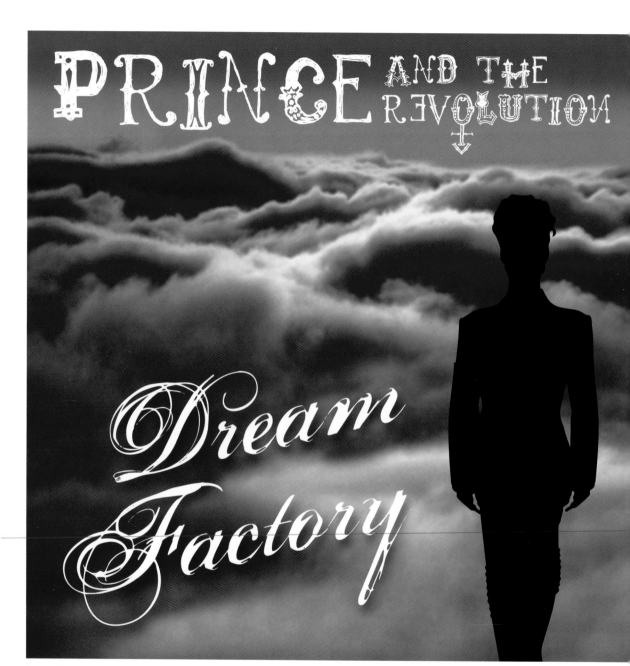

Cover: Herita MacDonald

DREAM FACTORY

Artist Prince & the Revolution **Year** 1986 **Country** US **Genre** R&B **Label** Paisley Park / Warner Bros.
What The Minneapolis maestro sows the seeds of *Sign 'o' the Times*

Pop's most prolific artist of the 1980s, Prince unleashed three hit albums in under two years: *Purple Rain*, *Around the World in a Day*, and *Parade*. In the same twenty-one months, he toured *Purple Rain*, masterminded albums by Sheila E, The Time, Apollonia 6, and The Family, gave the hit 'Manic Monday' to The Bangles, *and* made the *Under the Cherry Moon* movie. Just weeks before the release of the latter's soundtrack, *Parade*, in March 1986, he resumed recording at a new home studio. The following months brought personal and professional upsets, yet yielded both his greatest album and one of his most legendary unreleased collections.

BLACK, WHITE, STRAIGHT, GAY
'When we were working on it,' recalled guitarist Wendy Melvoin of the project, 'it wasn't called the *Dream Factory*.' Nonetheless, the mooted album wound up taking its title from a George Clinton-esque song of that name, recorded in December 1985 at sessions that also yielded *Parade's* 'Anotherloverholenyohead'. In March 1986, after committing his droll 'The Ballad of Dorothy Parker' to tape, Prince laid down the spine-tingling 'Power Fantastic', based on a piece by Melvoin and her partner, keyboardist Lisa Coleman. The latter also conjured the piano instrumental 'Visions'.

Melvoin, her sister Susannah (who sang with Prince's protégés The Family and with whom he was in a turbulent relationship), Coleman, and woodwind/ brass player Eric Leeds were his prime foils during this productive period – Lisa and Wendy having become key elements of his band since being enlisted for the *Dirty Mind* and *Purple Rain* tours, respectively. ('He didn't care if you were 'black, white, straight, gay, Puerto Rican, just a freakin'',' Melvoin told out.com, paraphrasing *Dirty Mind's* 'Uptown'. 'That guy wanted fans. So any way he could get them – and a more interesting way he could do it – appealed to him.')

Susannah Melvoin, her sister told *Vibe*, 'was doing a lot of vocals on that record, (while) Lisa and I brought the Fairlight (synthesiser) into the situation.' 'The Fairlight was just inspiration for a writer like Prince – for all of us,' Coleman explained. 'There were flute sounds, wind sounds, voice samples, handclap sounds. We would just build these songs around it.'

PRINCE
'I worked a long time under a lot of different people,' the star said in a 1986 interview, 'and, most of the time, I was doing it their way. That was cool, but I figured if I worked hard enough, and kept my head straight, one day I'd get to do it on my own. And that's what happened . . . My way usually is the best way.'

THE COST OF LOVING

'We were hoping that we would have the next fucking Grace Jones *Slave to the Rhythm* extravaganza,' declared Wendy Melvoin of her and Lisa Coleman's collaboration with super-producer Trevor Horn. 'We thought, "This is going to be genius! We're going to be musician freaks and experiment,"' she told out.com. 'And he, honest to god, wanted us to be the Spice Girls. My heart was broken.'

After the demise of the Revolution, the duo had earned a cult following with their albums *Wendy and Lisa* (1987), *Fruit at the Bottom* (1989), and *Eroica* (1990). By the end of the 1990s, however, their fortunes required a boost, hence the hook-up with Horn (to whose 1992 soundtrack *Toys* they had contributed). The sessions broke down when, according to Melvoin and Coleman, their working relationship with the producer became 'very uncomfortable'.

Fourteen songs were duly bootlegged as *Friendly Fire*. However, as manager Renata Kanclerz – later Coleman's wife – observed a decade later, 'The album was not named *Friendly Fire*. It never even evolved to a point of being named anything other than the inside joke name we had for it, which was *Costly Demos*.'

wendy & lisa

CRYSTAL BALLS

The 1998 anthology *Crystal Ball* included a handful of *Dream Factory* tracks from the archives. However, more recent songs dominated, leaving bootlegs as attractive as ever to fans of the era in which Prince created his finest work, the 1980s.

Within weeks, a first configuration of *Dream Factory* had been assembled and committed to cassette tape:

Side 1: Visions · Dream Factory · It's a Wonderful Day · The Ballad of · Dorothy Parker · Big Tall Wall · And That Says What?
Side 2: Strange Relationship · Teacher, Teacher · Starfish and Coffee · A Place in Heaven · Sexual Suicide

The sparse, drum-driven 'Big Tall Wall' boasted a chorus – 'I'm gonna build a big tall wall / stone circle so you can't get out' – aimed at Susannah, who had, around the time of its composition, fled Prince's castle (but nonetheless earned a rare co-writing credit for creating the lyrics of 'Starfish and Coffee'). The song was later considered for 1990's *Graffiti Bridge*, but both it and the largely instrumental 'And That Says What?' would remain unreleased.

(Susannah also inspired, as she told beautifulnightschitown.blogspot.co.uk, 'The infamous "Wally", which no one heard because he destroyed the tape. There's a huge story behind that. [I also inspired] 'Strange Relationship', [The Family's] 'Nothing Compares 2 U', 'In a Large Room with No Light', 'If I Was Your Girlfriend'. God, you know there's more and I can't remember . . .')

'It's a Wonderful Day' predated the *Dream Factory* sessions and, according to engineer Susan Rogers, may only ever have been intended as a placeholder. 'Strange Relationship' and 'Teacher Teacher' were resurrected from 1982, and revamped with Wendy & Lisa, in the latter instance creating a beguiling, quirky cocktail of his vintage new wave leanings and their psychedelic influence. 'A Place in Heaven' opened with Prince quipping, 'So, do you like environmental records? Crickets chirping, water rushing . . . S'posed to make you horny – just make me wanna go to the bathroom,' before evolving into a harpsichord-laden ballad. 'Sexual Suicide' was an addictively funky slice of sleaze that, had it remained as the closer, would have bucked Prince's penchant for ending albums with epics like 'International Lover' and 'Sometimes it Snows in April'.

CHARACTERISTICALLY QUEASY

Meanwhile, Prince & the Revolution played sporadic concerts in support of *Parade*. 'We were,' Lisa recalled, 'travelling and working every day.' As solo and group songs were added, *Dream Factory* grew into a double album:

Side 1: Visions · Dream Factory · It's a Wonderful Day · The Ballad of Dorothy Parker · It

Side 2: Strange Relationship · Teacher, Teacher · Starfish and Coffee · Interlude – Wendy · *(Life Is Like Looking For A Penny)* In a Large Room with No Light · Nevaeh ni Ecalp A *(a backwards portion of A Place in Heaven)* · Sexual Suicide

Side 3: Crystal Ball · Power Fantastic

Side 4: Last Heart · Witness 4 the Prosecution · Movie Star · A Place in Heaven · All My Dreams

Among the additions was the funk epic 'Crystal Ball', with characteristically queasy string arrangements by jazz and salsa veteran Clare Fischer. 'He never visits the studio when I am working for him,' Fischer told artistinterviews. eu, 'and I have never met him in person. He sends me memos and we talk

ME AND MRS JONES

Created alongside *Dream Factory* was the self-titled debut by former backing singer (and *Purple Rain* actress) Jill Jones. With Clare Fischer's strings, Prince engineer David Z's production, and songs from the man himself, *Jill Jones* (1987) is regarded as one of the finest Paisley Park albums.

> *'Crickets chirping, water rushing . . . S'posed to make you horny – just make me wanna go to the bathroom.'*
>
> Prince

over the phone. Once I sent him my *2+2* (album). I heard from people that were present at the time that, while he took out the disc, he looked away from the cover, saying, 'I don't want to know what he looks like. It is working just fine as it is.' Jazz also coloured the Stevie Wonder-esque 'In a Large Room with No Light' (originally prefixed with 'Life Is Like Looking for a Penny . . .') and the jaunty 'All My Dreams'. 'It reminded me of classic Kid Creole and the Coconuts,' recalled Wendy (whose 'Interlude' was a guitar instrumental).

The remainder was relatively straightforward funk, from the grinding 'It' and 'Witness 4 the Prosecution' to the delightful 'Last Heart'. The latter was a pristine, pre-*Dream Factory* demo, which Prince intended to re-record 'but never got around 2.' 'Movie Star' had been written for his (by now disbanded) protégés The Time and hence was laden with their characteristic wisecracking and arguing with female associates – a voice (assumed to be Susannah) demands, 'Are you wearing that Paco Rabbit or whatever you call it?'

SEXUALLY IRREVERENT

But for all the frivolity and creativity, mutiny was rumbling. Wendy and Lisa resented the heightened roles played by Susannah and dancers Greg Brooks and Wally Safford, especially as their own contributions to Prince's music often went uncredited. Longtime bassist Brownmark was similarly disenchanted. 'Wendy comes in the band one year, and she's famous because he made her famous,' he complained to Prince chronicler Per Nilsen, 'while you've got guys that have been hanging around with him for years. It's not fair.'

Melvoin suggested a further reason for the fallout. 'He had used up all he needed from us . . .' she told out.com. 'It might've been because he got Cat the dancer, and Sheila E to be in the band and be more sexually irreverent on stage with him, and that kind of played to his heterosexual side. Because, as a lesbian couple, we weren't playing that sexuality with him specifically, and I think that maybe he needed more of that playfulness, and that probably came from him wanting to exploit his heterosexual side more.'

The group survived to play two weeks of shows in the summer of 1986, by which time *Dream Factory* had been reconfigured once more:

Side 1: Visions · Dream Factory · Train · The Ballad of Dorothy Parker · It
Side 2: Strange Relationship · Slow Love · Starfish and Coffee · Interlude – Wendy · I Could Never Take the Place of Your Man
Side 3: Sign 'o' the Times · Crystal Ball · A Place in Heaven
Side 4: Last Heart · Witness 4 the Prosecution · Movie Star · The Cross · All My Dreams

Of the new songs, 'Train' was a churning soul oddity, 'Slow Love' a ballad co-written by songwriter Carole Davis (with whom Prince reportedly had a

WAKING FROM A DREAM

'He wanted to express himself completely,' said Wendy Melvoin (below, right) of the Revolution's demise. '(Lisa Coleman and I) were doing so much work. That's the way I rationalize it now. Prince may have other reasons . . . but we were led to believe that he needed to get back his mojo.'

brief relationship), and 'I Could Never Take the Place of Your Man', another playful cut resurrected from 1982. Most significant, however, were two very serious new songs, 'Sign 'o' the Times' and 'The Cross', which would ultimately become cornerstones of the album into which *Dream Factory* evolved.

SMASHED

Susannah designed two covers for *Dream Factory*. 'One of them was actually a dramatised version of myself,' she told beautifulnightschitown.blogspot.co.uk, 'opening up a door into this dream world, with images that were based on some of the songs. I remember that there was a lot of white space, because I couldn't fill up the background with colour. . . . Everything was kind of drawn onto white paper. But the doors were very ornate and I'm opening the door into the Dream Factory. The second album cover didn't have me on it. It just had the name *Dream Factory,* with some things hanging off the words.'

But the album was doomed when Wendy and Lisa confirmed their intention to leave, and Prince opted to disband the Revolution. At the end of a final show

WHAT HAPPENED NEXT . . .
After plotting a musical called *The Dawn,* Prince devised an album by his alter-ego Camille (whose sped-up vocals grace 'If I Was Your Girlfriend'). But its proposed January 1987 release date came and went, and cuts from it were combined with new songs to create *Crystal Ball* (unrelated to the 1998 anthology of the same name). When Warner balked at this proposed triple album, Prince cherry-picked from the past year's songs, including those on *Dream Factory,* to create the classic 1987 album *Sign 'o' the Times.*

> ## 'As a lesbian couple, we weren't playing that sexuality with him.'
>
> Wendy Melvoin

in Japan, in September, according to legend, the star smashed his guitar. 'His perception . . . was that *Dream Factory* equated Lisa and the Melvoins,' said Alan Leeds (Eric's brother and the Revolution's tour manager). 'You just simply don't make records with people like Wendy and Lisa . . . and then release that record after they've gone and go play those songs with somebody else.'

Several songs earned official releases: 'Power Fantastic' on *The Hits/The B-Sides* (1993); 'Dream Factory', 'Crystal Ball', 'Movie Star', Last Heart', and 'Sexual Suicide' on the *Crystal Ball* anthology (1998); 'Visions' on a bonus CD with Wendy and Lisa's *Eroica* (1990); and 'Train' on Mavis Staples' *Time Waits for No One* (1989). Others resurfaced only on bootlegs or occasional setlists. A few, however, survived to form the basis of his greatest album. And after years of strained relations between Wendy and Lisa and their former employer, détente was eventually reached. 'The three of us really had a special relationship and it's unbreakable,' Lisa told the *Guardian.* 'We did things that only happen in your dreams. They were some of the best times of my life.' **BM**

0/10   **WILL IT EVER HAPPEN?**
His tense relationship with Wendy and Lisa seems to have coloured Prince's view of the Revolution era. In 1998, he plotted a set called *Roadhouse Garden,* based on material recorded by the band around the *Dream Factory* era, including 'Witness 4 the Prosecution', 'All My Dreams', and 'In a Large Room with No Light'. 'The group needn't b 2gether 2 release an album,' he explained. But this never appeared and the *Dream Factory* remains closed.

THE MAN WHO STEPPED INTO YESTERDAY

Artist Phish **Year** 1987 **Country** US **Genre** Prog rock **Label** Self-release **What** Stonedhenge

TREY ANASTASIO
'Music is like a porthole into this other world, which is the world of truth,' Phish's leader told *Guitar World*. 'By listening to different types of music, you get a glimpse into the way the world is really lined up ... Bob Marley – he was on to something. So was Jimi Hendrix and Duke Ellington and Duane Allman and Bach and Brahms and Kurt Cobain and Bill Monroe.'

Somewhere on the other side of a conceptual door in the United States is a mystical, mythical land that draws revellers and acolytes in the same way Stonehenge does on the summer solstice in the United Kingdom. The land is called Gamehendge, and it is embodied in a travelling circus of Phish fans, dedicated to following the band on seemingly endless tours across the US. 'The Gamehendge Saga', as it is popularly known, is a strange tale first told on the concept album *The Man Who Stepped Into Yesterday,* whose lack of official release has proved no impediment to its elevation into rock lore.

A TERRIBLE TIME IN MUSIC
Customarily abbreviated to *TMWSIY* by fans (a.k.a. 'Phish heads'), the album was composed by guitarist and chief songwriter Trey Anastasio as his senior project to obtain a music degree from Goddard College in Vermont. As the first studio album by a youthful Phish – formed in 1983, and then all in their early twenties – the recording recounts, through narration and song, the quest of the retired Colonel Forbin, who steps through a mysterious door while walking his dog McGrupp. He encounters Rutherford the Brave – a knight 'in gnarly armour' – who draws him into a quest to release the people of Gamehendge (The Lizards) from the grip of Wilson, an evil dictator.

Forbin must recover *The Helping Friendly Book,* written by the prophet Icculus, stolen by Wilson, and containing 'all the knowledge inherent in the universe.' Wilson executes revolutionaries with the AC/DC Bag, a metal robot hangman. Forbin eventually locates Icculus on a mountaintop retreat, from where the holy man sends The Famous Mockingbird to retrieve the stolen tome. The colonel is warned, however, that, 'all knowledge, seeming innocent and pure, becomes a deadly weapon in the hands of avarice and greed.'

The piece was intentionally out of step with prevailing trends. 'Pop music had become, in the '80s, this horrible plastic thing where you had to make a video before you made music,' Anastasio remarked to *The Believer.* 'It was a terrible time in music, for me, other than some of the great punk bands like Bad Brains. I mean, there's always good stuff going on – Prince, Talking Heads – but, in pop culture, it was horrendous.'

Cover: Jayne Evans

PHISH UPON A STAR

Among Phish's most popular traditions is the Halloween show in which they don a musical 'costume', performing a classic album in its entirety alongside sets of their own material.

To date there have been six 'costumes': 'The White Album' by The Beatles (performed in 1994), *Quadrophenia* by The Who (1995), *Remain in Light* by Talking Heads (1996), *Loaded* by The Velvet Underground (1998), *Exile on Main St* by The Rolling Stones (2009), and *Waiting for Columbus* by Little Feat (2012). In 1998, two days after the Velvet Underground night, Phish surprised the crowd by performing another lysergic classic: Pink Floyd's *Dark Side of the Moon*.

The first four Halloween shows are available on CD as part of the Live Phish series.

THE VICTOR DISC

After a two-year hiatus, Phish returned for New Year's Eve 2002. Prior to the comeback shows, they cut an impromptu album of studio jamming in New York on 19 December. The raw result – named *The Victor Disc,* after its engineer – was never released but, like most Phish music, is available online. 'I called Mike (Gordon) and he was in bed,' Anastasio told *Rolling Stone.* 'But he (and the others) came down and we recorded another album. He's always up for anything bizarre.'

A GIANT IN-JOKE

Fans and band members have likened the Phish phenomenon to a giant in-joke (during a band hiatus, Stephen Colbert quipped, 'Marijuana is a gateway drug that can lead to awful things, like Phish getting back together'). In that spirit, *The Man Who Stepped Into Yesterday* does not take itself too seriously, with bewildering plot twists and deviations from its narrative to name-check college friends. Gamehendge is a land populated by 'spotted stripers', 'unit monsters', and 'multi-beasts'. The result is like a kaleidoscopic cross between *The Chronicles of Narnia* (the source of the song title 'Prince Caspian') and a self-aware Spinal Tap. (Although yet to perform in front of a scale model of Gamehendge, Phish have been known to play solos on vacuum cleaners and execute synchronised trampoline routines while jamming.)

For all the tongue-in-cheek trappings, the music of *The Man Who Stepped Into Yesterday* is remarkably accomplished. While Anastasio, bassist Mike Gordon, keyboardist Page McConnell, and drummer Jon Fishman are known today for extended improvisation, their early years were a more arranged affair. 'When I was doing that whole Gamehendge thing,' the guitarist told jambands. com, 'I don't think that there's ever been a time when I was working so hard. I was living alone in a little apartment and working from the minute I woke up

> *'It was important for us to play in odd time signatures and have lyrics about strange monsters.'*
>
> Mike Gordon

until the minute I went to bed. I was listening to a lot of Stravinksy and Ravel. I really was only listening to classical music . . . Ravel was an impressionist composer of sorts and it was music where there were flurries of notes that were big, broad strokes of sound. I was trying to do a lot of stuff like that: breaking ground in every direction. I don't think that the power of the simple tune was at the forefront of my mind at the time.' ('Back in the day,' Gordon told 7d.blogs. com, 'it was more important for us to play in odd time signatures – to play in 13 and have lyrics about strange monsters from other galaxies or whatever.')

The Man Who Stepped Into Yesterday was never officially released, as the then-unsigned band focused on honing their live act. (After two independently issued albums, 1989's *Junta* and 1990's *Lawn Boy,* they made their major label debut with 1992's *A Picture of Nectar,* on Elektra.) But all the songs on the album still feature in the band's vast in-concert repertoire, and the complete piece has been played live on a handful of occasions.

MAGICAL WORLD

Phish biographer Parke Puterbaugh has unashamedly likened *The Man Who Stepped Into Yesterday* to The Beach Boys' legendary *Smile* (see page 12), insisting that a formal recording would elevate the work to the level of *Dark Side of the Moon* and *Quadrophenia* (both covered by Phish – see opposite page). However, the full 'Gamehendge Saga' remains hard to pin down, partly because many songs have been added. Live favourites like 'Punch You in the Eye', 'Gumbo', 'Llama', 'Divided Sky', and 'Cavern' relate fragments of tales set in Gamehendge, but are never consciously played in order, so their relation to the narrative is left to the interpretations of 'phans'. Some songs in the original piece – including 'Wilson' and 'ACDC Bag' (the latter a reference to guitar chords rather than the Australian heavy metal legends) – were even written before Anastasio conjured up the album's concept.

Nonetheless, the name Gamehendge has evolved beyond its genesis in *The Man Who Stepped Into Yesterday* to signify the realm of the Phish-heads and Phish shows – a parallel, culturally alternative, magical world. **JF**

WILL IT EVER HAPPEN?

5/10 The band has always allowed fans to tape and circulate shows. And, since 2003, all concerts, as well as some archived shows, have been available at livephish.com – so there is a chance that *TMWSIY* could be released as a download. Meanwhile, copies circulated among friends and fans in 1987 have surfaced online.

WHAT HAPPENED NEXT . . .

The Man Who Stepped Into Yesterday became one of the seeds that grew into a social and musical phenomenon that is now in its fourth decade. Phish was once thought of as the next Grateful Dead, and the Deadhead model of a travelling fan community is mirrored by the devotion shown by Phish-heads. Many fans survive by selling goods and food to each other while following the band across the country, creating a nomadic festival atmosphere. Phish is consistently one of the top-grossing acts in the US, able to sell out four-night runs at New York's Madison Square Garden.

Among the attractions are the band's spontaneity and versatility: fans know they will never hear the same song two nights in a row, and the music encompasses rock, jazz, bluegrass, country, barbershop quartet, covers, and epic improvisation. The audience is part of the show, bringing juggling, costumes, and art to the mix. At the peak of a particularly inspiring jam, they might launch glowsticks into the air, creating a sparkling sea of colour (not to mention a 'health and safety' headache).

Over the years, many A-listers have joined Phish onstage, including Bruce Springsteen (left, with Anastasio), B.B. King, Jay-Z, Neil Young, Willie Nelson, Phil Lesh, Carlos Santana, Kid Rock, and George Clinton.

Chapter 4

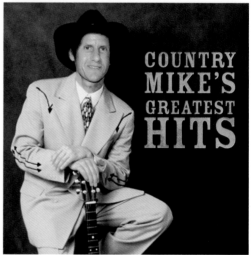

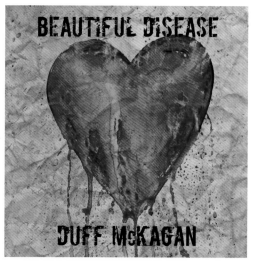

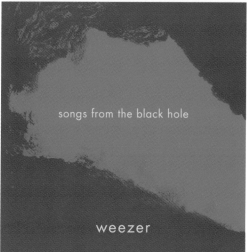

songs from the black hole

weezer

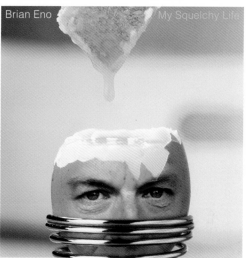

The Nineties

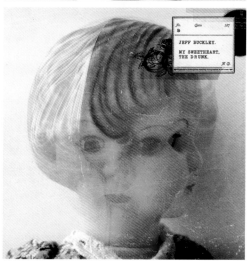

MY SQUELCHY LIFE

Artist Brian Eno **Year** 1991 **Country** UK **Genre** Left-field scuzz **Label** Opal/Warner Bros
What The boundary-pushing pioneer goes pop

BRIAN ENO
'We're not writing symphonies to sit around for 100 years,' the maestro told *Mojo*. 'We're making magazines, not novels, and it really makes a difference when it appears what mood the rest of the culture is in. For instance, (Eno and David Byrne's) *My Life in the Bush of Ghosts* would have been a total nonevent four years later.'

Late summer 1991, and Brian Peter George St John Le Baptiste de la Salle Eno's creative and commercial stock was high. He'd recently returned to the microphone for *Wrong Way Up,* a surprisingly accessible set with old sparring partner John Cale, while the fruits of his latest collaboration with a creatively revitalised U2 were imminent with *Achtung Baby.* The prospect of his first album of solo songs in almost fifteen years was made all the more tantalising by the array of projects that he had produced and composed since 1977's *Before and After Science.* But despite the distribution of promotional copies by record company Warner Bros, and even a couple of reviews in the music press, the album was shelved.

TREMENDOUS CONSTERNATION

The label was enthusiastic about *My Squelchy Life,* yet the two parties couldn't agree on a release date. Eno wanted a September 1991 launch, firmly believing that to be the right time and place. Warners, concerned by a potential surfeit of albums in the run-up to Christmas, favoured February 1992. 'They said, "Don't you believe in it?",' he told *The Wire.* 'I said, "Yes, well, I do *now.* But I'm sure I won't by February. . . . Even the delay that currently exists between finishing something and releasing it is too long for me."'

Convinced that *My Squelchy Life's* moment would have passed by the new year – and with his mind already focused on a fresh project, *Nerve Net* – Eno opted to withdraw the album altogether. 'Perhaps unadvisedly in retrospect,' he admitted to *Mojo,* 'because some of the things on *My Squelchy Life* I really like now.' As he good-humouredly explained to *Audio* magazine's John Diliberto in 1993, 'I also returned the advance, which is something you've never seen an artist do at all. This actually broke all known industry standards and caused tremendous consternation. This had never been heard of before.'

Of the trio of songs yet to officially surface, 'The Harness' – which slipped out on a Warners promotional CD – is scuzzy, left-field pop. 'I just didn't feel convinced about it any more,' Eno reflected later to the BBC. 'The only thing I wish I could release somehow are the synthesiser solos in it, with that really, really piercing sound.' 'Tutti Forgetti' showcases Eno's humorous side.

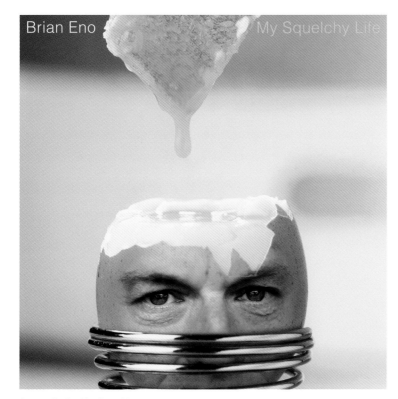

Brian Eno My Squelchy Life

Cover: Herita MacDonald

WHAT HAPPENED NEXT . . .
The creatively restless Eno moved on to *Nerve Net,* released in September 1992. Three of its tracks were culled from the *Squelchy* sessions: the terse, paranoid 'My Squelchy Life', the slightly comic 'Juju Space Jazz', and the piano piece 'Little Apricot', retitled 'Decentre'. Five further cuts – 'I Fall Up', 'Stiff', 'Some Words', 'Under', and 'Over' – bolstered 1993's *Brian Eno II: Vocal* box set.

Over propulsive percussion, comparable to 'Help Me Somebody' on his and David Byrne's *My Life in the Bush of Ghosts,* Eno exhaustively lists all he has forgotten ('Everything', it transpires, including his friends, dog, and teeth). 'Everybody's Mother/Step Up' opens with an eerie intro, which later surfaced within 1992's ambient set *The Shutov Assembly,* and segues into one of the album's most sublime moments. Demonstrating a remarkable ear for the obscure, the MTV Hive website listed this as one of Eno's five strangest songs.

With the album squelched, fans were denied a lush, warm, poppy collection. 'Some of the songs that were on that – very nice songs – were somewhat retrospective,' Eno told *Audio.* 'It's not a question of whether I like things or not. I pretty much like everything I do. But my feeling is that things don't come with intrinsic and timeless value.' His *Squelchy Life* was bygone. **JL**

WILL IT EVER HAPPEN?

4/10 Eno doesn't seem concerned with revisiting his past. Several songs were subsequently compiled, so he's unlikely to dust off decades-old work that he abandoned only months after it was recorded. As he told the *Telegraph* in 2010: 'I do sometimes look back at things I've written in the past and think, "I just don't remember being the person who wrote that."'

SWEET INSANITY

Artist Brian Wilson **Year** 1991 **Country** US **Genre** Pop **Label** Sire **What** The most aptly titled album in this book

BRIAN WILSON
'My name is Brian and I'm the man / I write hit songs with a wave of my hand,' ran the opening lines of a jaw-dropping rap on *Sweet Insanity*. 'Songs of surf and sun and sand / I make great music with my band,' sang the visionary who – via The Beach Boys' *Smile* – invented the notion of legendary unreleased albums. Sweet, no. Insanity, hmm . . .

By his early forties, Brian Wilson had been consigned to the sandpit of history. In the middle of the 1980s, he was a troubled relic – a genius no doubt, but one whose powers had been whittled away by drug abuse, mental health issues, and an ongoing war with his fellow Beach Boys. Cousin Mike Love, in particular, was a constant adversary. They had always fought for the soul of their band, but now they were grappling over the minutiae, with court disputes about writing credits. It looked like a sorry end to one of the greatest bands of the 1960s and their one-time creative beacon's fading light. Enter an unlikely saviour. His reputation would eventually lie in tatters, but clinical psychologist Eugene Landy bestowed a treasured gift on pop fans all over the world: a revitalised Brian Wilson.

CONSIDERABLE UNEASE
Landy's staggering degree of control over this renaissance may have been a necessity but, as the story unfolded, the overriding reaction was considerable unease. The psychologist nurtured Wilson towards a sort of equilibrium, but took a bizarre cut of the proceeds: chaperoning his charge through life, and appearing in the credits for 1988's comeback *Brian Wilson* as executive producer, co-writer, and even, on the epic 'Rio Grande', backing vocalist. He didn't so much re-write the doctor-patient rulebook as tear it up entirely.

Commercially, with heavy irony, *Brian Wilson* was overshadowed by the Brian-less Beach Boys' 'Kokomo', their first *Billboard* chart-topper since 'Good Vibrations' in 1966. Creatively, it was a success: Wilson sounded more committed, more inspired than he had since that same heyday. The feeling persisted that he was a marionette at Landy's fingertips, but his album met a rush of warmth for its reactivation of a special talent. Misgivings can be ignored in that atmosphere – but the follow-up would have to negotiate tougher terrain.

Work on *Sweet Insanity* began around the time of *Brian Wilson*'s release, its personnel largely retained from that album. Landy again took production credits to match his grip on Wilson's everyday life – albeit joined by producer Andy Paley and the Electric Light Orchestra's Jeff Lynne. The latter was now involved with The Traveling Wilburys – which, circuitously, meant guest appearances

BRIAN
WILSON

Sweet Insanity

Cover: Louise Evans

CHILD IS FURTHER AWAY

'Don't sit around on your ass / Smoking grass . . .' – it really is a mystery why The Beach Boys' *Adult/Child* failed to secure a release with a zinger like that in its opening verse. Brian Wilson had returned to fully-fledged Beach Boys duties in 1976 for *15 Big Ones* but, after the following year's *The Beach Boys Love You,* the band (*left to right* Dennis Wilson, Al Jardine, Brian Wilson, Mike Love, Carl Wilson) again began to split at the seams. Brian toiled on *Adult/Child* with various bandmates – including Dennis Wilson, then preparing his own *Pacific Ocean Blue* – coming and going. The patchy results, including jarring big band excursions, failed to impress Reprise and the album languished in the vaults, with only the occasional track – 'Hey Little Tom Boy', 'Shortnin' Bread' – popping up on later releases.

from fellow Wilburys Tom Petty and Bob Dylan, with Dylan taking a prominent role on the chugging, saxophone-peppered 'Spirit of Rock 'n' Roll'.

REALLY NOT HAPPENING

Setting their sights on the chart after *Brian Wilson*'s gorgeous 'Love and Mercy' fell short of the Hot 100, Landy and Wilson endeavoured to lure voguish hit-makers to the studio as work continued into the new decade. Among them was Matt Dike – who, in 1989, scored three top ten smashes in as many months, with rappers Tone Lōc and Young MC. To him they played 'Smart Girls', an ill-advised foray into hip-hop with clunky quotes from 'Surfin' USA', 'Help Me, Rhonda', and 'Good Vibrations' alongside a half dozen more Beach Boys favourites and a rap from Wilson himself. 'I'm thinking, "What are you – fucking *nuts?!*"' Dike marvelled to writer Dan LeRoy. 'But instead I said, "I'm a really big fan of The Beach Boys – and Brian, you gotta sing, man! People wanna hear you sing. This rap thing is really not happening." . . . They just stared at me – like, "You don't wanna be part of our million-dollar scheme?!"'

> *'An album of Brian's madness that no one wants to release and still everyone says he's a genius!'*
>
> Mike Love

Another big name was equally unimpressed: Was (Not Was)'s Don Was – who, having co-produced a chart-topping comeback by The B-52's, was now working with the likes of Iggy Pop and Bob Dylan. When he met Wilson at a party in 1990, Was reported, 'Brian had no idea who I was or what I'd done, but we began talking, and he invited me to come and hear the album he was making . . . It was difficult, though – listening to it with him – because, although a few of the hooks were good, I truthfully didn't like the songs. *Sweet Insanity* is well crafted, but kind of lazy at the songwriting end.' Was figured that being straight with Wilson would earn his respect and perhaps prove fruitful further down the line – a long game that paid off with 1995's *I Just Wasn't Made for These Times* album and documentary, which Was helmed.

SPLASHING COLOUR

Sweet Insanity in fact has plentiful merits, with bootlegs allowing us to imagine what might have been had the Sire label not balked at what they considered an underwhelming set. The production is more bombastic and opulent than the subtler shades of *Brian Wilson*. But Wilson's mojo remains in evidence, evoking former glories from the get-go with an introductory snatch of 'God Only Knows' before the big, brassy vamp of 'Someone to Love'. Wilson sounds unrestrained, if a little gruff, pepped by the happy response to his return.

There are, admittedly, missteps. 'Water Builds Up' feels like a garish festive song, working in whistles and fairground organ as sheer noise piles up. It's a similar tale on 'Do You Have Any Regrets?', which buries melodies and a sweet calypso rhythm beneath piano pings and extraneous effects. But the hooks and tunes throughout the remainder are enough to forgive any follies. 'Rainbow Eyes' is a gem: pizzicato synth strings and chimes combine as Wilson eulogises a girl 'splashing colour wherever you go,' his wide-eyed wonder as beguiling as ever, and the song soars on a killer bridge. 'Thank You (Brian)' also induces goosebumps with pretty musical motifs and a wandering trumpet solo. Even dumber fare like 'Hotter' has an irresistible swing.

And while 'Smart Girls' was a far from triumphant excursion into rap, Wilson's tongue was in his cheek. That – assuming it was his idea – is the message of the album title too: a frank indication that he was willing to poke fun at his own issues. Inevitably, there were some who didn't get the joke. 'Who wants to hear about Brian's mental problems anyway?' Mike Love asked *Mojo* in 1993. 'I mean, to call a record *Sweet Insanity,* imagine that. A whole album of Brian's madness that no one wants to release and still everyone says he's a genius!' He was right about one thing: no one wanted to release it. Sire shelved it and Wilson regrouped for better things. **MH**

WHAT HAPPENED NEXT . . .
The year after *Sweet Insanity*'s rejection, a court order arising from a suit by Wilson's family barred Landy from contacting him. When Wilson got his act together, 1995 saw the *I Just Wasn't Made for These Times* project and a welcome collaboration with his *Smile* co-writer Van Dyke Parks (see page 12) on the *Orange Crate Art* album (below). To Parks's frustration, Wilson refused to write, preferring only to sing. Nonetheless, the former told *The Independent,* 'I got a chance to register with him that I was grateful for what he had done for me, or to me, some thirty years prior.' A renewed creative impetus saw Wilson finally get *Smile* itself together for a lovingly arranged approximation in 2004.

WILL IT EVER HAPPEN?

4/10 The projected closing track 'Country Feeling' became the only one of the original recordings to see official release – on *For Our Children,* a compilation released by Walt Disney Records in conjunction with the Pediatric AIDS Foundation in 1991. Otherwise, 'Rainbow Eyes', 'Make a Wish', and 'Don't Let Her Know She's an Angel' appear in re-recorded and slightly rewritten form on Wilson's 2004 album *Gettin' In Over My Head.* That so few were salvaged suggests there was little faith in the overall quality of *Sweet Insanity,* dulling demand for a full release.

HELTER SKELTER

Artist Dr. Dre & Ice Cube **Year** 1994 **Country** US **Genre** Gangsta rap **Label** Death Row/Interscope
What A much mooted reunion of the N.W.A rap titans

ICE CUBE
'*Of course* we're exploiting violence, but there's nothing unusual about that . . .' the rap star told the *Los Angeles Times*. 'This country's national anthem is full of rockets' red glare and bombs bursting in air. That's just the way America is, so why shouldn't Dre and Cube be able to exploit a little violence every now and then?'

Cult leader Charles Manson, Paul McCartney marvelled, 'interpreted that (The Beatles' 1968 song) "Helter Skelter" was something to do with the four horsemen of the Apocalypse. . . . He interpreted the whole thing – that we were the four horsemen . . . and arrived at having to go out and kill everyone.' It's safe to say this association was on the minds of rap titans Dr. Dre and Ice Cube when they named their much-hyped joint venture after the Beatles classic. Unfortunately, over two decades after its conception, the album seems as likely to be released as Manson himself.

NIGGAZ WITHOUT EAZY

The reunion of Dre and Cube appeared as remarkable as the success of the quintet that made them famous: N.W.A, whose *Straight Outta Compton* (1988) put gangsta rap on the map thanks to the title track's aggressive video and the FBI-baiting 'Fuck tha Police'. But little over a year after the soon-to-be classic album's release, Cube walked out, having clashed with manager Jerry Heller over royalties that he felt were due him. Dre, MC Ren, DJ Yella, and founder Eazy-E persevered, scoring a US No.1 with 1991's *Efil4zaggin,* only to splinter that summer amid further financial acrimony.

The former brothers in arms waged war on wax. 'Started with five and, yo, one couldn't take it,' Dre sniped on N.W.A's '100 Miles and Runnin''. Most infamous was Cube's 'No Vaseline', which attacked Heller and his former bandmates so viciously that it was sliced from the UK edition of his *Death Certificate* album. 'We didn't break up the group,' he explained to *Rap City*. 'Somebody in the middle of us (i.e., Heller) broke the group up. So we just went our separate ways – my homies spittin' stuff in my ear, they homies spittin' stuff in they ear – and then we got this little feud goin'.'

By mid-1992, bridges had been built between the group's most creative members. 'N.W.A is finished . . .' Dre told *Yo! MTV Raps* in 1992, as his solo debut *The Chronic* began a rise to being as commercially successful and culturally influential in the new decade as *Straight Outta Compton* was in the late 1980s. 'I'm doin' my own thing. Me and Cube got together a few days ago and we're gettin' ready to start on our album.'

DR. DRE ICE CUBE

HELTER SKELTER

PARENTAL ADVISORY EXPLICIT CONTENT

Cover: Matt Reynolds

D.O.C. VS THE DOC

The D.O.C. grew dissatisfied with Dre (the pair allegedly arguing about the injured D.O.C.'s ability to rap), Death Row (whose accounts left much to be desired), and the on-off *Helter Skelter* saga. Eventually, he fled to Atlanta, taking his tapes and lyrics, and created his own *Helter Skelter* (1996) as a (subsequently disowned) spoiler. On its autobiographical 'From Ruthless 2 Death Row (Do We All Part)', he complained, 'From what I put out, I never got a fuckin' thing.'

'After he got away from that situation,' Cube explained of Dre's disentangling from N.W.A, 'we talked to each other, called each other, and just started dealin' with each other like men. We realised that there wasn't no reason for *us* to be feudin'. We family. So we just got back together.'

By 1993, there was no more successful sound in hip-hop than the G-Funk of the Death Row label. Dre had founded the Row with Suge Knight, whose persuasive deployment of baseball bats reportedly secured the doctor's release from his contract with Eazy-E's Ruthless label. (In August 1991, Eazy filed a state court complaint against Knight, alleging 'duress' and 'menace' was used to void his exclusive contracts with Dre and the D.O.C. – an N.W.A associate who, according to Cube, 'wrote the lion's share' of *Straight Outta Compton* with him). Hits from *The Chronic,* Death Row's first release, propelled the album to triple platinum and Dre's protégé Snoop Doggy Dogg to stardom.

> *'What would be the point of Ice Cube and Dr. Dre doing a project like this if we didn't freak people out?'*
>
> Ice Cube

Cube, meanwhile, had scored three platinum albums, including 1992's riotous, US chart-topping *The Predator.* In the wake of his old compadre's success, his 1993 set *Lethal Injection* had a distinctly G-Funkish air, not least in its enlistment of George Clinton, whose P-Funk empire was the source of many Dre samples. It too went platinum – making a reunion of the pair the hottest ticket in hip-hop. 'The plan is,' Dre announced, 'he's gonna do two solo cuts on the album, I'm gonna do two solo cuts . . . and the rest we're gonna do together. . . . It'll be Dr. Dre and Ice Cube, Ice Cube and Dr. Dre – we'll flip a coin to see whose name goes first. It don't matter to me. Just gimme the papes!' The good doctor evidently won: when the album, christened *Helter Skelter,* was announced on the liner notes of Snoop's solo debut *Doggystyle* in November 1993, it was credited to 'Dr. Dre/Ice Cube' – although they mockingly dubbed themselves N.W.E., or Niggaz Without Eazy.

APOCALYPTIC RACE WAR

Helter Skelter was apparently intended to feature an end-of-the-world theme. The same name had been given by Manson – inspired by the Bible and The

IN THA DOGG HOUSE

Another album trailed on *Doggystyle's* liner notes (right) – *Eargasm* by The Lady of Rage, a *Chronic* contributor and maker of the much loved 'Afro Puffs' – would follow *Helter Skelter* into unreleased oblivion, possibly owing to Death Row throwing all its weight behind 2Pac instead.

Beatles – to his vision of an apocalyptic race war. (Presumably Dre and Cube envisaged a different outcome to his predicted white triumph over 'blackies'.)

'We'll be a part of it,' Snoop assured MTV. 'Put my lil' two cents in, like I did on Dre's album.' Also on board was The D.O.C. Amid the N.W.A fallout, the Dallas-born rapper had remained tight with Dre, who produced his solo debut *No One Can Do It Better* (1989), then kept him on as a ghostwriter after a car crash rendered D.O.C. unable to take the mic himself.

However, with Dre distracted by Snoop and Death Row's success, and Cube consolidating his career in movies, work proved sporadic. The only confirmed recording was the George Clinton collaboration 'Can't See Me' (which subsequently passed to Snoop's compadres Tha Dogg Pound, before winding up, as 'Can't C Me', on 2Pac's 1996 bestseller *All Eyez On Me*). Rumoured cuts included 'Gimme Fifty Feet', an inevitable weed homage entitled 'Endonesia', 'Grand Finale 2' (the sequel to a cut featuring N.W.A on D.O.C.'s solo debut), and possibly an early version of 'Game Over' (a track on Scarface's 1997 smash *The Untouchable* that featured Dre and Cube).

BROTHERS IN ARMS
N.W.A captured on tour in Missouri in 1989: *standing, left to right* Dr. Dre, a member of the group's protégés Above The Law, The D.O.C., DJ Yella; *seated, left to right* Ice Cube, Eazy-E, MC Ren.

ON THE MACABRE TIP
'It's definitely gonna be one of the best hip-hop albums to hit the street . . .' Cube promised *Rap City* in 1994. 'We takin' our time with each and every song, so each an' every song will be doper.' 'The shit is the bomb,' agreed Dre. 'It's real different.' Hopes were raised when the Death Row showcase *Murder Was The Case* emerged in October 1994. This featured the first Dre/Cube collaboration in nearly five years: the horrorcore-styled 'Natural Born Killaz', which referenced serial killers – including Manson – and cultural flashpoints like the 1992 LA riots and Kurt Cobain's suicide. 'It's a b-boy gangsta record on the macabre tip . . .' Cube explained. 'What would be the point of Ice Cube and Dr. Dre doing a project like this if we didn't freak people out? The point of

TAKE IT, EAZY
Dr Dre and Ice Cube's reunion inspired fellow N.W.A. alumni Eazy-E and MC Ren to reconcile. 'Me and (Eazy) weren't talking for two years,' Ren told New York Times writer Neil Strauss. 'Then right after Dre and Cube did 'Natural Born Killaz', he called and was like, "Man, let's do a song together." At first I thought he was bullshitting. . . . But I called him back and we started working on it. We did that shit in three days. A week later, that's when he went in the hospital. Something brought us together to do that shit.'

The resulting 'Tha Muthaphukkin Real', produced by DJ Yella of N.W.A., appeared on *Str8 Off tha Streetz of Muthaphukkin Compton*— distilled from Eazy's own unreleased album: a sixty-track affair, originally scheduled for May 1993, entitled *Temporary Insanity,* whose guests included Slash and Duff of Guns N' Roses. Issued in late 1995, *Str8 . . .* proved a platinum-selling epitaph to Eazy, who died—aged just thirty-one—of complications from AIDS in March that year.

Prior to his death, Dre revealed, 'We made peace, and we were talking about doing something on his album.' Sadly, although The D.O.C. maintains that the reconciled rivals *did* work together once more, this plan never yielded released results.

NOT AGAIN . . .
Cube and Dre in 2000, the year the latter promised *Rolling Stone* an N.W.A reunion album entitled *Not These Niggaz Again* (featuring Snoop Dogg in place of Eazy-E). 'We've started a blueprint process,' Dre said. 'If it starts coming out hot, we'll continue it and finish it.' To little surprise, the album never got off the starting blocks.

the song is to poke fun at serial killers, like Oliver Stone's movie (*Natural Born Killers*) did. It's supposed to be humorous.'

The song originated as a collaboration between Dre, writer J. Flexx, and rapper Sam Sneed, but Cube was sufficiently taken with it to replace the latter's contributions with his own. Nonetheless, he didn't regard it as a precursor to *Helter Skelter:* '"Natural Born Killaz" was put together in two days. I'm pretty sure we're gonna have something doper in the mix than that.' (The video for the song features, right at the end, a cameo by 2Pac as a police marksman.)

CUT-THROATS INVOLVED
By mid-1995 – despite Dre contributing a cut to the first soundtrack for Cube's *Friday* film franchise – *Helter Skelter* began to look dead in the water. 'We had to put that on hold,' Dre told The 411 at the *Source* Hip-Hop Music Awards show. 'Cube went to South Africa to film a movie (1997's *Dangerous Ground*) for three months. . . . We can never seem to be in LA at the same time.'

What grabbed the headlines at the *Source* awards, however, was a deliberately inflammatory speech from Death Row's Suge Knight, suggesting that any artists tired of an executive producer 'trying to be all in the videos . . . All on the records . . . dancing,' come to his label instead. This barely veiled slight at New York-based producer Puff Daddy fanned the flames of a ludicrous and increasingly lethal East Coast-West Coast hip-hop war that would ultimately claim the lives of both 2Pac and Puff's protégé, The Notorious B.I.G.

Disgusted by how the label he co-founded had turned sour, Dre fled Death Row. 'You put out negative energy, it's gonna come back to you . . .' he observed. 'Live by the gun, die by the gun.' So keen was he to get out that, according to Knight, he forfeited residual profits he stood to earn from Death Row recordings. 'I went through *a lot,*' Dre noted. 'More than the public knows. The record business is, to me, the worst business you can be involved in. Because any Joe Schmo from off the block can make a record, which means you're gonna have more cut-throats involved.'

PUNK TRICK

'Quick to jump ship,' sneered 'Pac on 1996's 'Toss It Up'. 'Punk trick, what a dumb move.' But maybe not so dumb: Dre founded the Aftermath label – part of the Interscope giant – and, after a shaky start, soared to the greatest success of his career with a new protégé: Eminem. Meanwhile, Cube periodically returned to the studio; the results including the Dre collaboration 'Hello' on 2000's *War & Peace Vol.2 (The Peace Disc)*. However, his attention was concentrated on his *Friday* movies, the soundtrack to the 2000 instalment of

> ## 'The record business is, to me, the worst business you can be involved in.'
>
> Dr Dre

which boasted 'Chin Check' – the sole fruit of an N.W.A reunion (see opposite page) that featured Snoop Dogg in place of the deceased Eazy-E.

Of the now cobwebbed *Helter Skelter,* however, there was no sign. 'People ask me, "When's *this* gonna pop?"' Cube sighed to the hundredth question on the subject. 'It ain't gonna pop till Dre says it's gonna pop cos he gotta do the music. . . . It ain't like I got nothin' to rap about. He's like, "I'll sell no wine before its time." It's better to wait for his undivided attention than to do some shit that people'll be like, "(noncommittal) Yeah . . ."' **BM**

WILL IT EVER HAPPEN?

2/10 Given that Dre has been labouring on *Detox* – his alleged farewell – since 2001, and that Cube is now more successful as an actor and director than a rapper, only the bravest fan would bet on it. A full-length collaboration by the pair would excite veteran hip-hop fans, but probably not with the commercial rewards that would motivate two such savvy artists to finish it.

WHAT HAPPENED NEXT . . .

By 2010, the project had descended into myth. 'What happened to *Helter Skelter* was Eminem and 50 Cent . . .' Cube told Rap Radar, playing fast and loose with actual chronology. 'When we was thinking about doing that project, Eminem (left, with *left to right* Dre, Snoop and Cube) come in. . . . Dre has to turn his focus strictly on that. Which he should. Some shit that's poppin', you got to jump on that train. You can't be like, "Yo, I'll catch the next one. Let's create something that's popular." So he had to run on that train. As soon as that train started to die down, here come 50 (Cent) – which was a whole 'nother train. And then The Game. So a whole bunch o' good shit happened that put this project on the backburner, because you can't ignore that success. You can't be like, "Oh, I got a pet project over here . . ."'

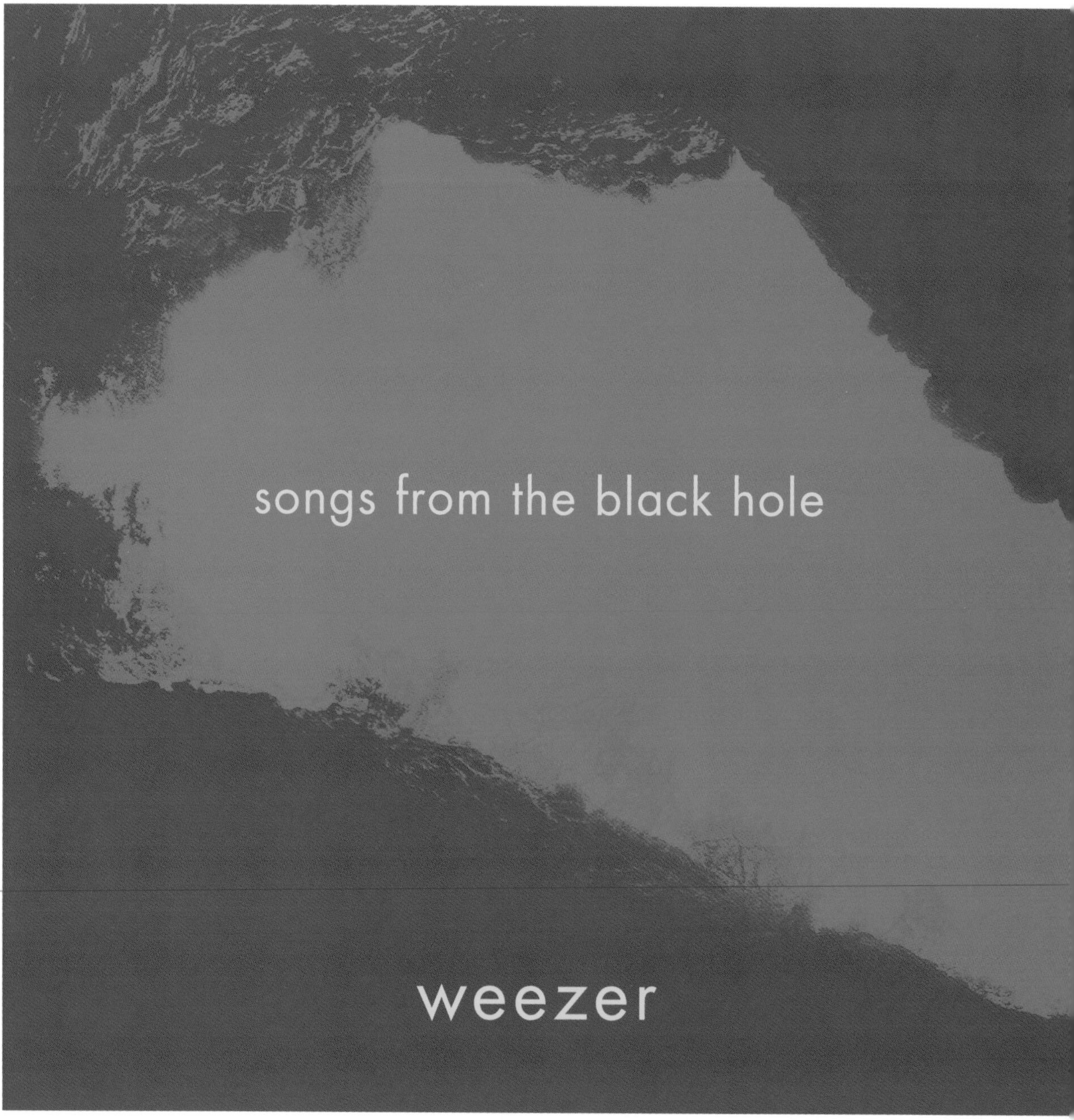

songs from the black hole

weezer

Cover: Ivan Markovic

SONGS FROM THE BLACK HOLE

Artist Weezer **Year** 1995 **Country** US **Genre** Garage rock **Label** DGC
What A space opera that has not attained escape velocity

oncept rock operas were mainly the preserve of established British acts who had earned the right to go loopy (The Who's *Tommy,* Pink Floyd's *The Wall*) or metal acts with well-thumbed copies of George Orwell's *Nineteen Eighty-Four* (Queensrÿche's *Operation: Mindcrime*). So who was the upstart planning nothing less than an opera set in the stars? Rivers Cuomo, still not twenty-five years old, had a one-album track record with Weezer to back up his ambition – although, admittedly, that one long-player was 1994's triple platinum *The Blue Album.* And while it requires a sense of proportion, there are parallels to be drawn between Cuomo's quest and the difficult journey Brian Wilson took three decades or so earlier with *Smile* (see page 12). 'Wilson is my ultimate hero,' Cuomo told *Vox* magazine of the lead Beach Boy in 1995. 'He's one of the standout talents of the century or of our culture. I think I'm a pea in comparison. But I certainly emulate him, as do countless others.' Both were young men in their mid-twenties with drive and direction. Both struggled to escape the monkey-on-the-back of acclaimed previous releases (*Pet Sounds* in Wilson's case). And both their long-abandoned projects were pursued with ever-intensifying interest – often bordering on mania – by fans.

BLAST OFF!

Cuomo had his issues with the spotlight trained on Weezer after saturation-point radio and MTV exposure of the hits 'Undone – The Sweater Song', 'Say It Ain't So', and 'Buddy Holly'. Much of what accompanied this raised profile seemed more a fame-based Faustian pact than the fringe benefits of success. When he holed up at his parents' place in Connecticut for a month over Christmas 1994, vaulting ambition and personal experience began to coalesce.

Without putting Cuomo on the couch – although his interviews from the mid-1990s suggest he might have been more at home there than on stage – it doesn't need Psychology 101 to equate the event horizon of the planned *Songs from The Black Hole* with a gaping void in Cuomo's life: what he saw as the vacuity of the rock star existence. 'For the previous year and a half, I'd done nothing but hang out and do photo shoots and play shows and drink,' he told *Addicted to Noise* in December 1996. 'And I just wanted to crawl into a hole

RIVERS CUOMO
'Usually there's some kind of crisis in my life, some conflict that I can't stop thinking about,' said Weezer's creative spring. 'I'm usually very confused about it and then I write a song about it, which tries to completely capture the whole conflict.'

HOME ALONE

The *Songs from The Black Hole* dam broke in late 2007 with Cuomo's demos collection *Alone I: The Home Recordings of Rivers Cuomo*. *Alone II...* followed a year later, and *Alone III: The Pinkerton Years* continued the cycle in 2012. Only after protracted negotiations did his record label Geffen grant see-the-light-of-day permission for these releases (modelled on Pete Townshend's *Scoop* sets).

Devoting one album to the full *Black Hole* suite was an option, but one Cuomo did not indulge. 'It was never finished, so it wouldn't really stand up,' he said. However, covering the bases non-sequentially across the three releases – with wry and candid sleevenotes – is closer than fans thought they would ever come.

This vault-opening spirit crossed over to his day job, with the release of Weezer's *Death to False Metal* (2010) – a round-up of rarities blessed with the slogan of metal band Manowar. 'We play power chords and guitar solos and we have that real basic enjoyment of playing through Marshall amps, playing loud power chords,' Cuomo said. 'And I think that's from heavy metal. But, probably, that's where we depart.'

ALONE
The Home Recordings
of Rivers Cuomo

WEEZER 0.39

Familiar to British TV viewers from the BBC *Tomorrow's World* logo, the typeface on a provisional *Songs from The Black Hole* cover – as shown on the artwork for Cuomo's first *Alone* collection – was also used on Vangelis's similarly space-themed *Albedo 0.39* (1976). There, admittedly, the resemblance ends.

and be alone and think and write songs for a while.' What better place than the galactic phenomenon that crushes everything and from which not even light can escape? Metaphorically, at least, it was the perfect spot for a retreat.

With 1995 upon him, home demos were worked on and added to at a week-long recording session in Hamburg, Germany. The story arc, Cuomo informed *Rolling Stone,* concerned 'three guys and two girls and a mechanoid that are on this mission in space to rescue somebody, or something. The whole thing was really an analogy for taking off, going out on the road and up the charts with a rock band, which is what was happening to me at the time I was writing this and feeling like I was lost in space.'

Two loose track lists were compiled (if nowhere near finalised):

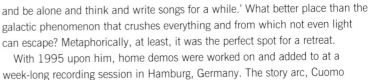

Blast Off! · You Won't Get with Me Tonight · Maria's Theme · Come to My Pod · This Is Not for Me · Tired of Sex · Superfriend · She's Had a Girl · Good News! · Now I Finally See · Getchoo · I Just Threw Out the Love of My Dreams · No Other One · Devotion · What Is This I Find? · Longtime Sunshine · Longtime Sunshine (Reprise)

Blast Off! · Who You Callin' Bitch? · Oh Jonas · Please Remember · Come to My Pod · Oh No, This Is Not for Me · Tired of Sex · She's Had a Girl · Dude, We're Finally Landing · Now I Finally See · I Just Threw Out the Love of My Dreams · Lisa · Superfriend · Superfriend Reprise · You Won't Get with Me Tonight · What Is This I Find?

Amid the chopping and changing, both launched with the same slice of turbo-charged garage rock. When *The Blue Album* broke Weezer in 1994, the slick sheen given to the songs by producer Ric Ocasek of The Cars served to mask darker lyrical content. Now those preoccupations were in place with *Songs from The Black Hole,* too. 'Somebody's giving me a whole lot of money to do what I think I want to, so why am I still feeling blue?' Cuomo sings as 'Blast Off!' achieves orbit. 'Go ahead and waste your life on silly fears / I hope you don't object that I crack another beer . . .' The other songs ranged from evocations of 'the safety, peace, quiet, simplicity, and family structure of my New England childhood' ('Longtime Sunshine') to one 'about a hypothetical girlfriend caught in a spiral of drug use ('No Other One').'

PROPULSION LOST

Band historian Karl Koch recalls feverish huddles as possibilities were thrown around for *Songs from The Black Hole*. 'I remember Matt (Sharp, bassist) and Rivers talking about it excitedly back when Rivers first revealed the idea,' he told the Songs from the Blog Hole webspace. 'The original idea was to really perform it as a rock opera – we'd have to have guest artists on the road with us to play/sing their parts.' The cast was mooted to include Joan Wasser (in pre-Police Woman days) and That Dog bassist Rachel Haden as crew members

> *'I just wanted to crawl into a hole and be alone and think and write songs for a while.'*
>
> Rivers Cuomo

Maria and Laurel, Cuomo and his bandmates Brian Bell and Matt Sharp as their male colleagues Jonas, Wuan, and Dondo, and Koch as the robot M1.

But Cuomo lost the propulsion to finish it. Another session in the second half of 1995, Koch recalled, 'failed to come together in a way that felt right for the *Black Hole* concept.' As Cuomo began a year as a self-confessed 'scum bag' at Harvard University, he began to be consumed with thoughts of instead basing the band's sophomore effort around Giacomo Puccini's *Madame Butterfly*. As the space opera faded, so a real opera came into focus.

Some songs survived the change of lanes. 'I Just Threw Out the Love of My Dreams' – possibly the closest approximation to musical methamphetamine in existence – surfaced on a B-side. Others made it to the initially criminally underrated *Pinkerton* (see What Happened Next). But Cuomo never reached the point of adding necessary layers of nuance and narrative. 'Calling it finished or complete I think is a major error,' said Koch. 'The total (running) time is so short. . . . I just think Rivers would have developed it more, had the *Songs from The Black Hole* thing really gone into the final stages.' **CB**

WHAT HAPPENED NEXT . . .
'Tired of Sex', 'Getchoo', and 'No Other One' were included on *Pinkerton*, as was 'Why Bother?', which dates from the *Songs from The Black Hole* period, although it didn't make it to either of the proposed rundowns. *Pinkerton* – 'An exploration of my dark side,' Cuomo explained – was met with a cool, even hostile, reception from those who wanted *The Blue Album Part Two*. But over the same period that *Pinkerton* was reassessed and elevated to its rightful status, *SFTBH* began to assume a legend of its own.

WILL IT EVER HAPPEN?

2/10 Ever the unforgiving self-critic, Cuomo said of *Songs from The Black Hole* in 2002, 'It was kind of a lame idea.' Five years after that – by then over a decade after the project began – the narrative was still amorphous, hence him telling *Rolling Stone* that it was about rescuing 'somebody, or something'. Demos have been drip-fed to fans via Cuomo's *Alone* albums, while persistent souls have pieced together releases and rumours in the ultimate DIY fan tribute: a full download of their own versions. Cuomo's original vision, however, has given in to gravity and remained firmly earthbound.

MY SWEETHEART THE DRUNK

Artist Jeff Buckley **Year** 1998 **Country** US **Genre** Rock **Label** Columbia
What The troublesome album that died with its author

JEFF BUCKLEY
'There's a lot of strength to the self-destructive soul,' the star told *Juice*. 'Not that it's wise to be self-destructive (but) I'm on the rapids. I see the waterfall ahead. I know I'll fall. I scream. It's never a result of the art form, but there's something about the social life of a musician who lives as a musician and nothing else.'

Crafted away from the prying eyes of the world and released without expectation or fanfare, Jeff Buckley's 1994 debut *Grace* was something of an unexpected success. He would enjoy no such luxury while preparing its follow-up. With a devoted fanbase and an expectant record company eagerly awaiting his next move, the thirty-one-year-old singer-songwriter agonised over the sessions for his second album. Initial attempts with producer and Television guitar hero Tom Verlaine were jettisoned in favour of a reunion with Andy Wallace, who had helmed his debut. But when Buckley waded, fully clothed, into Memphis's Wolf River for a swim, just after 9 p.m. on 29 May 1997 – a swim from which he would not return – the world was denied the chance to hear the album as he intended.

REALLY STALE – LIFELESS
According to girlfriend Joan Wasser, Buckley was uneasy with *Grace*'s success and the media's portrayal of him as a moody heart-throb. With its successor, she told writer Kevin Birsch, 'He was planning on losing a lot of fans.' In a 1995 interview with Australian radio's Triple J, Buckley promised his sophomore effort would be 'a really radical evolution from *Grace*.' The man to whom Buckley first entrusted this vision was Tom Verlaine, who he met when they both contributed to Patti Smith's 1996 album *Gone Again*. Across four sessions – three in Manhattan in mid-1996 and early 1997, one in Buckley's adopted hometown of Memphis in March 1997 – the band and producer cut the new material, but Buckley was dissatisfied with the results. The final session, drummer Parker Kindred told Birsch, 'was really stale – lifeless. We were learning how to play these songs, translating to tape, and hearing what wasn't working. When we came out of there, Jeff said, "Fellas, we're gonna burn over that tape next time you come down (to Memphis). We're going to have a fucking recording-over party . . . and we're going to erase all this shit."'

Speaking to *Rolling Stone* the following year, Buckley's mother, Mary Guibert, considered the reasons for her son's dissatisfaction with the demos: 'I think the primary issue for Jeff is that he had not really been able to develop the songs, the album, in the shape of the concept going on in his own mind.'

No.   Date   187

Ɓ

JEFF BUCKLEY.

MY SWEETHEART,
THE DRUNK.

M.D.

Physician's Prescriptions carefully Compounded at all hours.

Cover: Heath Killen

FOOT IN MOUTH

'There's a thin line between right and wrong,' Buckley's touring partner Juliana Hatfield (right) told writer Dan LeRoy about releasing material without its maker's permission. 'After Jeff Buckley (left) died and the record (*Sketches for (My Sweetheart the Drunk)*) came out, I knew Jeff wouldn't have wanted that – but I bought it anyway.' Hatfield had problems of her own: in 1996, in a bid to overcome near-suicidal depression, she went to Woodstock to record tracks for what should have been her fourth solo album, *God's Foot.*

After failing to meet the Atlantic label's demands for a hit, Hatfield asked to be released from her contract. The label agreed, but retained the rights to the recordings for which they had shelled out. Two tracks were later released on *Gold Stars 1992–2002: The Juliana Hatfield Collection,* and another was made available for download from her website. The rest have never been officially released and Hatfield rarely performs any of them in concert. **AG**

SOUND AND FURY
In the hype surrounding *Sketches for (My Sweetheart the Drunk),* much was made of the involvement of Soundgarden front man and Buckley confidante Chris Cornell. Although Mary Guibert credited him with helping her negotiate with her son's label, engineer Michael Clouse – who mixed Buckley's demos – was dismissive. Cornell, he told *Mojo,* 'listened to the mixes I'd done, gave his opinion, and then left. That was the extent of his musical involvement. Afterwards, all I read about was how he was involved, like "Doctor of Music" . . . He was a marketable name.'

To better realise his goals, Buckley remained in Memphis when his band and Verlaine returned to the East Coast. Echoing his early performances in New York cafés – immortalised on 1993's *Live at Sin-é* EP – he took a Monday-night residency at a local dive bar called Barrister's, where he tested new songs on crowds that often tallied no more than thirty. He recorded those new songs on a four-track in his one-bedroom, midtown house and sent the results to his bandmates on a cassette labelled *My Sweetheart The Drunk – Sketches For My Boys* (its title derived from a poem he had written entitled 'Sexpot Despair').

The singer reached out to *Grace* producer Andy Wallace to take over from Verlaine, and sessions were scheduled to restart in Memphis in June. 'It was significant that Andy came back into the picture . . .' Guibert told *Uncut.* 'I can remember Jeff's manager saying, "Are you sure you want Andy back in? Don't you want the album to be free of the artificial patina of production?" And Jeff said, "Don't worry: I got a pair of size twelve Doc Martens and I'll stamp on his wrists if I don't like what he's doing!"' But at the same time the band were making their way from New York to join their singer, Buckley was wading into the Wolf River. His body would be recovered four days later.

ERASE YOUR VOCALS
Upon leaving Memphis after his final session with Buckley in March 1997, Verlaine had offered the singer salient advice. 'I told him,' he recounted to *The Australian,* '"This stuff is multitracked now. If you don't want this out, *ever,* go and erase your vocals after I leave – because I can tell you, if anything ever happens, they are going to put this out. They might overdub trombones on it. Who knows what they'll do. It technically belongs to them . . ."'

Verlaine's words rang true when, a year after Buckley's death, Columbia released the double album *Sketches for (My Sweetheart the Drunk),* containing the Verlaine sessions on the first disc and demos the star had been working on at the time of his death on the second. Of the plans to burn the former, Wallace told *Mojo:* 'My feeling was, Jeff didn't want them released because he'd have another shot at them. But the parameters of that decision had changed radically, and what other opportunity was there for fans to hear those songs?' In any case, as bassist Mick Grondahl told Triple J, the fact that Buckley *didn't* erase his vocals or destroy the tapes meant the Verlaine sessions weren't necessarily bound for the scrap heap: 'Maybe he doesn't think it's perfect, but he likes it . . . I don't know if he would have really performed the incineration.'

AFTERMATH OF PAIN

Certainly those songs were received well, with *Rolling Stone* remarking, 'there is explosive garage rock theatre here – the barking vocals and twisted metal guitars in "The Sky Is a Landfill" – and breathtaking change-ups of melody and mood like "Witches Rave" . . . and "Opened Once".' Of the disc two demos, the song the band seemed best pleased with was 'Haven't You Heard', a rollicking, jagged track recorded in Manhattan in February 1997. 'That was the session they all loved the most,' Guibert told *Rolling Stone*. 'They felt in the groove, and

> *'If you don't want this out, ever, go and erase your vocals . . . Who knows what they'll do.'*
>
> Tom Verlaine

it was happening, and you can tell from Jeff's vocals, in the way he goes "Ha!" at the end of the song. That's not part of the song, that's him saying, "Ha! We got it! That's a take!" He felt on fire.'

The rest are so bare bones and ill-formed as to be inconclusive. A rambling Genesis cover (*The Lamb Lies Down on Broadway*'s 'Back in N.Y.C.') is an indulgence, while 'Murder Suicide Meteor Slave' is an effects-laden trip. (The album concludes with a 1992 recording of 'Satisfied Mind', which also played at Buckley's memorial.) 'I was asked to mix the demos,' Wallace told *Mojo*, 'but I didn't think I could bring anything else to them, and didn't think now was the time to release them because they were the thing that Jeff *wouldn't* want released. They were like notes on a scratchpad.'

In contrast to Wasser's claims about Buckley's intentions, Guibert said her son wanted these new songs to be about 'love – really enjoyable songs that people would hum and sing to themselves.' They would also, she added, 'be about damnation and salvation, loss and recovery, and the aftermath of pain, which is the healing, and the learning, and the growing.' **RY**

WHAT HAPPENED NEXT . . .
Sketches for (My Sweetheart the Drunk) was issued on 26 May 1998, almost a year to the day after Buckley's death. It debuted in the UK top ten and at number one in Australia. Wasser found fame in her own right as singer-songwriter Joan As Police Woman. Wallace continued his bewilderingly varied day job as mixer for artists from Slipknot to Natalie Imbruglia. Verlaine periodically reunited with Television – who, in 2013, revealed they have a 'lost album' of their own in the form of sixteen unmixed tracks cut in 2007. 'It might happen before we all die, I don't know,' drummer Billy Ficca told *Rolling Stone*. 'It's sort of laying there.'

WILL IT EVER HAPPEN?

0/10 There is evidence to suggest Buckley felt he was on the right path at the time of his passing. In the liner notes of *Sketches . . .*, Guibert recalls his last phone conversations, in which he declared he had it all down in 'black and white', and that the band just had to 'supply the colours'. They never got the chance, and the chances of *My Sweetheart the Drunk* appearing as its creator intended died with Buckley that night in Memphis.

GO FIGURE

Artist SSV **Year** 1997 **Country** UK **Genre** 'Perverse techno' **Label** EastWest
What The Sisters of Mercy self destruct

ANDREW ELDRITCH
'I still talk to record companies now that I
have never been signed to . . .' the singer
told heyheymymy.com.au. 'I can't agree
with their policies on very much at all.
They are not corporations that you need to
be successful but they *are* corporations that
you need to be famous. Luckily I've had a
lot of success but I don't really need fame.'

Andrew Eldritch, the driving force behind The Sisters of Mercy, once
remarked, 'A band that isn't doing what it's expected to takes an awful
lot of defending in the shark pool.' The goth god has spent much of his
career defying expectations: using drum machine Doktor Avalanche instead
of a drummer; covering Dolly Parton's 'Jolene'; playing a 'farewell' show two
months after his first album; and returning to the road with Sigue Sigue Sputnik
survivor Tony James. No episode, however, was as gleefully self-destructive as
creating a purposefully obtuse album for a company he despised.

SELLING DRUGS TO SCHOOLCHILDREN
Eldritch had rarely been enthusiastic about EastWest, the label to which the
Sisters were assigned in a reshuffle of the Warner empire. In the aftermath of
1990's *Vision Thing* and its accompanying shows – remembered for disastrous
co-headliners with Public Enemy – the relationship deteriorated further. Eldritch
cherry-picked two fine compilations but flatly refused to record a new album.

A Sisters associate, suspecting that writing block was a contributing factor,
approached Gary Marx, who had co-founded the band with Eldritch but quit in
1985. 'Andrew contacted me a couple of days later ...' Marx told side-line.com.
'He laid down the terms under which we might proceed and I wrote eleven
backing tracks for him to add vocals to.' To Marx's complete lack of surprise,
Eldritch bailed, 'without uttering a single word.'

The Sisters resumed touring in 1996, upon which EastWest agreed to
terminate Eldritch's contract in exchange for one album. 'They were perhaps
more worried that a judge would regard a seven-year strike as evidence that the
contract was dead anyway,' opined the singer, who had 'neither the money
nor the desire to spend years on a court case.' In any case, the wily front
man was not unused to recording spoiler albums: he issued 1986's *Gift* as
The Sisterhood, to prevent ex-bandmates using that name for *their* new group
(rechristened The Mission). Now he united with producers from his adopted
hometown Hamburg, including former Xmal Deutschland drummer Peter
Bellendir. Two days' work resulted in a seventy-four-minute 'techno without
drums' epic that bore 'no resemblance to any quality product.' Eldritch credited

Cover: Gerry Fletcher

WHAT HAPPENED NEXT . . .
The Sisters have never released
another album, but periodically
perform songs old and new. 'We
are not broke and we don't need to
fix it,' Eldritch remarked. 'We have
done so much better for ourselves
since we have stopped pandering to
anybody's idea of a release schedule,
even ours.' Marx's proposed material
surfaced as *Nineteen Ninety Five
and Nowhere* (below) in 2007.

it to SSV, abbreviated from SSV-NSMABAAOTWMODAACOTIATW. 'Could this,'
he wrote, 'possibly stand for 'Screw Shareholder Value – not so much a band
as another opportunity to waste money on drugs and ammunition, courtesy
of the idiots at Time Warner? Surely not. That would require a comma.' A
statement from the Sisters suggested that fans boycott it and wait for the songs
to appear online. In fact, as Eldritch expected, EastWest refused to release it,
and the album – titled *Go Figure* after the longest of its songs, but bootlegged
as *Feel No Pain* – was indeed circulated on the web. ('Bad – and expensive –
copies of the MP3s leaked from EastWest,' its maker complained.)

  This was, Ben Graham wrote for *The Quietus,* 'a shame, as taken on its own
terms – perhaps as a second Sisterhood album – the record definitely works . . .
threatening, pulsing, disconcerting . . . one long Bad Vibe.' Eldritch's mumbled
vocals – reportedly tales of shooting people and selling drugs to schoolchildren
– were mostly inaudible, bar the closing, self-explanatory 'Shut The Fuck Up'.

  'I would have been miserable dealing any further with the corporate world ...'
Eldritch reflected in 2010. 'Someone says, "Would you like to sign this record
deal for three and a half dollars and we'll put you under all the strictures that
you used to be under when we paid you millions of dollars?" I say, "No. You
haven't got a grip on the internet, you haven't got a grip on proper accounting,
Apple and Amazon are eating your lunch, and you are all dicks."' **BM**

WILL IT EVER HAPPEN?
2/10 'One day, EastWest may
      decide to release the SSV
album,' wrote Eldritch. 'We can't
recommend it.' An alternative version,
with drums, was once mooted
for release by a US independent
label – 'It's still not the Sisters,
and it's still a very perverse techno
record, but it's a whole lot better
than EastWest's' – but, as of 2014,
this has yet to appear.

COUNTRY MIKE'S GREATEST HITS

Artist Beastie Boys **Year** 1998 **Country** US **Genre** Country **Label** Self-release **What** No sleep till Nashville

MIKE DIAMOND

'At some point after *Ill Communication* came out,' said fellow Beastie Boy Adam Yauch, 'Mike got hit in the head by a large foreign object and lost all of his memory. As it started coming back, he believed that he was a country singer named Country Mike. The psychologists told us that if we didn't play along with Mike's fantasy, he could be in grave danger.'

Pinned down by MTV2, Mike Diamond protested: 'There happened to be a guy called Country Mike, and I've known the man. He's a bit of a lone, loose cannon.' The Beastie Boys were hardly the tightest of cannons themselves, punctuating hip-hop with hardcore punk, jazz-funk noodling, and dub breakdowns. So it's perhaps less surprising that their contribution to pop's unreleased canon was a surprisingly good country album.

DRUGS AND STUFF

Country Mike was born in the screenplay for *We Can Do This,* an ultimately aborted movie collaboration between the Beasties and their 'Sabotage' video director Spike Jonze. 'One of the characters in the script was this crazy country singer, played by Mike,' Adam Yauch told writer Dan LeRoy (whose meticulous research on the Beasties appears in his book, *The Greatest Music Never Sold*). 'The storyline was that he was this young country singer who became a big star, and then his life went down in the dumps because of drugs and stuff. And then later he comes back and gets his own TV show.'

Having conjured titles like 'Sloppy Drunks' for the movie, the band were inspired to create songs to match them. 'I might've had to write probably the lion's share of the lyrics . . .' Diamond told LeRoy, 'but Spike Jonze was involved.' When they recorded it, reported Gabby Glaser of the Beasties' Grand Royal label mates Luscious Jackson, '(Yauch and Diamond) were wearing full western outfits and Adam (Horovitz) was wearing a giant cowboy hat and cowboy boots. And they spoke in a southern accent. . . . They'd go downstairs outta the studio in their outfits and order pizza with the accents, 'cause they wanted to stay in character.' *Country Mike's Greatest Hits* was duly brought to life before the Beasties knuckled down to creating their fifth album. 'We really should've been making a record,' admitted Diamond.

With *Hello Nasty* in the can, Yauch noted, 'I thought it'd be funny to finish the (country) album and press some copies to give to our friends for Christmas.' William 'Bucky' Baxter – who had played with R.E.M. and Steve Earle before taking to the road with Bob Dylan – overdubbed pedal steel guitar on the tracks to bestow them with countrified authenticity. Mandolin and whistling by

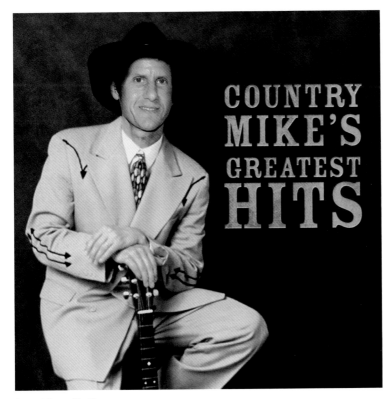

Cover: Dean Martin

WHAT HAPPENED NEXT . . .
'Railroad Blues' and 'Country Mike's Theme' graced the Beasties' 1999 anthology *The Sounds of Science*. (With characteristic perversity, they omitted the most obvious candidate: 'Country Delight', a pastiche of The Sugarhill Gang's hip-hop classic 'Rapper's Delight'.) The anthology's introductory video, 'Alive', featured Diamond – suitably attired and on horseback – boasting, 'Reading you the news 'cause I'm Country Mike.' This referred to lines from 'Sloppy Drunks' that evolved into the character's trademark threat – 'He went and cussed my papa, now that was downright rude / You get liquored up in my house, son, I'm gonna hafta read you the news.'

BEASTIE BOYS ANTHOLOGY
THE SOUNDS OF SCIENCE

associates of the band completed the illusion, and vinyl versions of the album were pressed, featuring thirteen tracks:

Sloppy Drunks • Railroad Blues • We Can Do This • Country Delight • Don't Let the Air Out My Tires • How Do You Mend an Achin' Heart • One Song a Night • Country Christmas • Kenny Jones (Country Knows Best) • Country Mike's Theme • On Your Way Up Again (The Fowl Song) • We Can Do This (live) • The Half-Wit

In due course, the album found its way to the internet and eBay. But, as Luscious Jackson's Jill Cunniff suggested in 1998, 'They should just put this stuff out – you know, Grand Royal, on a small level. It is classic.' **BM**

WILL IT EVER HAPPEN?

6/10 Diamond and Adam Horovitz are unlikely to make new music as the Beastie Boys without Adam Yauch, who died of cancer in 2013. More plausible is that they will unearth material from their archives, possibly for release online. 'Yauch,' Diamond told *Rolling Stone*, 'would genuinely want us to try whatever crazy thing we wanted but never got around to.'

BRING THE NOISE 2000

Artist Public Enemy **Year** 1998 **Country** US **Genre** Rap **Label** Def Jam
What It took a corporation worth millions to hold them back

CHUCK D

'Fuck 'em all,' Public Enemy's mouthpiece declared of the music industry as it scrambled to shut the lid on the Pandora's Box of downloading. 'Now they're all fucking scared. The means of distributing the product (is) in anyone's hands.'

By 1998, Public Enemy's glory days were behind them: after a four-year hiatus, their comeback set *He Got Game* proved only a modest success. Nonetheless, front man Chuck D remained a media magnet – his incendiary ranting becoming ever more dismissive of a music industry he had long distrusted. When downloads began to shake that industry's foundations, Chuck was happy to man the wrecking ball – but he had a fight on his hands.

INTO THE FIRE
Even before the Metallica-led Napster war that erupted in 2000, downloading was re-shaping the landscape. 'There are literally thousands (of MP3s) being downloaded,' one record company exec glumly conceded to *Wired*. 'The train has already left the station.' Chuck, however, viewed the internet as a means of discovering fresh acts, creating music with new technology, and subverting an industry that had sidelined himself and other socially conscious rappers in favour of gangstas and bling. In his online commentary 'The Terrordome', he even railed against the heads of his own label, Def Jam – re-christening Russell Simmons, for example, 'Hustler Scrimmons'.

David Bowie aside, no major artist had embraced the internet with such open arms: Public Enemy's website was packed with audio files, video clips, message boards, photos, and lyrics. The trouble began when Def Jam's parent, PolyGram, got wind of their plan to post free downloads of a twenty-seven song remix set called *Bring the Noise 2000,* featuring newly scratched mixes of classics like 'Welcome to the Terrordome', 'Don't Believe the Hype', and 'Fight the Power', plus album cuts and the self-explanatory new jam 'There Were More Hype Believers Than Ever in '97'.

Intending to post one track a day, PE made it to day four before alarm bells rang. 'The weasels have stepped into the fire,' Chuck fumed. 'PolyGram/ Universal or whatever the fuck they're now called forced us to remove the MP3 version of *Bring the Noise 2000.* The execs, lawyers and accountants who lately have made most of the money in the music biz are now running scared from the technology that evens out the creative field and makes artists harder to pimp. Let 'em all die. I'm glad to be a contributor to the bomb.'

Cover: Steve Clarke

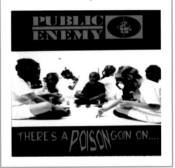

WHAT HAPPENED NEXT . . .
Public Enemy left Def Jam and, less than a year after the *Bring the Noise* battle, issued *There's a Poison Goin' On* (below) – the first of a succession of independently released albums – as, initially, a digital download. In 2012, they scored their biggest hit in over two decades with 'Harder Than You Think'. Meanwhile, online mix-tapes became the norm for big-league rap acts, who use them just as Public Enemy intended: appetite-whetters for official product.

Co-producer Gary G-Wiz admitted PolyGram were entitled to do as they pleased with the songs: 'We weren't selling them – they were just there for promotional purposes. But it's their call. They can make us take them down.'

'We don't like the way (PolyGram) has been handling the album, that goes without saying,' Chuck told *Billboard*. 'But the bigger picture is the entire industry and the legal aspect of the game skewing towards executives and against the creative. There are tons of artists that are having the same problems, but now we're in a situation where the industry can't pimp this technology like they've pimped every other form of technology. (The labels) invented the wild, wild west – and now that everybody's got a gun, what are they gonna do?' For Chuck himself, the answer was clear: 'I'm gonna ride the MP3 like a muthafuckin' cowboy riding a burro.' **BM**

WILL IT EVER HAPPEN?

2/10 Enterprising fans, possibly aided by sympathisers in the PE camp, ensured the entire set eventually ended up online, rendering an official release superfluous. 'We were looking for (PolyGram) to shut us down anyway,' Chuck declared. 'This industry is one-sided and Public Enemy has always been one to make a statement.'

VERONICA ELECTRONICA

Artist Madonna **Year** 1999 **Country** US **Genre** Dance **Label** Maverick/Warner Bros **What** A refracted *Ray of Light*

MADONNA

'Drug music without drugs' was how the star described her 1998 renaissance *Ray of Light* to MTV. So it was fitting that she planned to plunge further into club culture with a spin-off remix album – only for it to fall victim to her own restless creativity.

Remix collections have long proved lucrative stop-gaps in Europe. Soft Cell's *Non-Stop Ecstatic Dancing* (1982) followed its parent *Non-Stop Erotic Cabaret* into the UK top ten and earned a gold certification. The Human League's *Love and Dancing* (1982) went one better, matching *Dare*'s platinum status. Eurythmics – or, rather, their record label – weighed in with *Touch Dance* in 1984. But in the US, where twelve-inch singles were the domain of DJs rather than record buyers, they tended to be shunned: the Pet Shop Boys' *Disco* met such a poor reception that manager Tom Watkins told *Q* he wasn't sure whether it flopped or was simply never released. What the medium needed was a dance-oriented act whose name alone guaranteed multi-million sales. With Michael Jackson content to simply issue single after single from *Thriller,* that left the newly-crowned Queen of Pop.

WITCHY CHARACTER

In mid-1985, Madonna could hardly have been hotter. Reissued and new singles jostled each other in worldwide charts, *Like a Virgin* had sold five million in the US alone, and 'The Virgin Tour', on which she was supported by the then-unknown Beastie Boys, had been a resounding success. Warner Bros duly proposed *12'ers+2,* an EP-cum-mini album featuring 'Ain't No Big Deal' (which might have been her debut single had her label not opted for 'Everybody') and 'Into the Groove' (from the soundtrack of *Desperately Seeking Susan*), alongside remixes of 'Dress You Up', 'Angel', 'Lucky Star', 'Material Girl', 'Borderline', and 'Like a Virgin'. But with the *Virgin* album clinging limpet-like to charts, and *True Blue* looming in the not-too-distant future, the miniature's moment never came. It was issued as a promo cassette in Japan and thereafter became a Holy Grail for collectors.

Madonna finally bucked the Stateside fortunes of remix albums in 1987. Rather than simply repackage existing mixes, she worked with pet producers Jellybean Benitez and Pat Leonard to create *You Can Dance*. It promptly went platinum around the world – including, crucially, the US – and would remain the best-selling album of its type until, a decade later, Michael Jackson belatedly boarded the bandwagon with *Blood on the Dancefloor*.

Cover: Vaughan Oliver

WHAT HAPPENED NEXT . . .

Ray of Light kept selling and spawning hits in proportions that dwarfed its predecessors *Bedtime Stories* and *Erotica,* each of its singles (such as the title track, below) being accompanied by an avalanche of remixes. It's possible that neither Madonna nor Warner anticipated such a reversal of fortune, and envisaged *Veronica Electronica* as a stop-gap when sales dried up. Instead, as *Ray of Light* built towards a reported twenty million worldwide tally, Madonna began work on a follow-up with that album's producer William Orbit. When the results, like the remix project, began to seem retrogressive, she ditched them and re-started with French producer Mirwais to create what would become 2000's *Music* – another worldwide smash.

In ensuing years, her mixes would vary from dance workouts, through a religious reinvention of 'Justify My Love' dubbed 'The Beast Within', to an Orbital mix of 'Bedtime Story', co-written by Björk. The latter song proved the clearest pointer to the trip-hoppy *Ray of Light,* which introduced her alter ego Veronica Electronica – reportedly the witchy character she plays in the video for the album's first hit, 'Frozen'. (Veronica is Madonna's confirmation name.) A spin-off album, also entitled *Veronica Electronica,* was mooted in the early stages of promotion for *Ray of Light* – but, at the end of 1998, she told *Q:* 'I've abandoned the remix record because it's very time-consuming and there are other things I'd rather concentrate on.' Talking to the same magazine a few years later, she was more emphatic: 'I don't ever want to make the same record or do the same thing twice. Yuck!' **BM**

WILL IT EVER HAPPEN?

1/10 It's never been clear if *Veronica Electronica* was ever much more than an idea – of all the albums in this book, it's among the least likely to be sitting in a finished state in a vault. And with the exception of rather desultory reissues of her first three albums, neither Madonna nor Warner Bros seem especially interested in repackaging her past.

BEAUTIFUL DISEASE

Artist Duff McKagan **Year** 1999 **Country** US **Genre** Hard rock **Label** Geffen
What Proof that having Guns N' Roses on your resumé doesn't guarantee job security

DUFF McKAGAN

'They fuckin' took the record, man,' the ex-Guns N' Roses star told sputnikmusic. com. 'I don't even have access to it. . . . Universal came in and bought Geffen, Mercury, A&M, and a bunch of labels, and just freaked. I can't even get my record. I ain't into that 'asking nicely' shit . . .'

An exploded pancreas in 1994 was the legacy of bassist Duff McKagan's alcohol-fuelled world tours with Guns N' Roses. Equally agonising were ensuing years of waiting for Axl Rose to decide what the group should do next. However, McKagan had proved adept at juggling two careers: he cut his solo debut, 1993's *Believe in Me* – playing and producing most of it himself – while on the road with Guns. After a largely ignored album with Sex Pistol Steve Jones, Duran Duran's John Taylor, and fellow GN'R survivor Matt Sorum (1996's *Neurotic Insiders* [see page 228]), McKagan finally quit the dysfunctional superstars in 1997. He promptly re-formed his pre-stardom punk band 10 Minute Warning – who recorded a self-titled album, issued in 1998, and returned to the road. Barely drawing breath, as he later noted, 'By fall, I had an entire (solo) album done, which Geffen planned to release as *Beautiful Disease* on my birthday, February 5, 1999.' Fate, however, had other plans.

KICKED IN THE HEAD

Early signs were encouraging. McKagan's sidekicks included Black Flag guitarist Dez Cadena and Faith No More/Ozzy Osbourne drummer Mike Bordin. GN'R alumni Izzy Stradlin and Slash also made cameos, the latter on a remake of 10 Minute Warning's 'Mezz'. In his entertainingly candid autobiography *It's So Easy*, McKagan listed the album's lyrical themes: 'Number of lines about getting kicked in the head: 2. Number of veiled references to GN'R breakup: 2. Number of drug deaths mentioned: 2. Number of songs about a person whose drug habit imperils his or her ability to parent: 1.'

'I met the Geffen staff and everybody was really enthusiastic,' he told *Hard Force*. 'I started the promotion and tons of magazines reviewed the record.' Anticipating that a tour would follow, he formed a new band, called The Gentlemen. But then, in December 1998, came 'Black Monday'. In the biggest reorganisation to hit the record industry, the Seagram corporation bought Polygram and merged that recording giant with its own music arm, Universal.

As part of this consolidation, Seagram undertook to offload sufficient assets to save $300 million a year. Against this backdrop, and keen to learn the fate of his work, McKagan met a new paymaster: '"Here's the story," said the exec.

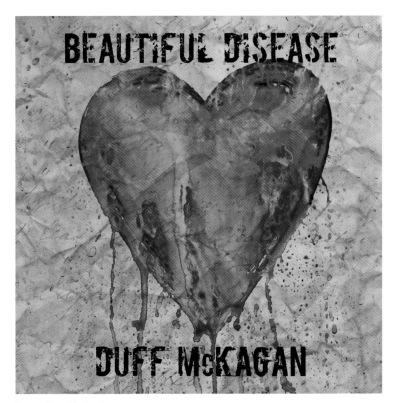

BEAUTIFUL DISEASE

DUFF McKAGAN

Cover: Ivan Markovic

WHAT HAPPENED NEXT . . .

In 2002, McKagan co-founded Velvet Revolver with Slash and Matt Sorum. Stone Temple Pilots' Scott Weiland completed a line-up that attracted immediate record company attention. Among interested executives was the one who booted McKagan from Geffen – but evidently didn't recall doing so. As the bassist wrote in his autobiography, Weiland 'started talking – seemingly off-the-cuff – about a friend who had been dropped one time without a call from the label . . . The guy took the bait: "No way, I treat my artists like family. That would never happen with me." Then Scott dropped the bomb: "That friend was this guy here," he said, pointing to me, "and you're the asshole who didn't have the decency to make the courtesy call. Get the fuck out of here."'

"I'm going on a ski vacation and I'm going to listen to all the upcoming releases with my kids. We'll decide whether they have a future with the label or not." . . . I never heard what his fucking kids thought of my record. In fact, I never heard from the guy again. On my birthday – the day of the album's supposed release – an intern from the label called and left a message on my answering machine to say it wouldn't be released that day or any other day.'

McKagan offered to buy the album back, paying the $80,000 recording costs. The record company's response, he reported, was, 'No, sorry, we will only sell it at a profit. You can have it back for $250,000. Otherwise we'll just keep it in the vault.' Down but not out, he took his band – now called Loaded – on tour, and recorded a live album in LA, the self-released *Episode 1999: Live*, including six *Beautiful Disease* songs. 'The result sounds very convincing to me,' said McKagan. 'Nothing happens without a reason.' **BM**

WILL IT EVER HAPPEN?

1/10   'The version with Slash, Izzy, and Mike Bordin will never come out,' McKagan confirmed. Loaded re-recorded the album with a view to releasing it themselves, but ultimately abandoned the idea, instead placing three of its songs on their next album, 2001's *Dark Days*.

'VAN HALEN IV'

Artist Van Halen **Year** 1999 **Country** US **Genre** Hard rock **Label** Warner Bros **What** Goodbye Gary, be good

GARY CHERONE/EDDIE VAN HALEN

'This guy's got elephant balls,' Eddie Van Halen told KLOS-FM of singer Gary Cherone, 'and he can sing like an angel.' Fans' reactions to this version of the band, however, tended less towards the angelic and more towards 'balls'. And when *Van Halen III* proved their poorest seller, the writing was on the wall for its follow-up.

Initial signs for the third incarnation of Van Halen were good. After the departure of singer Sammy Hagar – precipitated by an abortive reunion with his predecessor David Lee Roth – brothers Eddie and Alex Van Halen found a more malleable figurehead in the form of Extreme front man Gary Cherone (co-writer of that band's hits 'More Than Words' and 'Hole Hearted'). The first fruit of this new line-up, 1998's 'Without You', became the first-ever song to debut atop *Billboard*'s Mainstream Rock chart. And though their *Van Halen III* failed to match the chart-topping success of all four Hagar-era albums, it still went top five. That, however, was the last good news for a long time. The album took five months to crawl to gold status – a catastrophe for a band whose previous poorest seller (1981's *Fair Warning*) had turned double platinum – and the *III* tour proved commercially underwhelming. ('It wasn't like Extreme, where you were preaching to the converted,' Cherone told *The Phoenix*. 'With Van Halen, every town we went to it was, "Gary Cherone: Mr. More Than Words."') Meanwhile, Alex Van Halen sustained an injury that forced the cancellation of several dates, the tenure of bassist Michael Anthony hung by a thread (thought to have allied with Hagar, he had played on only three *III* tracks), and Eddie Van Halen was beginning to live at the bottom of a bottle. Not, it turned out, the best recipe for a career-reviving record . . .

A LITTLE BIT MORE MANIC

'The new songs we wrote after the tour were better,' Cherone told *Rolling Stone*. 'We were working with (Madonna/Pink Floyd collaborator) Patrick Leonard and did a couple of songs with him. It was really good stuff. . . . (*Van Halen III*) was really Eddie's baby and maybe we needed a little more guidance on the album. So by coming home and doing other stuff, it felt more like a band.' (Eddie and Leonard had collaborated on a song co-written by Ennio Morricone and Pink Floyd's Roger Waters for the movie *The Legend of 1900*.)

Early 1999 brought the news that the band were 'very excited' about their new songs. Working titles, revealed in the spring, included 'Left For Dead' (later reworked by Cherone's band Tribe of Judah), 'River Wide', 'Say Uncle', 'You Wear It Well', 'More Than Yesterday', 'I Don't Miss You . . . Much', and 'Love

Cover: Sarah Holland

WHAT HAPPENED NEXT . . .

Sammy Hagar (below right, with Eddie) announced, 'I only wish the best for Van Halen and Gary. I hope they all continue to make great music and have great success in whatever they do.' What the band did, in fact, was reunite with Hagar for a bad-tempered 2004 tour. In the interim, Eddie had been treated for cancer but lapsed into alcoholism. The guitarist, said Cherone of his time in the band, 'was fine for three years. Towards the end he started drinking, but he was no way close to how he was in 2004.'

Divine'. By the summer, Leonard had been succeeded by producer Danny Kortchmar, best known for his work with Don Henley, while 'Love Again' (possibly the same song as 'Love Divine'), 'Rock and Roll Cliché', and 'I Want Her Anyway' had been added to the prospective titles. 'All of them were cut at (Eddie's) 5150 Studios,' reported Cherone. 'All we had to do was turn on the mics and we had a pretty good demo.' But then the Van Halen camp fell silent – until November brought the news that Cherone was out.

'Eddie started drinking a bit,' the singer told *Rolling Stone.* 'It wasn't bad, but it wasn't going in the right direction. Also, I wasn't in a great place mentally. I had some things going on in my personal life that affected me. . . . The hours got more crazy, a little bit more manic. Not everyone would be around. I'd be hanging out with a producer and he'd say, "Write to this. . . . ," (Alex) was like, "We sense that you're unhappy and a little bit frustrated." I was playing the diplomat. It wasn't crazy dysfunction because we all could talk, but there was an unhappiness and they wanted to move in a different direction.'

Uniquely in the Van Halen story, the split was amicable. 'Gary is a brother,' Eddie declared, 'and he and I will continue to have a personal and musical relationship.' (Indeed, Cherone lived at the guitarist's house for another two months.) The album, however, bit the dust – and it would be another twelve years before a new Van Halen set appeared. **BM**

WILL IT EVER HAPPEN?

1/10   Even supposing there were a commercial motive, Van Halen have never shown any interest in issuing archive material. And when they resurrected unused ideas for 2012's *A Different Kind of Truth,* recorded with David Lee Roth, they returned to ones birthed in the 1970s and 1980s, bypassing the Cherone and Hagar eras entirely.

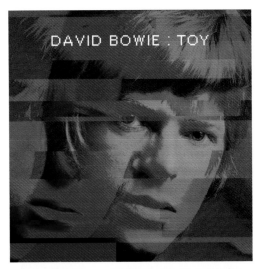

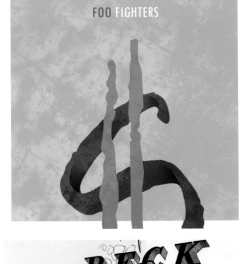

Chapter 5

The Noughties

'THE LILLYWHITE SESSIONS'

Artist Dave Matthews Band **Year** 2000 **Country** US **Genre** Jam rock **Label** RCA **What** *Billboard* or bust

DAVE MATTHEWS

The star's darkest songs, he told *Rolling Stone,* evoked only 'self pity, or pity for the sad bastard that wrote them . . . I was in the process of failing; in the process of letting everyone down; in the process of not supplying the band with songs, not giving the producer the music, not giving the record company tunes. So, (in) that environment, I was continuing to . . . come up with these sad bastard songs.'

By the dawn of the millennium, the Dave Matthews Band – though largely ignored in the rest of the world – were one of the most successful acts in the US and Canada. *Under the Table and Dreaming* (1994), *Crash* (1996), and *Before These Crowded Streets* (1998) had all sold millions, and all three were helmed by Steve Lillywhite, best known for shepherding U2 to the big time. With no reason to tamper with this winning formula, they cut an entire – and perfectly fine – new album, only to scrap it and start again.

HIDEOUSLY UGLY

'It's sort of a strange thing to be a musician . . .' Dave Matthews mused to *Rock's Backpages* in late 2001. 'You have to be an egomaniac to think that what you do is worth other people's time. . . . I never thought I'd have to struggle to hold on to "normal" and every once in a while it's more of a challenge, because there's also the temptation to become a glutton for the fame side of it. But it's so hideously ugly in so many ways, that sort of self-indulgence.' Two years earlier, as work began on a new album in a Virginia studio, these misgivings had manifested themselves in his bleakest songs to date. 'I was choking,' he said. 'Every song was about dying.'

Matthews dealt with his misgivings by vanishing to a room in which he lived above the studio, or drinking. His bandmates, sensing there was a problem but not wishing to rock the boat, 'felt kind of closed in', bassist Stefan Lessard told *Rolling Stone.* 'It seemed like we were playing more baseball and riding more ATVs, because no one wanted to go into the dark studio and get into this mood.' For his part, however, Lillywhite maintained, 'I didn't feel anything like that. These sessions were nothing compared to a U2 album.'

RCA, however, *were* prepared to sound the alarm, particularly as they heard nothing likely to be a hit. This, Matthews contended, 'pissed me off no end. Because what I was saying was, "Don't you think I'd love to be in a frame of mind to write something upbeat?" But I wasn't. I was feeling as if I had run out. And there was nobody around me – as far as I could see – who could help me.'

In June 2000, senior RCA A&R man Bruce Flohr sounded the band members out, then confronted Matthews for 'a very difficult conversation'.

Cover: Tom Howey

WHAT HAPPENED NEXT . . .
The Glen Ballard-produced *Everyday* (2001) topped the US chart, en route to selling two million copies in just over a month. But as the scrapped album – dubbed *The Lillywhite Sessions* by fans – leaked online, fans found they preferred its darker songs to Ballard's polished pop. *Everyday*, drummer Carter Beauford admitted to *Rolling Stone,* 'almost divided the five members . . . . (It) is Dave and Glen's record, really.' To Lillywhite – who would not reunite with the band for another eleven years – *Everyday* was 'all very alien . . . Part of the uniqueness of the band is what the four other members bring to it. That wasn't accented enough.'

'Dave was as upset by it as I was,' Lillywhite told *Rolling Stone.* 'If anyone tells you your songs aren't good enough, you're gonna get hurt.'

Ultimately, however, Matthews was persuaded to rework the album with producer Glen Ballard, whose co-creation of Alanis Morissette's *Jagged Little Pill* had led to work with heavy-hitters like Van Halen and Aerosmith. Inspired by this new partnership, Matthews junked the Lillywhite songs and co-wrote an entire new album – only to discover that, in the newly birthed file sharing age, his present couldn't escape his past. **BM**

5/10

WILL IT EVER HAPPEN?

Nine of the Lillywhite songs were reworked and re-recorded for 2002's *Busted Stuff,* leaving 'JTR', 'Sweet Up and Down', and 'Monkey Man' on the shelf. The last-named is the only one to not even be played live – its despairing lyrics ('I could weave a fairy tale / On a great Bible-thumping scale / When he stands, empty hands / on his empty land / That's what happened here') perhaps proving too stark a reminder of a troubled time. Nonetheless, as a bootlegged version by a recording engineer calling himself Karmageddon proved, the sessions were a fine addition to the DMB catalogue, and as such are prime candidates for a box set or *Busted Stuff* reissue.

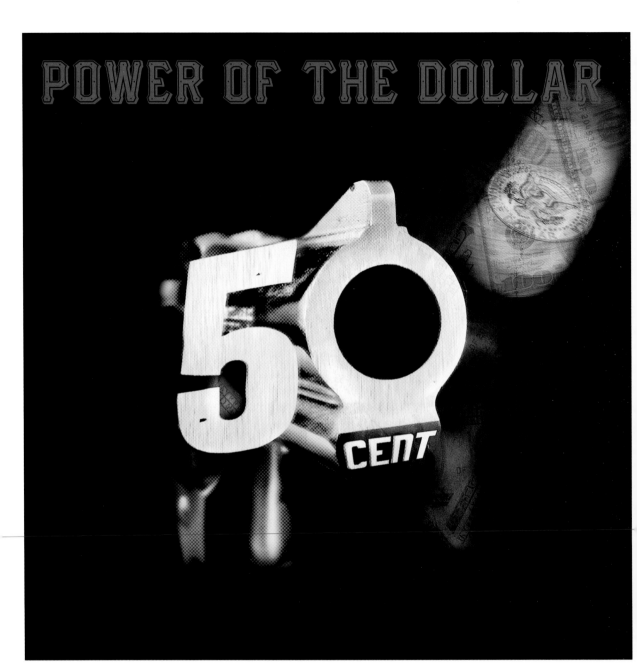

Cover: Simon Halfon

POWER OF THE DOLLAR

Artist 50 Cent **Year** 2000 **Country** US **Genre** Rap **Label** Track Masters / Columbia **What** Power cut

P issing off famous musicians might not seem the smartest career move when you're starting out. 50 Cent, however, shot from nobody to notoriety with 'How to Rob', which detailed how he would relieve forty celebrities – from Bobby Brown to Will Smith – of their riches. 'I had to make the kind of record that would make the entire music business say, "Who the fuck is this guy?"' he recalled in his autobiography. 'All the top dogs had an issue with me, and I didn't even have an album out. . . . The more they reacted, the bigger my name got.' But as his profile rose, so did his notoriety, the results of which eclipsed the irritation of fellow rappers: an assassination attempt, a cancelled record deal, a shelved album, and – if one theory is given credence – the murder of a onetime mentor.

A LOTTA ENEMIES

'I stood on the corner when that was my hustle,' 50 told *XXL*. Rapping, however, gave him 'a new hustle and a new concept of a corner to stand on.' Key to his evolution from amateur boxer and drug dealer to wannabe rapper was Run-DMC's Jam Master Jay, who produced a 1997 demo – never commercially released – that set out 50's stall with titles like 'Get Money' and 'You Don't Want War'. Most prophetic, however, was 'Slugs Gone Fly', which detailed the armed drug deals that had been a feature of his life since adolescence. Jay also united 50 with his protégés Onyx, on whose 'React' he made his commercial debut, spitting lines like, 'The gat (gun) blast left his brains on the glass / In a dash I snatched the cash . . .'

There was, however, little to suggest the twenty-two-year-old had a bright future. Run-DMC and Onyx were past their peak, rap was awash with MCs bragging about gangsta pasts, and 50's delivery was competent but undistinguished. Nonetheless, he was taken under the wing of producers Samuel 'Tone' Barnes and Jean-Claude 'Poke' Olivier – who, as Trackmasters, had helmed hits by Nas, Foxy Brown, Will Smith, R. Kelly, and Jay-Z. A reference to robbery in one of 50's songs fired the producers' imaginations and, Tone told complex.com, 'We said, "Why don't you make a whole record out of that?" We did it in one night . . . and we're like, "This is fucking crazy."' In

50 CENT
'The gangstas don't like that I do whatever the fuck I wanna do,' the rapper sneered to *Rolling Stone*. 'I'm movin' around, I'm all over the country, I'm makin' money, I'm a motherfuckin' star. That bothers a nigga. The people that dislike me have nothin' to lose. I'm from the bottom. They're uneasy about still bein' on the bottom.'

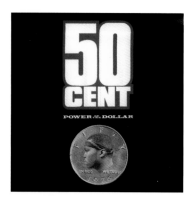

DOLLARS MAKE CENTS

The availability of promotional copies of *Power of the Dollar* meant there was no shortage of resources for bootleggers when 50 hit the big time. Many counterfeit copies use the original artwork, the coin of which is based on the Eisenhower Dollar issued for the American Bicentennial – hence the year of that event (1976) rather than that of 50's birth (the year before).

a bid to make 'How to Rob' 'a fun song that wasn't so serious', the producers added a chorus by The Madd Rapper, the terminally irate alter ego of Puff Daddy associate Deric 'D-Dot' Angelettie. They also excised a reference to Mariah Carey, the Columbia label's biggest seller and one of their clients.

Some of the stars named took the cut in good humour. Its suggestion that Missy Elliott 'put the hot dog down' inspired the then plus-size star to, she wrote, '(get) on the treadmill'. Others were less amused, particularly reigning rap kings Wu-Tang Clan, Big Pun, and Jay-Z. The latter, recalled 50, 'stood in front of all of New York and dissed me: "I'm about a dollar / What the fuck is 50 Cent?" The next day I was on the radio station talking about the dis. . . . I didn't give a fuck what he was saying. "Say whatever you want, motherfucker. Just say my name."' With airplay on the influential Hot 97, 'How to Rob' achieved Trackmasters' aim of putting the rapper on the map. But, as Jay-Z's lawyer Reggie 'Combat Jack' Osse noted, 'From day one, 50 made a lotta enemies.'

ATTEMPTED ASSASSINATION

In just two weeks, 50 created thirty-six songs, of which eighteen were assigned to *Power of the Dollar,* his debut for Trackmasters' own Columbia imprint:

Intro · The Hit · The Good Die Young · Corner Bodega (Coke Spot) · Your Life's on the Line · That Ain't Gangsta · As the World Turns · Ghetto Qu'ran (Forgive Me) · Da Repercussions · Money By Any Means · Material Girl · Thug Love · Slow Doe · Gun Runner · You Ain't No Gangsta · Power of the Dollar · I'm a Hustler · How to Rob

However, the best part of a year separated the August 1999 release of 'How to Rob' and the scheduled 4 July 2000 appearance of the album. 'I got $65,000 in advance from Columbia,' the rapper recalled. 'Fifty thousand dollars went to Jam Master Jay to negotiate the release from JMJ Records. Ten thousand dollars went to the attorney that drew the contracts up between me and Columbia, and the release between me and Jam Master Jay. That left me with $5,000 . . . So I was back selling crack.'

He also shot two videos, for 'Rowdy Rowdy', from the *In Too Deep* soundtrack, and the album cut 'Your Life's on the Line'. The latter was widely interpreted as an attack on another Queens, New York rapper, Ja Rule, with whom he fell out in 1999. Though they couldn't agree *why* the beef began, it simmered for years, and led to 50 being stabbed in March 2000 by Rule's label mate Ramel 'Black Child' Gill. Soon, however, that began to seem like small change. In May – two days before cameras rolled on a video for 'Thug Love', featuring Beyoncé's alma mater Destiny's Child – 50 was shot nine times in Jamaica, Queens. One bullet pierced his cheek, causing the slur that distinguishes his pre- and post-shooting delivery.

He would subsequently accuse Darryl 'Hommo' (Homicide) Baum of the attempted assassination (conveniently, Baum was himself shot and killed three weeks later) but was vague as to the motive. 'Me being shot is karma,' he remarked. 'I did some things that I got away with.'

What *did* concern him was how it would affect his career. 'I was in the hospital for thirteen days,' he told hip-hop DJ Davey D. 'It sounds crazy: it hurt more to not know what I was gonna do with myself *after* being shot. Like when I called Columbia Records and they didn't know what to do. I was supposed to do a video with Beyoncé and, as soon as I got shot, they just like moved it: "Well, Beyonce's doin' a record with (Jay-Z protégée) Amil ('I Got That')". . . There was no Plan B for me.' Indeed, the murders of rappers 2Pac, The Notorious B.I.G., and Big L were fresh in people's minds and, despite 'Pac and B.I.G.'s posthumous sales, Columbia remained unmoved. 'The industry would prefer a studio gangsta rather than someone who actually comes from that background, because it's less of a risk,' 50 told journalist Ethan Brown, ''cos you're investing money in this person as an artist – and shots could go off.' The label cancelled his contract and, just weeks before its scheduled release, shelved *Power of the Dollar*. The album, however, would not be silenced.

> *'Me being shot is karma. I did some things that I got away with.'*
>
> 50 Cent

STREET SHIT

'How to Rob' had been provocative but tongue-in-cheek. Another cut on *Power of the Dollar* was simply inflammatory. 'Ghetto Qu'ran' dared to name check people from 50's old Queens hood, including Thomas 'Tony Montana' Mickens (a drug dealer who laundered money through a chain of businesses that used his *Scarface*-derived name, and who was sentenced to thirty-five years in jail in 1990), Chaz 'Slim' Williams (a former bank robber who, at the time of the song's recording, was 50's manager), and Lorenzo 'Fat Cat' Nichols (a dealer convicted for the murder of his parole officer).

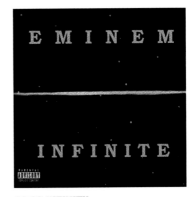

96 TO INFINITY

50 Cent's saviour Eminem has his very own greatest-album-you'll-never-hear-unless-you-have-no-problem-with-pirated-MP3s: his 1996 debut, *Infinite*. With only around 1,000 copies pressed on vinyl, it earned modest reviews and served more as a calling card than a chart contender, despite – according to its producer – the rapper's aim of 'trying to get on the radio.'

SNAP SHOT

Incarcerated for dealing heroin and crack, the nineteen-year-old Curtis Jackson is shown while serving time in New York. His reinvention as rapper 50 Cent was intended to provide a safer means of earning a living – a notion that proved sounder in theory than in practice.

JAM MASTER JAY

The DJ, 50 said, 'taught me about song format. I didn't even know how to count bars . . . I could rap but I didn't know how to put it in song format. And the melodies and cadences – I got used to it with Jay.' The result was 50's first demo, boasting cuts like 'Slugs Gone Fly'. He filled his room in his grandmother's house with promotional stickers for the set, reading '50 Cent Means Change'. Three years later, he was shot outside the same house.

The biggest names cited, however, were the kingpins of crack-dealing gang the Supreme Team: Kenneth 'Supreme' McGriff and his nephew Gerald 'Prince' Miller. 50 maintained that neither McGriff nor Miller were concerned when they heard the leaked song: 'Everybody who heard the record,' he told AllHipHop. com, 'appreciated it.' However, journalist Ethan Brown – author of *Queens Reigns Supreme: Fat Cat, 50 Cent, and the Rise of the Hip-Hop Hustler* – reported that they were very much concerned, with Supreme aggrieved that his nephew Prince was portrayed in the song as far more menacing: 'He conveyed a stark warning to 50 through a surrogate . . . "Stop rapping about me."'

Another associate of Supreme's – Tyran 'Tah-Tah' Moore, also cited in 'Ghetto Qu'ran' – was later rumoured to have been involved in 50's shooting; an allegation the latter addressed in his song 'Fuck You': 'Get back to questions like, "50, who shot ya? You think it was 'Preme, Freeze (another Queens dealer), or Tah-Tah?" / Nigga, street shit should stay in the street / So keep it on the low / But everybody who's somebody already know.' Adding fuel to the fire was Supreme's friendship with Irving 'Irv Gotti' Lorenzo – head of Murder Inc Records, the home of 50's rival rapper Ja Rule.

EDGY AS YOU GET

The rising heat suggested Columbia had been wise to cut 50 loose. 'Niggas call me a snitch . . .' he complained to AllHipHop.com. 'That's the worst thing you can actually be in the environment I'm from.' He duly retreated to Canada to work on mix-tapes with his G-Unit posse, the highlights of which were compiled on the 2002 album *Guess Who's Back?*. This also featured three cuts from *Power of the Dollar:* 'Corner Bodega',' the Ja Rule-dissing 'Your Life's on the Line', and, somewhat unwisely, 'Ghetto Qu'ran'.

> *'When you go through Jam Master Jay and his enemies, you have a long list.'*
>
> 50 Cent

For 50, the tale had a happy ending. *Guess Who's Back?* found its way to Eminem, who was intrigued by its maker's bullet-strewn biography. 'A story behind the music,' he told *XXL,* 'is so important.' Em's boss, Interscope label head Jimmy Iovine, was less convinced. 'He thinks the hood is so in me – so deep – that it might not ever get out . . .' 50 told Davey D. 'He might be right.'

When the 'Slim Shady' star went public with his admiration, a bidding war saw 50's worth skyrocket, but he signed to Em and Dr. Dre's Shady/Aftermath label. 'Way better than Columbia,' the beneficiary enthused. 'Dre understands, being from N.W.A, my lyrical content. And Eminem – picture *him* saying, "Yo, you can't say that." He's as edgy as you get on his level.' In fact, Dre – wary after his experiences at Death Row (see page 159) – counselled him to 'stay focused'. 'There's a possibility that they'd be purchasing the biggest problem that they've ever found,' 50 admitted to MTV. 'But because they believed me when I told them I wanted to make music, we were able to progress.'

WHAT HAPPENED NEXT . . .

'If I ain't rich by twenty-six,' 50 rapped on 'Ghetto Qu'ran', 'I'll be dead or in jail.' As rapgenius.com noted, 'He *just* made it! 50 was signed by Eminem and received a $1 million advance in 2002, when he was twenty-six.' His life story was brought to the screen in *Get Rich or Die Tryin'* in 2005 (left).

Jam Master Jay's murder, as of 2014, has not been solved. Kenneth 'Supreme' McGriff was convicted of murder conspiracy and drug trafficking, and sentenced to life imprisonment in 2007. 'Rappers and record label execs need to re-consider the strategy of using guys like 'Preme as props to express street cred,' opined Ethan Brown. 'The drug business has put hundreds of thousands of African-Americans in prison; it's not something that should be used as a marketing strategy for middle-class rappers.'

The newly crowned star made his major-label debut on Eminem's *8 Mile* soundtrack album in October 2002. That same month, Jam Master Jay was shot dead in his own Queens recording studio.

NOT AN ANGEL

The circumstances, motive, and culprit for Jay's murder have never been proved. In latter years, most weight has been given to the theory that the DJ – thought to owe up to $500,000 to the IRS – was unable or unwilling to settle a debt to a former friend and drug dealer (the implication being that Jay needed the money from a deal, rather than that he was a drug user himself). At the time, however, there was speculation that he had been shot for his association with 50 – despite that association having been contractually severed for three years. 'I can't say it's far-fetched . . .' an NYPD source told MTV. 'But is it the most probable scenario? Absolutely not.'

50, adamant that there was no connection and dismissive of the theory that the murder was intended as a warning to himself, refused the offer of police protection. 'When you go through Jam Master Jay and his enemies, you have a long list,' he informed AllHipHop.com. 'And when you go through his friends and I pop up, it's all, "Shit, he's not an angel." You've got to understand: if he wants to make an album, (Jay's studio was) right next to a precinct that has had chases, motorcycle chases, and different shit . . .' To the suggestion that Kenneth 'Supreme' McGriff might have been involved, his response was curt: 'I have no idea. And if I told you I *did* have an idea, I'd be a snitch.' **BM**

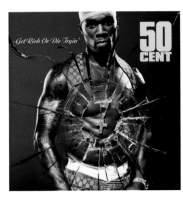

CENT OF VICTORY
In February 2003, 50's eventual major-label debut album – *Get Rich or Die Tryin'*, produced by Dre and Eminem – entered the US chart at No. 1, selling 872,000 copies in its first week.

WILL IT EVER HAPPEN?

4/10   The album is so readily available online that it scarcely seems worth releasing – and 50's commercial standing is not what it was. Nonetheless, a complete, mastered album is unlikely to gather dust forever.

MACHINA II/THE FRIENDS & ENEMIES OF MODERN MUSIC

Artist The Smashing Pumpkins **Year** 2000 **Country** US **Genre** Hard rock **Label** Virgin **What** Pumpkins, smashed

BILLY CORGAN
'Breaking up the band is like when Obi-Wan Kenobi falls on his sword,' the head Pumpkin told MTV. 'Sometimes the hero has to fall on his sword. With *Machina I* and *Machina II,* we fell on our swords. We literally died for rock 'n' roll, and it will mean something twenty years from now.'

D rugs, death, and dissent characterised the final years of The Smashing Pumpkins' original line-up. In 1996, at the height of their success, keyboardist Jonathan Melvoin fatally overdosed on heroin. Drummer Jimmy Chamberlin, Melvoin's drug buddy, was fired, to scare him into cleaning up. The Pumpkins soldiered on with 1998's morbid *Adore,* whose sales paled beside those of its predecessor, *Mellon Collie and the Infinite Sadness.* A club tour in April 1999 saw Chamberlin return but bassist D'Arcy Wretzky – allegedly the driving force behind the drummer's firing – grow increasingly dissatisfied. 'I'm glad that my band is back together . . .' leader Billy Corgan told the *Chicago Tribune* in August. 'How long that is going to last, I don't know.' Just weeks later, Wretzky walked out of both recording sessions and the band. (Her situation, she grumbled to launch.com, was 'like being married to three other people. Imagine being on a tour bus with them, living with them, and working with them – people you didn't pick. It's like people you didn't want to date. Except for James [Iha, guitarist], of course. I did date James.') Then, in January 2000, manager Sharon Osbourne quit after only four months at the helm. 'I must resign today due to medical reasons,' she announced. 'Billy Corgan was making me sick.' Amid all *this,* the Pumpkins made two of their finest, most tuneful albums. Only one, however, became available.

PERVERT ALL THE IMAGES
'Before we even started this album,' Corgan suggested, 'we had come to the end of our road – emotionally, spiritually, musically.' He duly envisaged *Machina* as 'an imitation of The Smashing Pumpkins. It will pervert all the images and all the energy that people think of the band.' Drawing on the messianic central characters of *Tommy, Ziggy Stardust,* and *The Wall,* he imagined himself as Glass, a rock star who believes he communicates directly with God. James Iha, he told *Rolling Stone,* 'would have been this super-aloof rock guy in high heels and a cape. D'Arcy would have been this super-space queen. And it would have been 24/7, (in) all of the interviews and language.' He drew a flow chart of the concept's seven acts, with arrows pointing to each song – of which there were enough to fill a double album. But when Wretzky –

MACHINA II
The friends & enemies
of modern music

The Smashing Pumpkins

Cover: Ivan Markovic/Sarah Holland

ZWAN AND ONLY
Billy Corgan, guitarist Matt Sweeney, and singer Linda Strawberry – under the name The Djali Zwan – created the soundtrack to video director Jonas Åkerlund's 2002 feature film debut *Spun* (starring Brittany Murphy, above). Sadly, this soundtrack – including covers of Pat Benatar's 'Love Is a Battlefield', Iron Maiden's 'The Number of the Beast', and UFO's 'Love to Love' – has never been released.

whose past mediation of Corgan's grander schemes had arguably been more important to the band's cohesion than her bass playing – quit, his priority shifted from theatrical conceit to 'internal spiritual survival'.

The band's label, Virgin, were, in any case, firmly against the idea. *Mellon Collie* had become modern rock's best-selling double album (four million in the US alone), but its successor hit platinum and then a plateau. '*Adore* was a great record,' Sharon Osbourne observed to *Q*, 'but, as soon as it wasn't a massive commercial success, (Corgan) blamed the record company, sacked his previous management, and ignored the fact that it wasn't a particularly commercial record.' The new album would be a single disc, decreed Virgin – who shot down Corgan's suggestion that purchasers receive the second as a free download. And when *Machina/The Machines of God* – issued in February 2000 – achieved only gold status, the chances of a physical release for *Machina II/The Friends & Enemies of Modern Music* were fatally torpedoed.

CUTTING MY OWN WRIST
Corgan's solution – in 2000, still a novel one – was to press a limited number of discs for fans, and spur them to put the songs online. 'I'm thinking, "This is pretty fucking good, I want this music out,"' he told *Rolling Stone*. Twenty-five songs were distributed this way, including outtakes, provisional B-sides, and the fourteen that would have made up the actual album (as *Mellon Collie* and *Machina I* also had fourteen per disc, the number was probably intentional):

> Glass · Cash Car Star · Dross · Real Love · Go · Let Me Give the World to You · Innosense · Home · Blue Skies Bring Tears · White Spyder · In My Body · If There Is a God · Le Deux Machina · Atom Bomb

'Glass' – possibly inspired by a Joy Division song of the same name – and the irresistible 'Cash Car Star' got the album off to an explosive start, while other highlights included the rapturous 'Real Love' and piano-led 'If There Is a God'. But the one that might have reversed the band's fortunes was 'Let Me Give the World to You', first cut during the *Adore* sessions under Rick Rubin's direction, but omitted because it 'didn't fit' that album's mopey electronica.

FIXING A HOLE
D'Arcy Wretzsky was replaced by bassist Melissa Auf Der Maur (far left, next to Chamberlin, Corgan, and Iha). A protégée of Corgan's, she jumped ship from his ex-girlfriend Courtney Love's group Hole.

'I knew it was a hit,' Corgan told *Rolling Stone.* 'There's no better example I can give you of the integrity that I tried to put into that record. I knew I was cutting my own wrist. But it's like a test, and I stayed the course.' That act of self-sabotage, however, was to be eclipsed by one much more dramatic.

FIGHT AGAINST THE BRITNEYS

In May 2000, just weeks into the *Machina* tour, Corgan told KROQ that the outing would be their last. The Pumpkins, he quipped, were tired of 'fighting the good fight against the Britneys of the world.' (Subsequently, he groaned, 'Everywhere I went in Europe, I heard that: "Your band is breaking up because of *Britney Spears?*"') 'Deep down, our fans really knew this was the end,' he explained. 'If you really listen to the album, it's in the album.'

'I kinda just got cross,' drinking buddy Bono grumbled. 'I thought, what the fuck are you guys doing, letting this go?' Iha was similarly unimpressed by the burden of significance now attached to the tour. 'It makes me self-conscious,' he complained to *Rolling Stone.* 'I would have just announced it after the last

> ## 'Everywhere I went, I heard that: "Your band is breaking up because of Britney Spears?"'
>
> Billy Corgan

concert. I would have sent out a fax: "To whom it may concern . . ."' At the shows, fans were alternately enraptured and enraged by set lists that mixed moments of greatness with deliberately obtuse selections like *Adore*'s 'Blank Page', a hideously rearranged version of 'Bullet with Butterfly Wings', and an unrecognisable cover of Talking Heads' 'Once in a Lifetime'.

Little was read into insults that Corgan and Iha traded onstage, as the two had a history of jokey asides in concert. Behind the scenes, however, the former was frustrated by Iha's 'real unhappiness with me. Many times I said, "Please tell me what's wrong. Let's just fix this thing and move on," and he wouldn't let go. He wouldn't quit the band, but he wouldn't fix it.' Iha never discussed his misgivings in public, beyond allowing that he was 'burned out from touring'. It seems fair to deduce, however, that years of sharing stages, studios, and tour buses with Corgan – who replaced Iha and Wretzky's parts on 1994's *Siamese Dream* and included his own name fifty times on the *Adore* artwork – might test anyone's patience. Still, for all their dysfunctional strife, the Pumpkins' first incarnation left an extraordinary legacy, to which *Machina II/ The Friends & Enemies of Modern Music* was a fitting conclusion. **BM**

WHAT HAPPENED NEXT . . .
At the final *Machina* show – at the Metro, in the band's home town of Chicago – Iha thanked the absent Wretzky. Corgan simmered for years before unleashing in 2004: 'The truth of the matter is that James Iha broke up The Smashing Pumpkins... Many friends at that time suggested letting James leave, so Jimmy and I could continue on under the name, but I was too loyal to the man I had started the whole thing with, and I protected him until the very end – right up until the last show on Dec 2, 2000, when he thanked D'Arcy on stage, but not the two men standing next to him. And I was loyal until he left the Metro without even saying goodbye.' When Corgan and Chamberlin revived the Pumpkins for 2007's *Zeitgeist*, Iha and Wretzky were conspicuous by their absence.

WILL IT EVER HAPPEN?
10/10 Corgan's admirably lavish, annotated, and outtake-packed series of Smashing Pumpkins reissues is to include a merged repackaging of both *Machina* albums. The Rubin-produced 'Let Me Give the World to You', meanwhile, has been mooted for the *Adore* reissue.

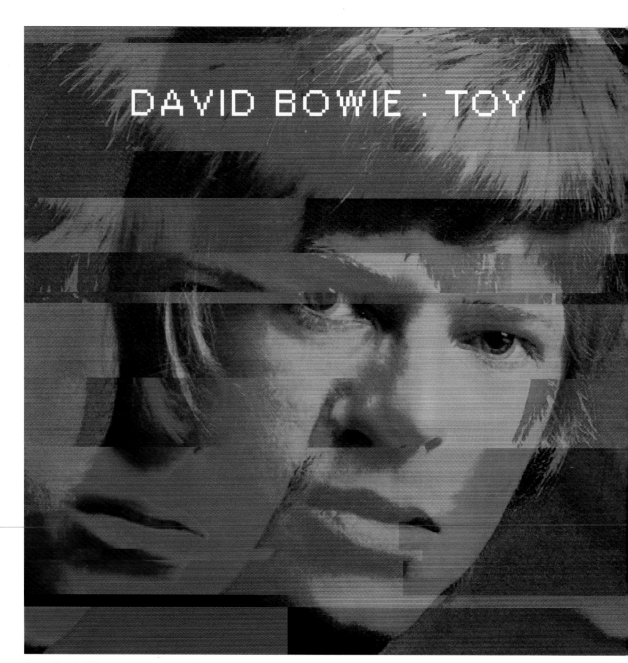

DAVID BOWIE : TOY

Cover: Heath Killen

TOY

Artist David Bowie **Year** 2001 **Country** UK **Genre** Rock **Label** Virgin
What Bowie delves into his past and previews his future

After 1999's dour and under-achieving *'hours . . .'*, it's safe to assume that Virgin would have liked a hit-making David Bowie. On signing to the label, he had intoned, 'I have enjoyed my affiliation with Virgin Records America over the last four years, and look forward to working with the coordinated efforts of the Virgin Music Group on a worldwide basis.' For its doubtless substantial investment, however, the label was rewarded with a mortality-themed album that made *Low* sound positively chipper and which was Bowie's first to fall short of the US top forty since 1972. A light on the horizon was his subsequent reunion with Tony Visconti, who had helmed smashes like *Young Americans.* But one can only imagine how boardroom alarm bells rang when it turned out that, far from crafting potential hits, the star and his team were exhuming songs from a pre-*Ziggy Stardust* era that was almost entirely free of commercial success.

BREATHE NEW LIFE
During live shows from 1999 to 2001, Bowie surprised fans who had only just acclimatised to his drum and bass stylings by reviving 'I Dig Everything', 'Can't Help Thinking About Me', 'The London Boys', and 'Silly Boy Blue' – songs that pre-dated the hit-packed 1970s. They were originally recorded for the Decca and Deram labels – a part of his back catalogue customarily associated only with the novelty number 'The Laughing Gnome'. Meanwhile, in September 2000, the long anticipated *Bowie at the Beeb* collection contained several early, obscure numbers. Four of these Bowie planned to resurrect for *Toy* – a project intended to breathe new life into a neglected era of his past.

Recording commenced in New York, Bowie co-producing with Mark Plati, a key collaborator on stage and in the studio. The sessions reunited most of the trusted musicians who had taken *'hours . . .'* on the road, including guitarists Earl Slick and Gerry Leonard, bassist Gail Ann Dorsey, drummer Sterling Campbell, and pianist Mike Garson. Multi-instrumentalist Lisa Germano would later add violin, recorder, and more to many of the recordings.

As the touring band were familiar with some of the material from rehearsals, the songs were cut at speed. 'Liza Jane' was Bowie's first single in 1964 (as

DAVID BOWIE
'I've had one too many years of bumping heads with corporate structure,' the star grumbled in 2001 about his involvement with major record labels. 'Many times I've not been in agreement with how things are done and, as a writer of some proliferation, (I've been) frustrated at how slow and lumbering it all is.'

OVER AND OUT

Bowiedom features numerous unrealised projects. In 1994/1995, sessions for *1.Outside* spawned a surfeit of material, inspired by a character-driven art murder tale (a 'non-linear Gothic Drama Hyper-cycle') that Bowie envisaged had the potential to spawn up to five albums. With as many as twenty-seven hours' worth of recordings borne out of Brian Eno-produced sessions, there was certainly scope for the mooted sequels, proposed titles of which included *2.Contamination*, a.k.a *2.Inside*. But when the parent album met a decidedly mixed reaction, these often challenging outtakes were put aside, although some surfaced in bootleg form, derived from the so-called 'Leon Tapes'.

Davie Jones with The King Bees); 'You've Got a Habit of Leaving' and 'Baby Loves That Way' were the A- and B-sides of a 1965 seven-inch (as Davy Jones & the Lower 3rd); 'Can't Help Thinking About Me' and 'I Dig Everything' were 1966 A-sides; 'The London Boys' was a 1966 B-side; 'Silly Boy Blue' hailed from his self-titled 1967 debut; 'Karma Man' and 'Let Me Sleep Beside You' from 1967 were his first songs to be produced by Tony Visconti; 'In the Heat of the Morning' dated to sessions in 1967; and 'Conversation Piece' was the flip side of 1969's breakthrough, 'Space Oddity'.

Two tracks broke free of the 1960s. 'Hole in the Ground' probably dates to a demo recorded circa 1970, while 'Shadow Man' – transformed into one of *Toy*'s most transcendent moments – hailed from the *Ziggy* era.

Characteristically, Bowie wasn't content to dwell purely in his past. Having composed the new 'Afraid' (which name-checks The Beatles), 'Uncle Floyd', and 'Toy', he explained they were inspired by – and in keeping with – the 1960s concept. (A fourth song – 'Miss American High', registered by Bowie's publishing company – remains elusive.) 'Some of the songs from the sixties were never recorded, let alone released,' he told Bowienet web users, 'so will be as new to you as any of the new ones that I've written.'

VERY ODD

The latter stages of recording cultivated his revived working relationship with Tony Visconti. The producer had been unceremoniously snubbed in favour of Nile Rodgers for 1983's *Let's Dance* and gave invigoratingly candid interviews in its aftermath. When he dared to comment on Bowie's relationship with his son, the star excommunicated him for over a decade. 'Things stabilised in the nineties and we all grew up,' Visconti told the *Daily Telegraph*. 'I wrote to him several times and said, 'Whatever I did, let's talk it over.' Then one day I got a phone call from him. I just started to cry, because I'd really missed him.' With the problem 'glazed over', Visconti took baby steps by mixing a live version of Placebo and Bowie's 'Without You I'm Nothing' for a possible B-side, then added string arrangements to a couple of *Toy* tracks. By the mixing stage, he was fully back in the Bowie camp. Mark Plati could see the writing on the wall: after *Toy*, his role shifted entirely from producer to bandleader.

In August 2000, prior to further mixing and the album's submission to Virgin, Bowie celebrated a welcome diversion: his supermodel wife Iman gave birth to their daughter, Alexandria. And by October, when he discussed *Toy* online, his enthusiasm bubbled: 'It really has surpassed my expectations already. The songs are so alive. . . . It's really hard to believe that they were written so long ago.' He suggested a March 2001 release date and spoke of the 'very odd' artwork for the album's cover, featuring his face morphed, to disquieting effect, onto an image of him in his infancy.

However, the proposed release date came and went, and statements from Bowie over the ensuing summer revealed that *Toy*'s prospects were diminishing. 'EMI/Virgin have a lot of scheduling conflicts this year, which has put an awful lot on the back burner' was followed by the rather more nuanced 'unbelievably complicated scheduling conflicts.' October brought an emphatic change of plan: 'Virgin/EMI . . . are now going for an album of "new" material over the *Toy* album.' He made no definitive statement on the reason for its demise, but theories suggest Virgin were indifferent to an album dominated by old songs; that Bowie was increasingly frustrated by its stalled release and lost interest as he began to work on new songs; and that the project was victim to EMI's then turbulent fortunes. Meanwhile, in the spring of 2001, Bowie lost both his mother Peggy and one-time collaborator Freddie Burretti, which may have dissipated his appetite for battling corporate interests.

HURT TERRIBLY

Immersing himself in a fresh, Visconti-helmed project – *Heathen* – Bowie went so far as to tell fans that *Toy*'s fate was 'fine by me. I'm extremely happy with the new stuff.' Visconti, however, maintained the star was 'hurt terribly' by the label's decision. Accordingly, the Bowie camp seized on Virgin's alleged overlooking of an option to renew his contract. In a letter to them in 2002 – helpfully shared with the public by *Billboard* – his business representatives said, 'We respectfully decline your attempts to negotiate a new contract in light of the missed option pick-up.' Bowie formed the ISO label and signed a deal

> *'The songs are so alive. . . . It's hard to believe that they were written so long ago.'*
>
> David Bowie

with Columbia to distribute his new material. *Toy* duly slipped beneath the radar as the acclaimed *Heathen* and *Reality* were issued in swift succession.

Resigned to the album's fate, fans were surprised in March 2011 when an unsanctioned version leaked, attracting much media attention at a time when 'new' Bowie product seemed unthinkable (a decade elapsed between *Reality* and 2013's bolt-from-the-blue *The Next Day*). Featuring an unfinished mix – as comparison with the handful of officially released recordings attests – this version has no confirmed track listing, and includes songs that were earmarked for contemporaneous B-sides. Nonetheless, it provides a tantalising and revelatory insight into a missing piece of Bowie's discography. How it would have been received by press and public remains unknown. Perhaps it would have been seen as a creative resurgence and a work of inspired revisionism, or perhaps as a dalliance, an indulgence . . . in effect, a toy. **JL**

WHAT HAPPENED NEXT . . .
Heathen included 'Uncle Floyd' – re-recorded as 'Slip Away' – and an augmented mix of 'Afraid'. Four other *Toy* cuts surfaced on B-sides and a limited-edition, two-disc version of the album. The title track – renamed 'Your Turn To Drive' – was made available as a download, while fans could hear an excerpt from 'The London Boys' on Bowienet. As the star noted in 2003, '*Toy* has actually started now to become a reservoir of B-sides and bonus tracks, so it's much depleted.' However, the rest remain officially unreleased, while 'Karma Man' and 'Can't Help Thinking About Me' are unheard.

WILL IT EVER HAPPEN?

7/10 It seems unlikely that an album's worth of songs by an artist of Bowie's stature will remain officially unreleased, even if his undertaking in 2001 to not 'let that material fade away' has thus far proved unfounded. Although little rare Bowie material dating beyond the mid-1970s has surfaced, *Toy* could prove the exception, given its status as the now elusive superstar's only fully-fledged unreleased album.

'THE MILLION DOLLAR DEMOS'

Artist Foo Fighters **Year** 2002 **Country** US **Genre** Hard rock **Label** RCA **What** Hard-won battle

DAVE GROHL

'The Foo Fighters are like my family,' the band's front man told *Spin*. 'I can play drums with another band, and that's fun. But, at the end of the day, you come home to this thing that's yours.' For Foos drummer Taylor Hawkins, however, these years were rather more dramatic: 'We almost broke up and I almost died.'

By the end of 2000, the Foo Fighters' star was in the ascendant. *The Colour and the Shape* (1997) had shifted more than two million copies in the US; *There Is Nothing Left to Lose* (1999) earned two Grammys. But in 2001, as they reconvened to begin a fourth album, a professional and personal dark cloud was hovering – with near fatal consequences.

MUSIC EQUALLED DEATH

When British rock bible *Kerrang!* caught up with the quartet at LA's Conway Studios in March 2002, they seemed in good spirits. 'The Foo Fighters are finally comfortable as a band,' said Dave Grohl. They had, he said, cohered as a live act after two years on the road in support of *There is Nothing Left to Lose,* and were trying to bring that into the studio. The star, however, was putting on a brave face. As *Kerrang!*'s writer and photographer waited outside, preparing their photo shoot, inside the band erupted in an argument. 'People were making little jabs and comments and I said, "Okay, do you want me to go out and tell those guys we're gonna break up right fucking now?"' the singer recounted to *Mojo* in 2009. '"Because we can if you want . . ."'

The sessions actually began in the spring of 2001 at drummer Taylor Hawkins' home studio in Topanga Canyon, California, before the band flew to Europe for summer festivals. But on 20 August, Hawkins overdosed on drugs in his London hotel room, leaving him in a coma for two days and scuppering the final four dates of the tour. 'I was just becoming a clichéd rock idiot,' he later confessed. 'Our soundman at the time,' remarked then-new guitarist Chris Shiflett, 'he was like, "Oh yeah, Taylor fucked up. He's gonna die."'

'It was the first time in my life I ever considered quitting music, because I was wondering if music equalled death,' Grohl told biographer Paul Brannigan, the echoes of Kurt Cobain all too obvious. Once Hawkins had recovered, the band decamped to Grohl's home studio in Virginia in late 2001, then shifted to LA in the spring of 2002. 'We weren't ready,' Grohl admitted. Tensions mounted as ideas failed to materialise. 'Nobody,' Hawkins confessed to *Rhythm,* 'had their studio chops together – especially me.' Rather than sparking their creativity, Conway Studios simply cost them $3,000 a day, and

FOO FIGHTERS

Cover: Gerry Fletcher

TOO LATE

Over two sessions in 1990 and 1991, Dave Grohl – working under the monicker Late! – recorded ten tracks on his friend Barrett Jones's eight-track tape machine. Dubbed *Pocketwatch,* it was released on cassette on indie label Simple Machines, who were never permitted to put it out on CD. Several of its songs surfaced as Nirvana and Foo Fighters B-sides ('Color Pictures of a Marigold' became 'Marigold', the flip side of the former's 'Heart-Shaped Box'), while 'Friend of a Friend' was re-recorded for the Foos' *In Your Honor* and *Skin and Bones* albums.

brought them face to face with relatively new software: Pro Tools, a programme that enables mistakes to be quickly and easily corrected. 'We gave the drums, vocals, and guitar facelifts with Pro Tools, so everything was perfect,' Hawkins said. 'About three-quarters of the way through, I just stopped caring – I think everyone did. It didn't matter what I did, it was going to be perfect anyway.'

'The first four months we recorded ten songs,' Grohl told *Spin.* 'Five of 'em we liked. The other five we thought were okay, but we were basically just making songs that we thought people would want to hear . . . Our manager, John (Silva), actually made the call. He said, "You know what? I like half of it. The other half just sounds like singles to me. And I don't think that's what you guys are all about, and it's not what you guys should do" . . . That's when I sort of called it and said, "Okay, let's stop, let's back away from it, re-evaluate."'

> *'I was supposed to be happy that Dave's having such a good time. I wasn't. I wasn't fucking happy.'*
> Taylor Hawkins

Fears that Grohl was mooting something more permanent than a temporary halt were exacerbated when he agreed to spend the summer of 2002 touring with alt-rockers Queens of the Stone Age, on whose *Songs for the Deaf* album he'd played drums, and with whom he'd undertaken a US club tour in May 2001. 'I remember thinking, "Oh shit,"' Chris Shiflett told *Arena.* 'It's like breaking up with your girlfriend. You say, "We should take a break." And what you mean is, "I don't want to go out with you any more."' With their future seemingly hanging in the balance, the Foo Fighters abandoned their recordings, despite having accrued nearly one million dollars in studio costs. Hawkins duly dubbed them the 'million dollar demos'.

AWFUL TRAUMA

Four years later, while promoting the Foos' fifth album, *In Your Honor,* Grohl reflected to *Kerrang!* on the demos and the album they became, *One by One.*

TAYLOR MADE

The drummer takes out his frustrations at the Foo Fighters' career-saving Coachella set in 2002. Dave Grohl, he told *Rhythm,* 'is an awesome frontman. He knows how to connect with the audience, how to sing to people and how to be honest, musically. We hadn't played in a long time and it really hit home. I remember thinking, "He can't quit doing this."'

'If you were to listen to the original version of our last record, we wouldn't be sitting here talking about a new album right now,' he said. 'When I go back and listen to that original version, it just sounds wrong.' Of the songs cut during the aborted sessions, the two that have leaked in their entirety both ended up on *One by One,* in slightly different forms: the demo of 'Have It All' has a lengthy instrumental outro, while 'Come Back' is shorter than its final incarnation. Visiting Conway Studios in March 2002, *Kerrang!*'s Ian Winwood was played a track called 'Walking a Line', which featured backing vocals by former Nirvana bassist Krist Novoselic, but didn't end up on *One by One.* Winwood's description – the song 'doesn't grab your ear' – is telling.

The turning point came at the Coachella festival in California in April 2002, featuring Grohl playing with both Queens of the Stone Age and the Foos. During the latter's strained rehearsals, recalled bassist Nate Mendel, 'Chris at one point says, "Hey, I don't know if I'm the only one, but you can cut the air in here with a fuckin' knife. What the fuck's going on?" And then it was just *on.*' In the ensuing row, Hawkins let Grohl know exactly what he thought of his moonlighting. 'Taylor,' the latter realised, 'totally resented me for that.' 'I just went through this awful trauma,' marvelled the drummer, 'and I was supposed to be happy that Dave's having such a good time. I wasn't. I wasn't fucking happy for (him) to go play with another band.'

A TRIUMPHANT MOMENT

Assuming the Coachella appearance would be the band's last, they hit the stage and, as Hawkins recalled, 'played great'. Fences were promptly mended. (Grohl and Novoselic were then embroiled in a legal battle for control of Nirvana's legacy, which may have strengthened the former's resolve not to let his own band crumble. When the duo's request that Courtney Love undergo psychiatric evaluation was refused, a court battle loomed. 'I like to think that there's good in everything and that there's light at the end of every tunnel,' Grohl told *Spin.* 'But . . . you have to be dealing with rational people.')

The track listing of the 'million dollar demos' remains unclear, though two of *One by One*'s biggest songs – 'Times Like These' and 'Low' – were written after the initial sessions were abandoned. Both emerged when Grohl and Hawkins reconvened at the drummer's home studio following Coachella. 'In two takes we had 'Times Like These' and it felt great,' Hawkins told *Rhythms.* 'The next day we did 'Low' and then we re-did 'All My Life' and 'Have It All'. It was a triumphant moment, musically – for me personally, for the band, and for Dave and me. We threw the rules out the window and got excited about our music again. You can hear that excitement on the record.' **RY**

WHAT HAPPENED NEXT . . .
One by One emerged in October 2002 and Grohl boasted to *Kerrang!* that it was 'the best album we've ever made.' His enthusiasm has since cooled, but it was a critical and commercial success, earning two Grammys and debuting atop the British and Australian charts. Comparing the original and remade versions of its hit 'All My Life', Grohl remarked: '*This* one cost a million dollars and sounded like crap. *This* one, we did in my basement in half an hour and (it) became the biggest fuckin' song the band ever had.'

WILL IT EVER HAPPEN?

7/10 'We spent four months and nearly a million bucks recording that record and we threw it away,' Grohl told *Classic Rock.* 'We just fucking scrapped the whole thing. It was not good enough.' Nonetheless, this kind of material is what twentieth anniversary re-releases were made for.

Cover: Bill Smith

'ROBERT SMITH'

Artist Robert Smith **Year** 2002 **Country** UK **Genre** Rock **Label** Fiction
What Cure man goes solo. And then he doesn't. And then he does. And then . . .

Contradiction has long hallmarked pronouncements by Robert Smith. In 1989, for example, he announced that his band's Prayer Tour would be their last – an assertion he cheerfully reiterated with each new album and outing for the ensuing decade. 'I've seen The Cure on about eight different farewell tours,' observed Trent Reznor in 2013. No aspect of Smith's career, however, has proved as elusive as his oft-discussed, never finished solo album.

COCAINE AND VIDEO NASTIES

To all bar hardcore fans, Robert Smith *is* The Cure. Yet writing credits on the band's first albums, issued 1979–84, had been shared by all its members. The group spirit, however, was in tatters by the final encore of 1982's *Pornography* tour. Smith refused to sing and insisted on drumming, while bassist Simon Gallup played guitar, bequeathing his instrument to drummer Lol Tolhurst. 'The ensuing racket,' reported *Mojo,* 'was further enlivened by roadie Gary Biddles, who staggered on stage, grabbed the microphone, and began shouting about what a cunt Robert Smith was.' Punch-ups followed. Gallup quit.

By the end of 1982, Smith had been recalled to Siouxsie & The Banshees, with whom he had toured in 1979. Dismayed by the dissolution of its biggest act, the Fiction label insisted on a new Cure record. Smith and Tolhurst duly conjured the electronic disco of 'Let's Go to Bed', intending to smash their group's glum image (Fiction refused to put it out as a Smith solo single).

Fuelled by cocaine and video nasties, Smith and Banshee Steve Severin cut 1983's *Blue Sunshine,* credited to The Glove. The pair mooted an instrumental follow-up – *Music for Dreams* – but instead rejoined Siouxsie for a hit stab at The Beatles' 'Dear Prudence'. Banshees duties busied Smith into 1984, while one-off Cure singles 'The Walk' and 'The Lovecats' turned his own band into a pop phenomenon. But this dual duty, twinned with chemical and alcoholic indulgence, took an inevitable toll. 'I had all these boils and my skin started to fall off,' Smith recalled. 'It was like my body saying, "If you refuse to stop, I will stop you."' He duly produced a doctor's note to get out of a Banshees tour.

Back in Cure-land, Smith had two albums prepared: one a set of hit-type songs 'with really crass choruses.' Customarily contrary, he completed the

ROBERT SMITH
'During the last twenty years, I began to work on it two or three times,' The Cure's iconic frontman told Italian newspaper *La Repubblica* of his much-mooted solo album, 'but then I always stopped. I still have some songs up my sleeve.'

4:13 NIGHTMARE
Previewed in concert in October 2007,
4:13 Dream eventually staggered into the
marketplace a year later. In the intervening
months, it had occasioned the postponing
of a US tour, sailed through deadlines,
and been trimmed from a double to a
single album. The latter Smith blamed
on the 'fucking idiots who were around
me.' It was suggested that leftover songs –
dubbed the 'Dark Album' – might emerge
unfinished, but the chances of them
doing so were skewed by the commercial
performance of the parent collection. With
woeful promotion and mixed reviews, the
feisty *4:13 Dream* became The Cure's
worst charting set in almost thirty years.

'deranged' *The Top* instead. 'I've thought about releasing (the others) under a
pseudonym,' he mused, but concluded, 'You could write a shopping list, but
you don't want to be best known for your shopping lists.' With Tolhurst having
quit drums to take keyboard lessons, *The Top* became 'the solo album I never
made.' It also became The Cure's first to enter the US chart. And when *Kiss
Me Kiss Me Kiss Me* cracked the US top forty in 1987, the re-solidified band –
now a quintet – joined Depeche Mode at alternative rock's pinnacle.

VERY UNDEMOCRATIC
Along the way, as Tolhurst told writer Dave Thompson, 'The whole ethos of
The Cure . . . became very undemocratic, and a lot of people around the band,
like the record company, found it better that way because they only had to
deal with one person.' That one person considered a solo album in the run-up
to 1989's *Disintegration,* an evocation of 1981–82's axis of angst, *Faith* and
Pornography. Smith presented the songs to the band, 'knowing that if they
were resistant to the idea of going back to the Cure of eight years ago, I would
use them myself.' Demos produced in the spring of 1988 had their origins in
Music for Dreams, a descendent of The Glove's mooted second album. 'I'm
very happy that it has never been released and I'm the only person with a copy
of it,' Smith told *Soundi*. 'Let me put it this way: it isn't very good.'

Among songs mooted for inclusion was 'Ariel', which The Cure performed
on BBC Radio 1 in 1982, then abandoned. (A demo of it graced a reissue of
The Top.) Could Smith, *Melody Maker* enquired, be trusted on his own? 'Not
really,' he admitted. 'But . . . there were all these bits that had been rejected by
various Cures over the last five or six years, and I wanted to use them.'

Smith denied that the solo project simply became *Disintegration:* 'Of the
twelve songs on the CD, I think I only wrote six. . . . So it couldn't have been
a solo album and, if I'd done it on my own, it wouldn't have sounded anything
like The Cure.' (Meanwhile, a third option slipped by. 'Tim Burton had asked

> *'I played it to the others and they're not
> that impressed.'*
> Robert Smith

Robert for The Cure to do the soundtrack to *Edward Scissorhands,'* wrote new
keyboardist Roger O'Donnell, 'and the script was lying around the studio. I don't
know why we didn't or what happened. I don't think we knew who he was.')

NOT THAT IMPRESSED
The solo album trail went cold for the next decade. But just as the end of the
1980s and Smith's impending thirtieth birthday yielded the abandoned solo
project and the gloomy *Disintegration,* so the end of the millennium, and
his fortieth birthday, inspired fresh soul-searching. The *Disintegration*-esque
Bloodflowers cleared the decks for another stab at a solo album, this time
inspired by Prokofiev's *Peter and the Wolf,* whose characters are represented

by different instruments. The motivation for going it alone, he told Dave Thompson, was two-fold: 'One is the instrumentation that I've got in my mind from my demos, because they require instruments that no one in the band can play, including string and wind instruments, and I want them to be played live – I don't want them coming out of a machine. (And) I don't intend singing on it. . . . I'm not naïve: it will still be "Robert Smith of The Cure" whatever I do, but it will, in my mind, distance it from the body of work.'

The band was unfazed by being sidelined. 'I played it to the others,' Smith remarked of his wordless wonder, 'and they're not that impressed.'

Thereafter, plans changed on a biannual basis. By October 2000 – the end of the *Bloodflowers* tour – a planned start date for the solo album had passed. 'Most of the new songs I've written this year have turned out sounding like they should be played by us, not me,' Smith told fan site chainofflowers.com. However, he also remarked on the solo album: 'My home demos are pretty much complete – now I just have to change my mind about the whole thing.'

Change his mind he did. By November 2001, he was announcing plans to 'pick it up again after Christmas.' Much of 2002 was duly spent tinkering with other musicians in his home studio. Against a backdrop of rolling eyes, Smith even suggested that two concerts in Berlin in November might be The Cure's last, freeing him to go it alone. However, he later reflected, 'I didn't take into account how I'd feel about the band six months later.'

A BIT UNRELIABLE

'Things didn't quite go according to my plans,' Smith told *Soundi*. 'They are a bit unreliable at the best of times. I solemnly promised myself that . . . I would finish the solo album by Christmas, release it at the beginning of the new year, and review whether there's a future for The Cure. . . . I have sung all the parts and completed the instrument bits I play, but it's still not finished.'

An unlikely protagonist scuppered Smith's plans. Ross Robinson – the producer who effectively invented nu-metal by unleashing Korn and Slipknot – was delighted to meet the head of a band he adored; less so to learn that said head wanted him to helm a solo album. 'He insisted the next album should be a Cure album. . . .' said Smith, who faced 'the difficult choice of sticking to my solo career plans or working (with) a producer who seems to understand The Cure and who has a connection with a younger generation. . . . Ultimately I chose the last option, thinking, "There's a chance I'm going to regret this."'

In fact, the self-titled, Robinson-produced result returned The Cure to the US top ten, and earned the band their first British silver award since 1992. But with almost seasonal inevitability, no sooner had Smith finished the ensuing tour than he was declaring, 'I wanted to finish my solo album . . .' **BM**

WHAT HAPPENED NEXT . . .
Music for Dreams evolved into an instrumental set by the band, considered for an ultimately shelved bonus disc to accompany the Ross Robinson album. Solo work by Smith (below, with Tim Burton) occasionally saw the light: a cover of 'World in My Eyes' for a 1998 Depeche Mode tribute; a re-make of 'Pictures of You' for 2004's *One Perfect Day* movie; and a cover of Disney's 'Very Good Advice' for the soundtrack of Burton's *Alice in Wonderland*. Meanwhile, despite 2008's *4:13 Dream* sinking (see opposite page), The Cure continue to command vast audiences.

WILL IT EVER HAPPEN?
5/10 Perhaps Smith will release a solo album online. The work may be instrumental, this being the only constant in all his discussions of it. However, he said he would publish lyrics 'so fans can sing along anyway!'

CIGARETTES & VALENTINES

Artist Green Day **Year** 2003 **Country** US **Genre** Pop-punk **Label** Reprise **What** American idiocy

BILLIE JOE ARMSTRONG

'It made us look at our music and say, "Are we being ambitious enough?"' recalled Green Day's front man of the alleged theft of *Cigarettes & Valentines*. But this implausible event wasn't even the nuttiest twist in the story of the band's lowest point, before they became *the* stadium-filling rock sensation of the past decade.

Rarely can a tour have sounded so bittersweet to its stars. As Green Day embarked on the 'Pop Disaster' outing in April 2002, they were second on the bill to Blink-182: another pop-punk trio who had emerged in their wake. Adding insult to injury, where Green Day's most recent album – 2000's *Warning* – had stalled at gold status, the young pretenders' *Take Off Your Pants and Jacket* was hurtling towards its two millionth sale. 'There's a lot of Blink's fans that have never seen us live,' bassist Mike Dirnt rationalised wistfully, 'and I would love to connect with a lot of those kids.' Green Day, in fact, often stole the show, but were clearly in a slump. The solutions? A near-split, a ludicrous fairytale, a fictitious band, and an astonishing resurrection…

BURN IT ALL DOWN

When Dirnt, drummer Tré Cool, and front man Billie Joe Armstrong returned to the studio in 2003, they had worked together for a decade, created five albums, and played over eight hundred shows. 'The old jokes were getting old,' Armstrong told *Q*. 'I couldn't communicate with Mike and Tré.' And when the notoriously irreverent Cool took to describing Armstrong's compositions – specifically the hit and audience favourite 'Welcome to Paradise' – as 'shitty,' the front man 'got to the point where I was afraid to bring my songs to them.' The gravest fissure was between Armstrong and Dirnt, the childhood friends who had founded the band (with a different drummer) in California in the late 1980s. 'Billie called me and said, "Do you wanna do this any more?"' the bassist told *Q*. 'I said, "Yes, but you got to let us in. We're not, like, staff. You're the president . . . but we're the cabinet and you've gotta consult us."'

Against this fractured background, the trio began desultory work on a new album, christened (possibly retrospectively) *Cigarettes & Valentines,* at Oakland's Studio 880. To this day, no one has confirmed – though fans have conjectured at length – what was actually recorded. 'It was cool,' shrugged studio owner John Lucasey to Green Day biographer Marc Spitz. 'It was a punk album, that's for sure.' 'Hard and fast,' Dirnt confirmed. What it *wasn't*, however, was worth persevering with. 'Good stuff,' was Armstrong's verdict, but not – as a soon-to-be coined fan mantra had it – 'maximum Green Day.'

GREEN DAY

CIGARETTES & VALENTINES

Cover: Isabel Eeles

GREEN DAZE

While they never dropped the conceit of The Network (bottom left) being an entirely different band, Green Day have been open about their other side projects. Billie Joe Armstrong has played in Pinhead Gunpower (top right) since 1991, and Dirnt has intermittently led The Frustrators (bottom right) since 1999.

Neither, however, made as much impact as Foxboro Hot Tubs, who issued *Stop Drop and Roll!!!* (top left) in 2008 and who provided an opportunity for lighthearted leg-stretching between Green Day's increasingly weighty outings.

'We are the same band,' they confessed to MTV. 'That is basically the only similarity. We are Jason White, Jason Freese (both members of Green Day's live incarnations), Michael Pritchard (Dirnt), Frank Edwin Wright the Third (Cool), and the Reverend Strychnine Twitch (Armstrong). . . . We are five guys who love to play music and be spontaneous. After a few late night jams and a few too many bottles of wine, we were inspired to record some rockin' eight-track recordings.'

Adding to the intrigue, the Hot Tubs – whose garage-rockin' spirit informed Green Day's *¡Dos!* in 2012 – have been known to play songs by The Network during their occasional live outings.

When the material failed to find favour with producer and A&R supremo Rob Cavallo, it was abandoned – but this prosaic case of a band realising it needed to up its game was about to take a stupendously dopey turn.

'I got a call at home, explaining to me that the tapes went missing,' Warner Bros's then-CEO Tom Whalley smirked to VH1's *Behind the Music.* 'One morning we just showed up and the hard drive was gone,' Armstrong added. 'I just remember wanting to burn the whole studio down.' 'It was either one of the millions of people who were in and out of the studio . . .' Dirnt suggested to Fuse TV, 'or they're buried in a warehouse of equipment somewhere.'

The stolen tapes scenario wasn't without precedent: in 1980, British band Dexy's Midnight Runners spirited away their own debut album and held it to ransom until record label EMI upped their royalties. And, in 1991, U2's demos for *Achtung Baby* were bootlegged long before the album emerged. Nonetheless, it is unthinkable that material looted from a band of Green Day's stature in the era of file sharing would not have been available online within days. Significantly, this alleged larceny went undiscussed in public until the following year – when, conveniently, the trio had a new album to promote.

'It was not taken from here,' Studio 880's Lucasey protested to Marc Spitz. 'Everybody's fuckin' writing that it was taken from here. It was not. I mean, they took their drives with them at the time. There was nothing that was ever stolen from here. There are safes, everything, you know? Surveillance, safes – I mean, there's multiple steel doors that you would have to get through, too.'

EXTREMELY MYSTERIOUS

The band's mischievous self-mythologising took another bizarre twist in 2003. Presumably to rid themselves of the burden of expectation, they quickly cut *Money Money 2020,* credited to The Network – a sextet featuring, among others, Fink (Armstrong), Van Gough (Dirnt), and The Snoo (Cool). Its robot-fixated new wave bore little relation to the trio's punky heritage, suggesting they had not simply recycled the abandoned *Cigarettes & Valentines* material. But Armstrong's vocals were unmistakable – and the album's release on his Adeline label, not to mention publishing credits that confirmed Green Day members as the songs' authors, made it clear that their insistence the project had nothing to do with them was entirely tongue in cheek. Lest anyone miss the joke, an

> *'I just remember wanting to burn the whole studio down.'*
>
> Billie Joe Armstrong

official website described The Network as an 'extremely mysterious' band who 'never show their faces to humans or cameras. The members hail from all corners of the world and were brought together by an ancient prophecy, which predicted their rise to world power and eventually their demise.'

These pranks evidently reinvigorated the band. 'All of a sudden,' Lucasey noted, 'they just started having fun.' That meant consigning the *Cigarettes & Valentines* songs to history. 'Do we wanna go back and record those? I don't think so,' Dirnt mused to *Behind the Music.* 'We'd just written 'American Idiot' and that song seemed to set a new bar.' In fact, the song that planted the seed was the bassist's own 'Nobody Likes You', which he worked up while waiting for Armstrong and Cool to arrive at the studio. His bandmates were suitably inspired by the short but singalong tune to compose vignettes of their own that they wove into the medley 'Homecoming'. Over the ensuing months, thirty further songs emerged, which were whittled down to create one of the most creatively and commercially triumphant albums of its era, *American Idiot.* **BM**

WHAT HAPPENED NEXT . . .

Green Day returned to the top of the pop-punk tree, rendering the stolen tapes hype entirely superfluous. The tale was duly downgraded to the masters having been, as Armstrong told *Q,* 'mislaid'. Meanwhile, Dirnt suggested to *Billboard* that they were accidentally deleted from a hard drive. 'We still have some burned CDs,' he said, 'but those are not good enough to release.'

American Idiot eventually went platinum six times in the US alone, dwarfing everything the trio had released since 1994's *Dookie.* It also eclipsed Blink-182's brilliantly ambitious, self-titled 2003 album – which sold a million but divided that band's fanbase and ultimately contributed to their four-year split.

WILL IT EVER HAPPEN?

3/10 'If somebody's got (the tapes) and they put them out,' requested Dirnt in 2003, 'just put a good cover on it. Don't put a lame cover on it.' But if, as seems reasonable, the stolen tapes story is dismissed as a publicity stunt, the demos must exist and therefore could be released. However, it is unlikely Green Day would wish to revisit legendarily mediocre material from the lowest point in their history. ('It wasn't *American Idiot,'* sniffed John Lucasey.) It's more plausible that those songs have been or will be reworked as bonus cuts and album tracks: a song called 'Cigarettes and Valentines', for example, wound up on 2011's live set *Awesome as F**k.* However, it's not clear if this genuinely dates back to the album that shares its name, or if Armstrong is simply contributing to his band's murky mythology.

TAPEWORM

Artist Trent Reznor *et al* Year 2003 Country US Genre Industrial Label Nothing What Nine inch tools

TRENT REZNOR

'If you're gonna combine Tool and Nine Inch Nails,' observed Reznor of the alt-rock 'supergroup' led by himself and Tool singer Maynard James Keenan, 'it has to be ten out of ten. Not seven out of ten . . . It felt like it was landing in the seven range, and I kinda put a stop to it.'

Of the spawning of Tapeworm, Trent Reznor recalled, 'I was trying to waste time, because I was afraid to do a Nine Inch Nails record. So I was taking on other projects . . . to kinda feel busy, but not have the pressure of doing it all myself.' Happily, his keyboardist Charlie Clouser and bassist Danny Lohner were stockpiling ideas while their boss was producing Marilyn Manson's *Antichrist Superstar* in 1996. 'When we listen back to a lot of our stuff,' Clouser told *Alternative Press,* 'we go, "This is cool. We'd like to use this, but it's obviously not NIN."' As the project evolved, Reznor christened it Tapeworm – a jokey reference, said Lohner, to 'a parasite feeding off the bigger organism.' But, like any parasite, it eventually needed to be killed off.

HUGE EGO

Between the end of NIN's 'Self Destruct' tour in 1996 and their return to the road in 1999, the collaborators accumulated, Reznor recalled, 'millions of tracks.' Contributors included Pantera frontman Phil Anselmo and Helmet guitarist Page Hamilton, but most attention focused on the role of Maynard James Keenan. With NIN out of the spotlight, Keenan's band Tool had become the thinking metal fan's misanthropists of choice, with 1996's *Ænima* debuting in the US top three, en route to earning triple platinum status. With him, Tapeworm's music – 'heavy stuff and hip-hop stuff to Kate Bush songs,' said Clouser – evolved into something 'more electronic-y, but with heavy guitars.'

By 2001, Reznor reported, producer Alan Moulder had marshalled the tracks into 'more than an album's worth' of demos. The results, he promised, were 'very unlike' NIN's chart-topping 1999 set *The Fragile* (although Curve singer Toni Halliday was among several Tapewormers to contribute to that album too).

One track, 'Be Kind to Them', Phil Anselmo told *Rolling Stone,* 'was more atmospheric . . . It would be Nine Inch Nails' take on blues. . . . Danny (is) a great producer – he'll ask you to sing something twenty different ways, twenty different times. Then he'll take it and run with it, and build what he wants out of it: take certain textures and add them to vocals, and then the really beautiful orchestrations in the background.' (More predictably, Anselmo's other contribution was an 'aggressive-type song' entitled 'Ignorant'.)

Cover: Gerry Fletcher

WHAT HAPPENED NEXT . . .

Tapeworm's 'Vacant' was performed live by Keenan's other band A Perfect Circle before evolving into 'Passive' on their 2004 album *eMOTIVE* (below). The singer hailed Puscifer, another side project featuring Danny Lohner, as 'kind of becoming what I thought (Tapeworm) should have been.' Puscifer's 2009 EP *'C' Is for (Please Insert Sophomoric Genitalia Reference HERE)* features Tapeworm's 'Potions' – resurrected, Keenan suggested, as a wedding gift to Reznor, who married in October that year. It has been speculated that Lohner has used the project's material for his soundtrack work as Renholdër, while Reznor used drums from an unnamed Tapeworm cut on 'Convict Colony', from *The Inevitable Rise and Liberation of NiggyTardust,* an album he produced for hip-hop poet Saul Williams.

In 2003, despite Clouser's exit, Lohner told *Kerrang!* the album was 'ready to mix.' According to him, the stumbling blocks were legal issues between Reznor and Keenan's paymasters (further complicated by the former's deteriorating relationship with the co-founder of his Nothing label). 'There was a real element of pressure from record companies to make money,' Reznor reported. The result was what Anselmo described as 'a logistics nightmare.'

Reznor was also troubled by the collective's music being 'kind of just mediocre . . . I think through lack of focus.' Keenan agreed: 'Everybody involved with the project wasn't quite ready to do it,' he told MTV Hive. 'With my huge ego coming to the table, and everybody else's ego coming to the table, that really polluted the project. We just weren't ready.' In 2004, Tapeworm officially stopped wriggling. **BM**

WILL IT EVER HAPPEN?

2/10 'I'm not sure if I want people to hear it today or tomorrow, but in the next ten years or so, I don't mind,' Phil Anselmo told *Rolling Stone.* Trent Reznor, however, regards Tapeworm as dead and buried. 'I love Maynard and he's a good friend,' he declared, 'and I'm certain we're gonna do something together that *will* be ten out of ten.'

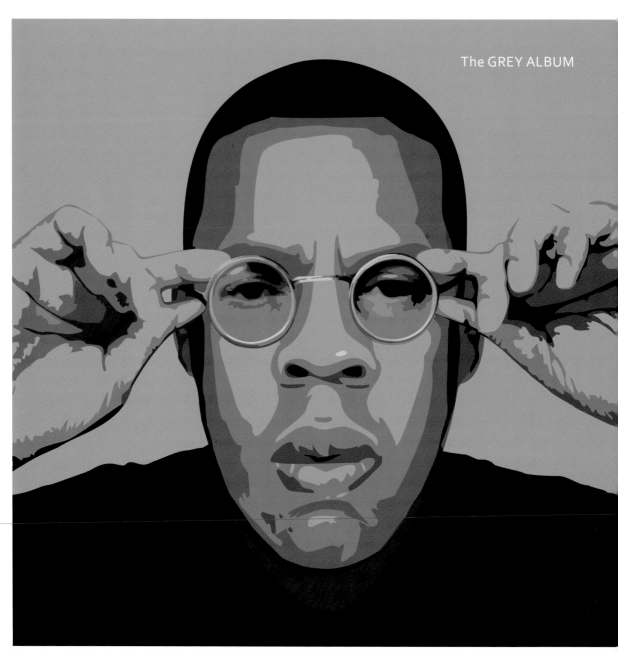

The GREY ALBUM

Cover: Isabel Eeles

THE GREY ALBUM

Artist Danger Mouse **Year** 2004 **Country** US **Genre** Mash-up **Label** Self-release **What** Fab Four, fresh to def

The title must have hit Danger Mouse like a freight train. *Of course.* Mix The Beatles' iconic 'White Album' and Jay-Z's self-mythologising *The Black Album,* and what do you get? Brian Burton – Danger Mouse in plain clothes – said he had the idea when listening to the Fab Four's self-titled 1968 opus soon after picking up the a cappella/beats edition of Jay-Z's 2003 album, but the potential name surely gilded the lily. It was a marketing coup waiting to happen. If, that is, you could market an unsellable item.

UNDERGROUND PROJECT

The legal ramifications involved in mixing The Beatles and Jay-Z were almost unthinkable. In the end, *The Grey Album* had to settle for being a simple work of art: the product of a wild imagination and a determination to see a smart idea to its natural conclusion. 'It was supposed to be an underground project,' Burton protested to Reuters, 'not playing in clubs.' Even if the benefits had been financial, for all the work he put into making a cohesive whole from Jay-Z rhymes and Beatles tunes, the pennies would have gone to the major players. ('I didn't see any money out of it,' he confirmed to djtimes.com. 'I pressed up like a few hundred copies on CD, handed them out to my friends and DJs . . .')

Burton himself was not yet a major player. He had surfaced a year earlier with *Ghetto Pop Life,* his hook-up with rapper Jemini, which earned kind reviews but did little to mark him out as someone to watch in hip-hop. More significantly, he had made overtures to Cee Lo Green of Goodie Mob some time before his debut release, but any chemistry there would take a while to come to fruition. *The Grey Album* would be the catalyst that alchemised Burton's future, putting his skills in stark relief. 'I was always a huge fan of classic rock,' he explained, 'and I had always done mash-ups. I had sent mash-ups to the guys at Warp Records, which helped me get a record deal.'

With *The Grey Album,* Burton achieved the ultimate goal for an artist: matching his imagination with deeds. 'It came to me one day as an art project,' he told the makers of the Danish copyright documentary *Good Copy Bad Copy* (2007). 'I wanted to challenge myself to do it. I had always mixed up different genres of music; I just hadn't done this particular thing yet.' Burton circulated

DANGER MOUSE
'I was actually honoured that someone took the time to mash those records up with Beatles records,' Jay-Z told NPR. 'I was honoured to be on – quote, unquote – the same song with The Beatles.' Paul McCartney, meanwhile, told the BBC: 'It's exactly what we did in the beginning: introducing black soul music to a mass white audience. It's come full circle.'

A DARK AND SPARKY NIGHT

Dark Night of the Soul represented further corporation-defying antics from Burton, with Mark Linkous of Sparklehorse and guests from the Shins, Cardigans, Super Furry Animals, and Pixies. A contractual dispute with EMI saw the album shelved – but Burton leaked it alongside a book of David Lynch photographs, also titled *Dark Night of the Soul,* that came with a blank CD-R. The inference was clear.

EMI finally sanctioned an official edition of the spectral set in July 2010. By then, however, both Linkous and Vic Chesnutt – who wrote and sang the album's 'Grim Augury' – had committed suicide.

The Beatles/Jay-Z mash-up to friends and they did the rest, springing *The Grey Album* onto the internet in February 2004 and watching it be downloaded in its millions. At which point, Burton noted drily, he 'got a call from EMI, saying that I had to stop.'

SOMETHING SINISTER

The genius of the mix is in the different shapes Burton moulded from his disparate source materials. The popularity of the two albums created pressure, but also opportunity. Burton took almost every track from *The Black Album* but was necessarily more sparing with the double set *The Beatles,* snipping sometimes the smallest elements from a song and weaving them through new arrangements. That's standard hip-hop practice, but there was something apt about The Beatles' sprawling jigsaw being sliced and diced like this.

The effect can be soothing, taking the edge off Jay-Z's embattled – and battling – rhymes and creating a sound palette unlike any hip-hop outside Prefuse 73's psychedelic meanderings. 'Public Service Announcement' is prettied up by a looped organ from George Harrison's 'Long, Long, Long', and the inspired use of 'Mother Nature's Son' on 'December 4th' brings a pastoral quality to Jay-Z's tales of boyhood in the projects, with Paul McCartney's acoustic picking adding poignancy to the rapper's mother's reminiscences. The almost unrecognisable pieces of 'Dear Prudence' on 'Allure' turn hip-hop soul into a kind of funky country groove, while the bouncy harpsichord of 'Piggies' makes the Neptunes production 'Change Clothes' near-comical.

But it's not all beauty and light. As there are dark corners to *The Beatles* – and Jay-Z's own patter – so is there an unsettling shade to *The Grey Album.*

SCRAMBLED LEGENDS

Utterly unfazed by corporate concerns over *The Grey Album,* Jay-Z and Paul McCartney teamed up with Linkin Park's Chester Bennington at the Grammy award ceremony in 2006. The improbable trio performed a mash-up of 'Yesterday' with Jay-Z and Linkin Park's 'Numb/Encore'.

It doesn't take a genius to make something sinister from 'Helter Skelter', but its cut-up cascade on Burton's reworking of '99 Problems' turns a forthright piece of braggadocio into a banshee wail of torment. A similarly uncomfortable trick is achieved on 'Dirt Off Your Shoulder', with John Lennon's yearning 'Julia' so chopped up that the whole track feels like a panic attack.

Unmoved by *The Grey Album*'s artistic merits, EMI tried to halt its distribution, but the digital genie was out of its cyber bottle. 'I'm one of the few people who has a ton of fans that don't have any product of mine,' said

> *'The record company minded. They put up a fuss. But it was like, "Take it easy, guys – it's a tribute."'*
>
> Paul McCartney

a bemused Burton, as downloads proliferated in the absence of a physical record. 'This wasn't supposed to happen . . .' he told Reuters. 'Online stores are selling it and people are downloading it all over the place.' But his reputation was being enhanced by the click.

As for the artists whose work had been purloined, ripped up, and chucked in the pot – well, it didn't bother them in the least. 'It was a really strong album,' Jay-Z told NPR. 'I champion any form of creativity and that was a genius idea to do it. And it sparked so many others like it. . . . There are other ones that, because of the blueprint that was set by him, I think are a little better, but him being the first and having an idea, I thought it was genius.' Interviewed for a BBC documentary, Paul McCartney was equally sanguine: 'I didn't mind . . . the record company minded. They put up a fuss. But it was like, "Take it easy, guys – it's a tribute."' And that's the way *The Grey Album* turned out – a love letter to two great artists with a healthy sprinkling of cheek thrown in. For all Burton's protestations about a nobler purpose – 'What I'm trying to do is change people's perceptions about music and what you can do,' he told *Good Copy Bad Copy* – the album stands up as a scintillating bit of mischief. **MH**

WILL IT EVER HAPPEN?

0/10 *You* try clearing Beatles samples. An official release could have made it one of the biggest albums of the decade, but EMI's stance never wavered, despite Burton seeking no recompense for his efforts. The closest *The Grey Album* got to an official release came in 2012 when sound engineer John Stewart took it upon himself to remaster the original and throw it out for free again on download sites. How many bootlegs get a remastered edition? This time, EMI didn't seem to have the appetite to close it down again – perhaps, with ninety-nine problems of their own at the time, it seemed less important.

WHAT HAPPENED NEXT . . .

Although Burton pocketed nothing for *The Grey Album*'s seismic statement of his abilities, it would swell his bank balance one way or another. The immediate result was a call from Damon Albarn, who was looking for the right man to hone the hip-hop-pop of the second Gorillaz album *Demon Days* (2005). Burton's dusty, gritty, hear-the-joins style was just the ticket. But he really hit pay dirt a year later with a long-mooted collaboration with Cee Lo Green as Gnarls Barkley, scoring big with the ubiquitous 'Crazy' (left), whose download figures dwarfed even *The Grey Album*.

Later years would see Burton work on Albarn's The Good, The Bad & The Queen project (2007), produce The Shortwave Set's classic *Replica Sun Machine* (2008), form Broken Bells with James Mercer of The Shins (2009), partner Italian composer Daniele Luppi for *Rome* (2011), and even produce a U2 album (see page 235). Meanwhile, Jay-Z came out of retirement and Paul McCartney quit EMI, claiming the label was 'boring'.

I/O

Artist Peter Gabriel Year 2004 Country UK Genre Art rock Label Real World What The lost temptation of Peter Gabriel

PETER GABRIEL

A self-confessed 'master of distraction', Gabriel has spent over a decade avoiding finishing an entirely new studio album. Having publicly christened it even before all the tracks were written, he was still fielding questions about the title in 2012. 'I can see if I still like it when we've got the appropriate collection of songs . . .' he told *Rolling Stone*. 'I think it's been used in other things since, but that's okay.'

Deadlines, Peter Gabriel once remarked, are markers on the way to achieving your goals. Consequently, nearly eight years elapsed between 1992's *Us* and 2000's *OVO*. But the dawn of the new millennium seemed to signal a fresh burst of energy. A mere two years after *OVO* came *Up* – and, with it, a promise that his *next* album would be out within eighteen months. Over a decade later, that promise is beginning to look a little rash . . .

BIRTH, DEATH, AND SEX

Widely overlooked owing to its promotion as a soundtrack for the opening of London's Millennium Dome, *OVO* in fact contained ravishing songs, notably the lovely 'Father, Son'. Gabriel had been productive in the post-*Us* years, and suggested several albums might ensue. But by *Up*, this had been refined to one mooted successor; to emerge – tour plans permitting – in 2004. 'Burn You Up, Burn You Down', a last-minute omission from *Up*, seemed a shoo-in – until it instead appeared on the 2003 best-of *Hit*. (A promo for which included a new instrumental, 'Wild' – which, with vocals, might too have bolstered a new album.) And given that he took to playing the song live, it's likely Gabriel envisaged a higher-profile home for another off-cut, 'Animal Nation', than that provided by 2002's soundtrack for *The Wild Thornberrys Movie*.

As the *Up* tour stretched into 2004, the new, sprawling 'Baby Man' and a re-recording of 'Curtains' – originally the B-side of 1986's 'Big Time' – were added to the list of contenders (the latter instead wound up on the soundtrack of the video game *Myst IV*). But, to no one's surprise, the provisional release date came and went with no hint of an album. Equally fruitless were talks with his old Genesis bandmates about a live reunion. 'He's a very busy man . . .' Tony Banks told *Rolling Stone*. 'Going out and performing *The Lamb Lies Down on Broadway* thirty-five years after the event is not high on his list.'

In 2005, after a fire at his Real World Studios briefly halted progress, Gabriel resolved to focus on *I/O*, its title derived from the computer term 'input/output'. Further additions included 'Amazing' and 'Silver Screen', but Gabriel was circumspect about a release date. It would appear, he told *Mojo*, 'when it is finished – however long that is going to take.' To *Rolling Stone,* he revealed its

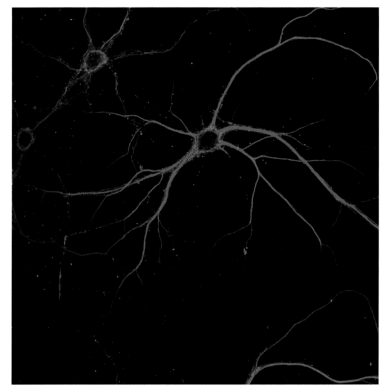

Cover: Heath Killen

WHAT HAPPENED NEXT . . .
In 2008 came news of an entirely different project: the covers album *Scratch My Back* (below), and a companion set – originally *Another Tongue,* eventually *I'll Scratch Yours* – on which acts whose songs he had recorded would perform songs from the Gabriel oeuvre. The former appeared in 2010, and in turn spawned the following year's *New Blood,* featuring orchestral interpretations of his back catalogue. The accompanying tours gave way to a 2012–13 outing that celebrated his most successful album, *So.* Determined not to live entirely in the past, Gabriel opened the shows with a new piano ballad, 'Obut'.

Up-esque themes were birth, death, and sex, and suggested he might road-test its songs on a tour featuring just himself, a bassist, and a percussionist.

While Genesis – minus Gabriel – announced a reunion tour, the singer delved into the archives with the mooted release of *Big Blue Ball,* a collaborative set whose cast stretched from Sinéad O'Connor to Living Color's Vernon Reid. Recorded in the 1990s, it languished in Real World's vaults for over a decade before producer Stephen Hague was called in to fashion it into an album. Announced in 2006, *Big Blue Ball* finally emerged two years later. Meanwhile, although snippets of new songs were teased on Gabriel's website, *I/O* slipped ever further down the list of priorities. **BM**

WILL IT EVER HAPPEN?

3/10 Of the 130 ideas accumulated for *I/O,* 'Some I'd probably like now and quite a lot I'd just leave by the wayside,' Gabriel told *Rolling Stone* in 2011. 'A lot of them are starting points and some more are fleshed-out recordings.' If these do eventually coalesce into a new album, there's no guarantee the title will be retained. 'With *I/O* I was thinking of a particular batch of material, which is sort of half-finished,' he noted. 'So, if it becomes something else, I might look at it and see if it still seems relevant.'

'FUGEES'

Artist Fugees **Year** 2006 **Country** US **Genre** Hip-hop **Label** Sony Urban Music **What** Three's a crowd

LAURYN HILL
~~In 2005, the year she toured with her old~~ band, Hill told *USA Today,* 'The Fugees was a conspiracy to control, to manipulate, and to encourage dependence. I took a lot of abuse that many people would not have taken in these circumstances. As a young woman, I saw the best in everyone, but I did not see the lust and insecurities of men. I discovered what a lie was, and how lies manifested themselves.'

When hip-hop trio Fugees fell apart in 1997, they were one of the world's biggest bands, the previous year's *The Score* having notched up six million sales in the US alone. Solo efforts by Lauryn Hill (the eight-million-selling *The Miseducation of Lauryn Hill*), her ex-boyfriend Wyclef Jean (the double platinum *The Carnival*), and his cousin Pras Michel (the smash 'Ghetto Supastar') confirmed their enduring appeal. By the mid-2000s, however, Wyclef and Pras had fallen out, and their commercial fortunes had waned. Meanwhile, Hill had reportedly spent over $2 million on an unreleased studio follow-up to *Miseducation.* 'Lauryn is not happy with herself . . .' Pras told *Rolling Stone.* 'It just so happens that she's done something that captured a moment in people's lives. They want more of that, but she's not ready to give that.' A Fugees reunion was an obvious solution – but also a recipe for disaster.

DOCUMENTING MY DISTRESS
Initial signs were promising. Invited to comedian Dave Chappelle's Block Party – a live show in Brooklyn in late 2004 – Hill opted to reunite the trio. 'Me and Clef went through our little bullshit . . .' Pras admitted, 'but to err is human, to forgive is divine. So we just came together. 'Cos I'm a fan of both Clef and Lauryn. . . . When she starts singing 'Killing Me Softly,' I almost wanted to cry.'

Hill had in fact long made fans want to cry, albeit for rather different reasons. Uneasy with fame, she followed the buoyant *Miseducation* with a downbeat set for *MTV Unplugged.* 'I was,' she told *USA Today,* 'documenting my distress.' Poorly received shows and 'long periods of separation' from Rohan Marley, son of Bob and the father of her children, compounded the impression of a downward spiral. In fact, the latter relationship hadn't had the best of starts, coming so hot on the heels of her split from Wyclef that, when she first fell pregnant, even insiders weren't sure whether he or Marley was the father.

At the Chappelle show, Hill threw in lines from her 'Lost Ones' ('It's funny how money change a situation / Miscommunication leads to complication / My emancipation don't fit your equation') that had been interpreted as a jab at Wyclef. His benign reaction suggested old wounds had healed, and the trio began a new album – but, by the close of 2005, all they had to show for it

FUGEES

Cover: Herita MacDonald

WHAT HAPPENED NEXT . . .

The Fugees were usurped by the Black Eyed Peas. 'I signed an autograph for a kid, "Clef from the Fugees",' Wyclef rapped on his *From The Hut, to the Projects, to the Mansion* (below) in 2009. 'The kid looked at me and said, "What the hell is the Fugees? / Ain't you will.i.am from the Peas?"' Pras swapped music for filming documentaries, while Hill's shows and personal life became ever-increasing causes for concern. Over a decade after 2002's *MTV Unplugged No. 2.0,* there was no sign of a new album, and she was jailed for tax evasion in 2013. The wilfully uncommercial 'Consumerism', recorded while she was incarcerated and issued on the eve of her release in October that year, suggested that radio-friendly hip-hop is low on her list of priorities.

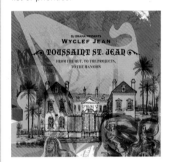

was the indifferently received 'Take it Easy.' Nonetheless, they embarked on a month-long European tour – on which the group's biggest star, it was widely reported, insisted on being addressed as 'Ms. Hill' and had apparently taken lessons on punctuality from Axl Rose. 'Those Fugees reunion shows shouldn't have been done,' Wyclef told *Blues & Soul,* 'because we wasn't ready. I really felt we shoulda first all gone into a room with Lauryn and a psychiatrist.'

Ensuing silence spoke volumes. 'Me and Clef, we on the same page,' Pras told *Billboard,* 'but Lauryn is in her zone, and I'm fed up with that shit. Here she is, blessed with a gift, with the opportunity to rock and give, and she's running on some bullshit? I'm a fan of Lauryn's but I can't respect that.' **BM**

WILL IT EVER HAPPEN?

2/10 'Before I work with Lauryn Hill again,' Pras told allhiphop.com in the aftermath of the aborted reunion, 'you will have a better chance of seeing Osama Bin Laden and Bush in Starbucks having a latte.' However, he did pop up at a Hill show in 2011. Unruffled by the lack of an invitation to that event, Wyclef told usmagazine.com, 'There's an energy and a buzz about the Fugees that everyone likes. I think that it would be exciting to see that happen again. I don't know if it would be another album – but maybe a song!'

SIRENS

Artist May Jailer (aka Lana Del Rey) **Year** 2006 **Country** US **Genre** Alternative folk **Label** Self-release
What The *Born to Die* belle before she dropped beats – and her voice

LANA DEL REY
'I come from a place that, geographically, isn't that stimulating,' Del Rey told *The Quietus.* 'But New York's architecture alone is enough to inspire a whole album. In fact, that's what happened at first – my early stuff was mostly just interpretations of landscapes. . . . When I was in New York I had nowhere to live, and I was trying to find a way to be a musician – just trying to survive, which is fucking hard by the way. So I got myself into a lot of situations I didn't plan on. What I was going for was something beautiful, but I kinda got myself into trouble along the way.'

Before she was Lana Del Rey – self-appointed 'American Poet/Angel Headed Hipster' – Elizabeth Woolridge Grant was Sparkle Jump Rope Queen. Before that, Lizzy Grant. And before *that,* May Jailer. Having learned six chords on the guitar, she realised she could 'probably write a million songs.' Fifteen of those – simple folk ballads about the loves of her life (sex and drugs and homicide) – wound up on the debut album that never was.

FLEDGLING HEROINE

At fourteen, Del Rey was sent to boarding school: a means of dealing with her alcohol dependence. She has since admitted booze was 'the first love of my life.' New York City beckoned when she was nineteen. 'That's when I found Bob Dylan, Frank Sinatra, Jeff Buckley, Leonard Cohen – my masters,' she told the *Daily Star.* 'I've never really listened to anything else since.' *Sirens* was conceived around this time at the Jim Cushman Studio in Lake Placid. Moldy Peaches bassist – and the singer's then-boyfriend – Steven Mertens is thought to have been in the producer's chair. (Post-Peaches, Mertens wound up in a band called Spacecamp. 'We were (Del Rey's) back-up band once cuz her and Steven used to make out sometimes, for like a year,' frontman Jon Wiley told syffal.com. 'Well, turns out *it wasn't him, it wasn't him, it wasn't all for him,* cuz she wanted to make out with someone else one week. I mean, look at her. If you had those lips, you would want to press them up against a lot of stuff.' Spacecamp's 'Alibi' is about the short-lived couple. 'They're friends now,' Wiley said, 'and laugh and joke about where their lips have been.')

Del Rey has never officially acknowledged that she was responsible for *Sirens* – which some commentators regard as a collection of demos – but concedes, 'I think I have over 120 songs that have been leaked online.' Only four of the album's tracks have confirmed titles ('A Star for Nick', 'Out with a Bang', 'Pride', and 'Birds of a Feather'), the remainder being gleaned from lyrics or fans' imaginations. But those fans that have heard them are in no doubt that they are indeed the work of their fledgling heroine.

'For K', the opening track, provides *Sirens* with its title, as she ponders the fate of a friend doing time for a double murder. Intriguingly, her true debut

SIRENS

MAY JAILER

Cover: Isabel Eeles

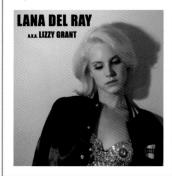

WHAT HAPPENED NEXT . . .
She recorded more acoustic demos, six of which appeared online and were compiled – either by Del Rey or her fans – onto an EP entitled *No Kung Fu*. These were handed to producer David Kahne, who recorded the three-track EP *Kill Kill,* issued on iTunes in 2008. That acted as a trailer for 2010's *A.K.A. Lizzy Grant* album (below), which included three of the *No Kung Fu* songs, but with full backing arrangements, hinting at the cinematic sound that is now Del Rey's stock-in-trade.

LANA DEL RAY
a.k.a. LIZZY GRANT

album – *Lana Del Ray A.K.A. Lizzy Grant* – features a track entitled 'For K, part two', in which she auditions for a bar band, then admits, 'I don't play a good guitar.' But the songs appear to share nothing bar a title – a head-scratcher that adds to the eerie mystique that is a major element of Del Rey's appeal. The same friend is the subject of a *Sirens* song thought to be titled 'Westbound', and the later hits 'Video Games', 'Blue Jeans', and 'Born to Die'.

The sound of her voice on the album is light and airy. 'I actually used to sing much higher,' she confessed when stardom hit, 'but I felt people weren't taking me very seriously, so I lowered my voice, believing that it would help me stand out. Now I sing quite low . . . well, for a female anyway.' Graduating from pink and fluffy to blue and velvety proved a smart choice, but it would leave *Sirens* languishing in obscurity until devoted fans began digging. **AG**

WILL IT EVER HAPPEN?

3/10 The *Sirens* songs are homogenous and uneventful, making it unlikely that they will be officially released with Del Rey's blessing – she will probably leave them online for the curious to unearth. It's possible, however, that she will revisit the songs in concert or, as she has done with 'Yayo' (twice), in the studio. The worst-case scenario – given her preoccupation with death and dying young – is that *Sirens* will comprise part of a posthumous set.

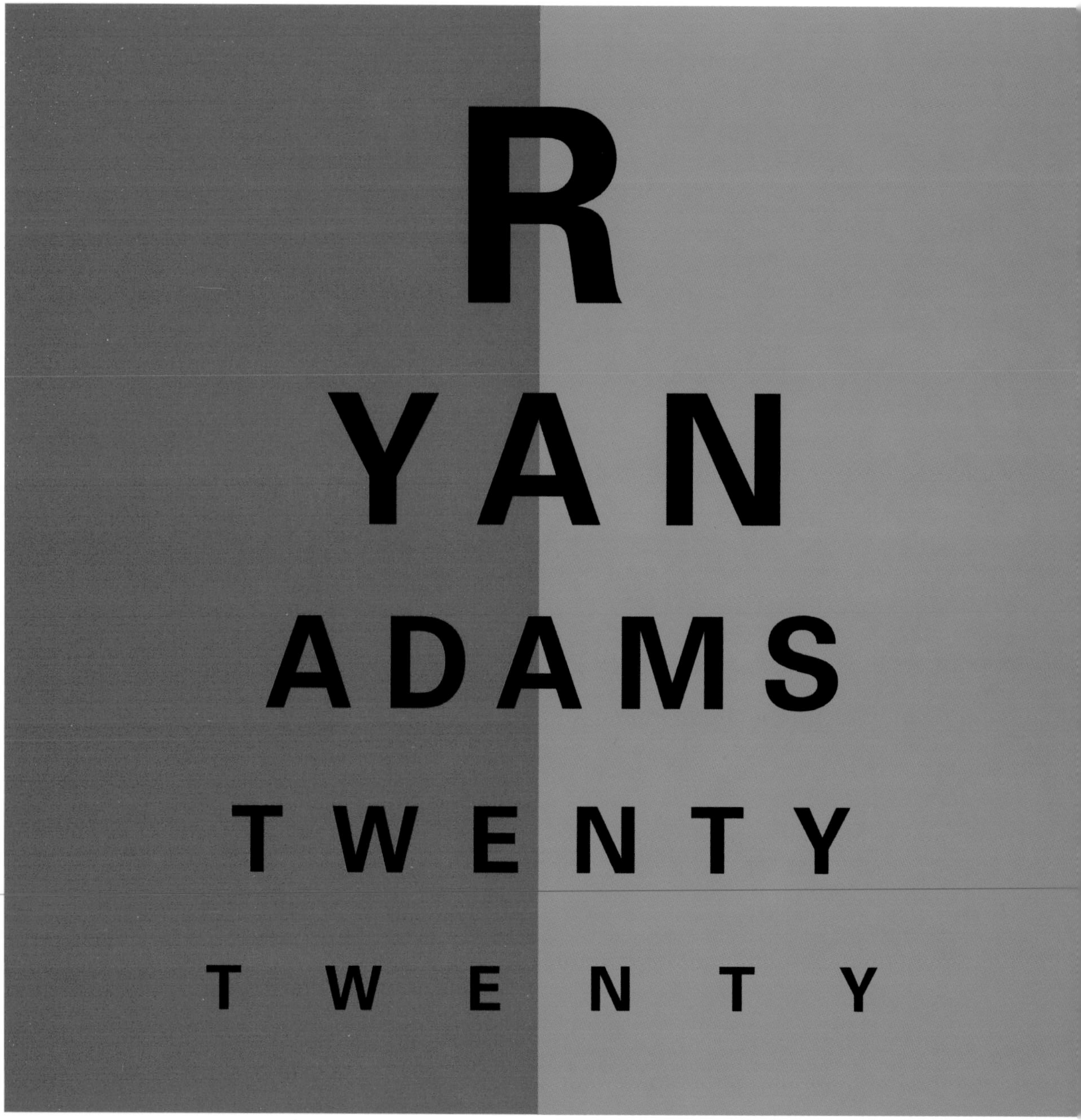

R

YAN

ADAMS

TWENTY

TWENTY

Cover: Tom Howey

20:20

Artist Ryan Adams **Year** 2007 **Country** US **Genre** Folk / country / alternative rock **Label** Lost Highway
What A box of by-products from a chemical romance

Egomania, drugs, and an inner ear disorder may have snared him along the way, but Ryan Adams has never suffered from writer's block. During the 2000s, the North Carolina-born singer-songwriter released at least one album a year – three in 2005 – and recorded enough songs for a dozen more, most of which are still sitting in the vaults. 'I just work too fast for any label to be able to put records out as I've needed them,' he told biographer David Menconi in 2000. 'If I could do two records a year, I think everybody would be happier, especially me.' But in 2007, his label Lost Highway announced it would catch up with this ever-growing backlog with *20:20,* a box set containing five 'lost' albums: *The Suicide Handbook, 48 Hours, Pinkhearts, Darkbreaker,* and *Black Hole.*

MOST MAJESTIC

Adams originally hoped to release *The Suicide Handbook* as the follow-up to his acclaimed solo debut, 2000's *Heartbreaker.* The two-disc set of delicate melancholy featured him on guitar and piano, accompanied on pedal steel by former Bob Dylan sideman William 'Bucky' Baxter (who also appears on the Beastie Boys' *Country Mike's Greatest Hits* – see page 170). It was inspired by an ill-fated fling with actress Winona Ryder. 'Songs like "She Wants to Play Hearts" and "Cry on Demand" . . .' Adams observed to *Entertainment Weekly,* 'I don't think you have to throw a fucking penny to fucking find out what that's about. "Cry on Demand" . . . acting . . . *hello?* I love the line, "She dies every night with her face on the news / Nobody cries, they just smoke and stare at their shoes." That's how I really felt about her. And then, weirdly, shit happened *(Ryder's 2001 arrest for shoplifting)* and she *was* in the news.'

(Years later, Adams blogged, 'I never dated Winona Ryder, but . . . I will always love her. She is so fucking smart and so fucking under the microscope I can't imagine how she pulled through. . . . She is as hot as the sun in a hot tub on itself though and everybody knows that. Also, who she is as an actress totally inspired me and helped me form what kind of artist I wanted to be.')

The Suicide Handbook, Adams boldly declared to *Q* in 2007, 'is *amazing.* If anything, it's my most majestic piece ever.' Lost Highway disagreed and

RYAN ADAMS
'I just really love playing guitar and coming up with these funky songs,' the wayward star told *Mojo* by way of an explanation for his prolific recording. 'I like it the way people like sex and food. That sounds boisterous, but I enjoy it and it's something I need to do.'

DUKE IT OUT

In a 2003 *Spin* magazine profile entitled 'Who the fuck is Ryan Adams?' producer James Barber complained: 'In every interview you read with Ryan, he talks about growing up on hardcore and Black Flag and punk rock. It's like, "Where's that in your music?"' Barber had clearly never heard the Patty Duke Syndrome – the short-lived North Carolina punk trio Adams fronted before joining alt-country legends Whiskeytown. The group's only official release amounted to one side of a seven-inch record (right), but an eleven-track demo recorded in 1993, filled with glorious Hüsker Dü and Replacements-inspired power-pop, can be found on fan sites. Adams doesn't have positive memories of this period: following the Syndrome's breakup in 1994, he penned a song about his ex-bandmates. Its title: 'Bastards I Used to Know'.

Adams subsequently indulged his punk and hardcore leanings by teaming up with Jesse Malin to form The Finger (whose sole album is 2003's *We Are Fuck You*), and reinventing himself as The Shit (whose self-released catalog includes *General Ulysses S. Grant Hospital, Christmas Apocalypse (Part 2), Slef* (sic) *Portrait,* and *Holy Shit!*

THE STROKES IS THIS IT

IS THAT IT?

While recovering from surgery for a tooth abscess in 2002, Adams recorded a cover of *Is This It,* the debut album by The Strokes, on a four-track recorder. That session has since become the white whale of Ryan Adams completists. 'But it's not that good,' he confessed to *Q.* 'It sounds like a crazy person. I'd just had dental surgery and I was on all these painkillers. So I got the banjo and mandolin out, playing along to *Is This It.* I'm laughing and my mouth is messed up bad. We're not talking unseen Van Goghs here.'

declined to release it; deeming the album, said Adams, 'too sad.' Cuts from it would be scattered across later releases: the wistful 'La Cienega Just Smiled' and the bluesy 'Touch, Feel and Lose' on 2001's best-selling *Gold;* 'She Wants to Play Hearts', 'Dear Chicago', and 'Cry On Demand' on the following year's off-cuts collection, *Demolition.* A bootleg of the acoustic *Suicide* session has since appeared online, but Adams told *Rolling Stone* that the *20:20* version would include previously unheard strings, bass, and drums.

Two weeks after finishing *Gold,* Adams headed back to the studio and laid down *48 Hours:* 'My stab at a real honest California country-rock record, minus the California part,' he told *USA Today.* Dashed off in two days at a reported cost of $1,200, *48 Hours* sounded more commercially viable than *The Suicide Handbook.* Tracks like the stomping, harmonica-led 'Hallelujah' and the tender, slow-building 'Desire' – both of which ended up on *Demolition* – seemed engineered to be radio hits. But Lost Highway, already tied up promoting *Gold,* weren't prepared to push yet another album.

Still, Adams refused to slow down. Soon after *48 Hours,* he threw together an 1980s-inspired rock record, *Pinkhearts,* with musicians who played on the *Gold* tour. The album, he explained to *USA Today,* was 'somewhere between The Replacements, but not as good, and The Rolling Stones, but not as good-looking or talented.' Tracks like the raging 'Mega-Superior Gold' proved Adams could write arena-sized anthems as well as gentle, alt-country laments.

LARGE QUANTITIES OF SPEEDBALLS

But there was a dark side to this extreme productivity. 'What terrified me was that at any moment the ability to make records would be taken away,' he told *Q.* 'At the back of my mind was this voice going, "You're only one bad gig away from being a plumber so work, work, work!"' Figuring that 'the only way to maintain it was to take drugs in order to write continuously,' Adams knocked back buckets of mind-melting chemicals. 'My thing was doing large quantities of speedballs, which is heroin and coke mixed together,' he said. 'Then I'd eat Vicodins (a painkiller) and have a bottle of champagne for dinner.'

The damage wrought by this chemical cocktail can be heard on the morbid acoustic dirges that fill 2005's *Darkbreaker*. Exhausted from recording three albums back-to-back – the honky-tonking *Jacksonville City Nights,* the Grateful Dead-style rock of *Cold Roses,* and the ethereal, folky *29* – Adams returned to the studio when director Cameron Crowe asked him to pen an 'uplifting' track for his romantic comedy, *Elizabethtown*. 'This depressive brain muck is all I could muster,' Adams wrote of *Darkbreaker* on his web site. He was similarly damning of *Black Hole,* a collection of raw and ragged rock that has never

> ## 'My thing was doing large quantities of speedballs, which is heroin and coke mixed together.'
> ### Ryan Adams

appeared even as a bootleg. 'It sounds like The Strokes, but if they sucked,' he told *Rolling Stone*. He later revised his opinion, telling avclub.com that *Black Hole* 'has the feeling of the one fucking thing all of my records were missing, the one part of the story, which is a record that's sort of just revelling in youth.'

SHIT HITS THE FANS
But Adams knew it was time to grow up, and in 2006, kicked his bad habits. 'It was part epiphany, realising that I was going to die,' he told *Q,* 'and partly that I'd have these people come around – people who are fucked-up drug vampires – *they* were saying I should go to rehab. So I quit.' As a goodbye to those tumultuous years, Adams decided to remaster the material from his druggy days for *20:20* and approached horror author Stephen King, who shared his prodigious work ethic, to write liner notes for the box set. '(Critics) always trash (King) because he works harder and twice as fast and has more valid ideas than many people know how to deal with,' Adams told *American Songwriter*. 'He works like (Henry) Rollins and Black Flag and the Minutemen – a punk rock work ethic, which is, "Get out of the house!"'

As 2006 closed, Adams put eleven album pastiches online: four by his rap alter ego DJ Reggie, and seven by his hardcore and metal parodies The Shit and Werewolph, their titles including *A Reginald Gangster, The Shit Hits the Fans,* and *Hillbilly Joel*. But *20:20* was terminated in 2008 when, after years of disputes, he quit Lost Highway and launched his own label, PAX AM. **TB**

WHAT HAPPENED NEXT...
Diagnosed in 2009 with Ménière's disease – an inner ear disorder that affects balance and hearing – Adams took a much-needed break from touring and recording. During this hiatus, he put out three previously unreleased (and sadly mediocre) albums – *Cardinology, Orion,* and *III/IV* – through the PAX AM label. Then, in 2011, he headed to the studio with legendary producer Glyn Johns and laid down *Ashes & Fire,* full of fragile songs about love, forgiveness, and healing. 'It felt good to ask: "What am I really capable of?"' Adams told the *Guardian*. 'I felt competitive again, to write great songs.' He followed that with *Live After Deaf* (its title inspired by his ear disorder and Iron Maiden), an in-concert set that filled fifteen discs.

WILL IT EVER HAPPEN?

3/10 Since leaving Lost Highway, Adams has shown little interest in revisiting *20:20*. He has, however, talked about releasing individual albums from the set – telling avclub.com that he spent four months in the studio mixing *Black Hole*. 'By the time it was done, we got it down to eleven songs, leaving a bunch of shit off,' he said. 'A few of my friends have it, and it reduced a few of them to tears. . . . It has beauty, but it has a darkness.'

REPORTAGE

Artist Duran Duran **Year** 2007 **Country** UK **Genre** Pop **Label** Epic **What** Four and the ragged release schedule

JOHN TAYLOR
'That whole project was a fucking nightmare,' the bassist (above, with Simon Le Bon) groaned to *The Quietus*. 'We delivered an album to Sony that was a natural-sounding, almost *rock* album, and they were like, "We need something a bit pop – do you fancy doing a couple of tracks with Timbaland?"'

And then there were two. The squeeze on Duran Duran's fortunes that had tightened through the 1990s took a terminal grip in 1997. Bassist John Taylor – who had stayed the course despite the exits in the previous decade of guitarist Andy Taylor and drummer Roger Taylor, and his and Andy's success with The Power Station in 1985 – jumped ship, beset by drugs and disillusionment. His departure meant Duran, once giants, were in a sorry state, their breakthrough line-up down to just keyboard player Nick Rhodes and singer Simon Le Bon. The pair forged on with former Frank Zappa and Missing Persons guitarist Warren Cuccurullo – a member for longer than his predecessor Andy Taylor, but never regarded as part of a classic line-up. This incarnation spawned 1997's *Medazzaland* (unreleased in Europe) and 2000's *Pop Trash,* but interest waned to infinitesimal levels. Major surgery was required.

PRETTY HORRENDOUS

Le Bon had the answer. He, Rhodes, and Cuccurullo were in Los Angeles in 2000 to promote *Pop Trash* and bumped into John Taylor at a restaurant for a tearful reunion. Within days, Le Bon and Rhodes went for lunch at Taylor's house, where Le Bon floated the idea of a reunion of the famous five. Drummer Roger Taylor, who had retired in 1986 to enjoy the country air but contributed to the band's covers album *Thank You* in 1995, was receptive. Andy Taylor was a more daunting proposition. Always a square peg in Duran's round hole, he had been an inevitable escapee and there had been a touch of relief about his 1986 withdrawal. Nonetheless, he too was keen on Le Bon's scheme.

Cuccurullo stepped aside: there was no stopping the juggernaut. Vintage fans took the quintet's comeback *Astronaut* to their hearts in 2004, sending it to top three in the UK and top twenty in the US. '(Reach Up for the) Sunrise' became their biggest British hit in two decades, and a sell-out tour confirmed the affection that Durannies reserved for their heroes. It was time to capitalise.

Work on *Reportage* began in September 2005. In time-honoured style, sessions were scheduled on a luxury yacht owned by Microsoft co-founder Paul Allen, but sadly the similarly seafaring 'Rio' video was not to be reenacted. The project moved to tennis star Andre Agassi's mansion in San Francisco. From

DURAN DURAN
REPORTAGE

Cover: Isabel Eeles

NEUROTIC, MOI?

In his autobiography *In The Pleasure Groove – Love, Death & Duran Duran,* John Taylor recalls the *Guardian* reporting, 'The *NME* in the '70s was responsible for creating a generation of neurotic boy outsiders.' As one of those outsiders, the name struck a chord with Taylor, who dropped the 'boy' when, in the fertile environs of Los Angeles' Viper Room club, he formed a supergroup with ex-Sex Pistols guitarist Steve Jones and Guns N' Roses' rhythm section Matt Sorum and Duff McKagan in 1995.

A self-titled album emerged in 1996 but, for Taylor, the band 'lost its mojo' when it became a career rather than four old boys having a laugh. Meanwhile, McKagan and Sorum were recalled to their day job by Axl Rose. 'Every time we all try to run off to do something . . .' the drummer told *Kerrang!,* 'it all happens. When it rains it pours! I really think a lot of the reason we're getting back together as a band is because he heard we were so good.' (Both, however, were out of GN'R within a year.) The Outsiders disbanded but performed no-strings reunion shows in 1999. Their album is a hard-to-find curio.

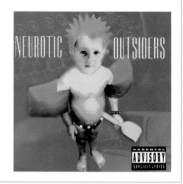

the outset, the album had a different flavour to their reunion set. *Astronaut* had been a studio concoction, with its makers acclimatising to each another again, but *Reportage* had a head start. After months on the road, Duran were ready to come up with something more organic and more 'rock'.

'When we begin writing, we have no idea where we're going,' Rhodes told Gavin Elder – regular director of Duran's promotional documentaries – early on in the San Francisco sessions. 'We just get in a room, plug in, and see what sound comes out when we start playing – which can be pretty horrendous, but we've got ten pieces of music that are, aside from lyrics and a few overdubs,

> *'The label were quite shocked that it wasn't all dancing and uplifting, but more political.'*
> Nick Rhodes

pretty close to completion.' Le Bon was enthusiastic about the location ('I always work better with a bit of sunshine getting to my brain') and could feel the new sound shaping up, calling the songs 'very natural, very powerful, very raw-sounding. We wanted to recapture the rawness and energy of our first album and I think we've got it with songs like "Traumatized" and "Nobody".'

TIMBERS, TAYLORS, & NERDS
The reunited Duran at 2003's MTV Video Music Awards, with Justin Timberlake, who would contribute to *Reportage*'s successor, and N*E*R*D. *Left to right* Roger Taylor, Timberlake, Andy Taylor, Nick Rhodes, Simon Le Bon, Chad Hugo, Pharrell Williams, and John Taylor.

In October 2005, they relocated to London with producer Michael Patterson, who had worked with Jay-Z. In April 2006, discussing a new cut, John Taylor told the band's site, 'We have been working on around fifteen songs over the last couple of months, so by the time Simon got the lyric polished off . . . we had probably been listening to the rough idea for twelve weeks or so. It's all about fine tuning, but without losing the energy and attitude of the original take.'

SIFTED OUT THE CRAP

Things went awry within weeks, when Sony rejected the album. 'It was an indie record, much more rock and angrier . . .' Rhodes explained to *TNT*. 'We were looking at the war and you couldn't avoid Iraq, America, Britain, Blair, and Bush. We took it to the label and they were quite shocked that it wasn't all dancing and uplifting, but more political. They said, "Well, this is amazing, but what are we going to do for singles?" And we said, "Well, we hadn't really thought of that. We just made the record."'

Youth – then between engagements with his alma mater Killing Joke – was sounded out to salvage the production, but the main contender was R&B guru Tim 'Timbaland' Mosley. 'We had spoken with Tim over the years,' Rhodes noted, 'and said, "We must do something together," which is what you say but it never generally happens.' Diaries were synchronised for September 2006, but another spanner was thrown in the works: Andy Taylor didn't turn up to the studio. 'Youth and Duran Duran – that woulda worked,' the guitarist observed to thedivareview.com. 'Sifted out the crap, got the good bits, and worked on some more material with someone who was a real clean, smart producer who really had made some great records.' The hiring of Timbaland he dismissed as 'an Emperor's New Clothes thing.'

The rest got down to work with their new helmsman and the sessions bore fruit, but the writing was on the wall for *Reportage*. 'When Timbaland saw the guitar and the bass and the drums come in to the studio,' Rhodes noted, 'I think he was mortified, because everything's in a box for those guys.' The result, John Taylor rued, 'sounded hugely different' to the original sessions.

Five years later, Le Bon sounded regretful in a chat with *The Quietus,* citing *Reportage*'s '48 Hours Later' as 'one of the best Duran Duran songs I've ever heard . . . it would work well with what we're doing now.' It's not over yet. **MH**

WHAT HAPPENED NEXT . . .
With Andy Taylor out of the frame, a virtue was born of necessity. Duran cut their losses and veered from the rock direction the guitarist naturally steered them in, using their new relationship with Timbaland to explore more R&B-related music. At the end of the aborted *Reportage* sessions, the band took the tracks they had worked on with the producer and built on them to create *Red Carpet Massacre*. The album, released in 2007 on Epic, featured further contributions from Timbaland and Justin Timberlake, as well as production from Danja. It did little to arrest the band's commercial decline, but found some favour with critics.

WILL IT EVER HAPPEN?

7/10 The signs are good, with Le Bon still misty-eyed and Rhodes talking about revisiting tracks to see if anything can be salvaged. It would be a welcome move for the fans, who devote message boards to Duran's great lost album. Rhodes' plan is to get it out there, clearing the decks. 'It was a really strong album,' he told the *Richmond Times*. 'It was never quite finished so we'd need to do some cosmetic work on it. But the songs are intact.'

A sticking point may be the band's relationship with Andy Taylor, who would presumably be able to exercise a veto. 'Hell is going to have to freeze back over first,' he told thisisnotretro.com. 'I don't really think it was our best work.'

EROS

Artist Deftones Year 2008 Country US Genre Nu-metal Label Reprise What Full of promise, halted by tragedy

CHI CHENG
'I would like to see it out,' guitarist Stephen Carpenter told metalsucks.net of the Deftones' *Eros*. 'Mostly because I think people would like to hear it because Chi (above) is on it. He has a family and I'd like to see it do something for them as well. That would be nice.'

Dysfunctional is the word that would best have summed up Sacramento metallers Deftones in 2006. The band's fifth album, that Halloween's *Saturday Night Wrist,* had taken more than three years to complete, a reflection of disharmony in the ranks. By the end of 2007, however, work had started on a new set, *Eros,* amid talk of renewed spirits. Then tragedy struck.

HEAVY AS FUCK
Saturday Night Wrist nearly brought the Deftones' career to an end, eighteen years after it began. With its members struggling through what vocalist Chino Moreno termed 'divorces, money problems, life' – not to mention his decision to put the band on hold during the recording to pursue his Team Sleep side project – it looked like album number five could be their last. 'I remember telling myself . . . that I don't know if I want to make another Deftones record,' the singer told *Kerrang!* magazine in 2010, 'because it has to be one of the most stressful, unhealthy experiences ever.'

Life on the road seemed to galvanise the quintet: by mid-2007, they were speaking publicly about their renewed vigour. This extended to converting their rehearsal room, The Spot, into a studio so they could, as turntablist Frank Delgado said, record their sixth album 'at our place, on our time, on our dime.' Writing began in earnest in September 2007 – and, when the band began recording the following April, they reunited with producer Terry Date, who had helmed their first four albums. 'The songs are definitely weird,' Moreno assured *Kerrang!*. 'There's a lot of atmosphere and a lot of soundscaping.'

In June, bassist Chi Cheng was quoted on metal website Blabbermouth saying they were finishing drum tracks on a song tentatively titled 'Trempest' that was 'heavy as fuck with a shitload of groove.' Guitarist Stephen Carpenter would later claim he'd been trying to create club-like grooves over heavy riffs, a reflection of his love of The Neptunes and Timbaland. On 18 September, the band debuted the new 'Melanie' during a performance in LA. YouTube footage reveals jerky, almost maths-like verses butting heads with a spacey, melodic chorus and frenzied mid-section – in a way making sense of each member's disparate descriptions of the music.

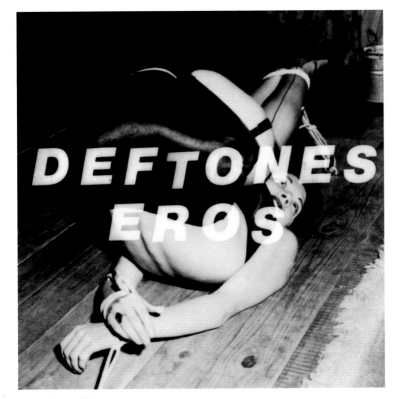

Cover: Heath Killen

WHAT HAPPENED NEXT . . .

Deftones have issued two albums since Cheng's accident – 2010's *Diamond Eyes* and 2012's *Koi No Yokan* (below) – but the partially-completed *Eros* remains in the vault. Prior to the crash, Cheng spoke of his excitement about it on Deftones' website: 'I truly believe this album to be well worth the wait. The idea of finishing the album and getting out to play in front of y'all is a nice light at the end of my tunnel.'

THE GOOD FIGHT

Eros ground to a halt on 4 November 2008: a car accident in Santa Clara, California, left Cheng in a coma. Work on the album was halted instantly. Seven months later, the band released a statement updating fans on Cheng's condition and their future plans: 'The songs recorded for *Eros* are very special to us as they are the latest with Chi (and we certainly hope not the last). However, as we neared completion on *Eros*, we realised that this record doesn't best encompass and represent who we are as people and as musicians.'

Accordingly, they opted to begin a brand new record with stand-in bassist Sergio Vega, claiming it was 'a creative decision' that had 'no connection with Chi's condition or anything associated.' But on 13 April 2013, aged just forty-two, Chi Cheng passed away. 'He fought the good fight . . .' his mother wrote to fans. 'He knew that he was very loved and never alone.' **RY**

8/10

WILL IT EVER HAPPEN?

At the 2013 *Revolver* Golden Gods awards in LA, Moreno confirmed the chances were 'more so now probably than ever.' To Philippines New Blog that May, he clarified: 'There's only like six songs that are finished . . . but I feel more positive now that it will see the light of day.'

Cover: Isabel Eeles

SONGS OF ASCENT

Artist U2 **Year** 2010 **Country** UK **Genre** Rock **Label** Island **What** No sign on the horizon

Not for the first time, U2 found themselves, in 2010, having to defend an album that had topped charts worldwide. 'I'm a little bit baffled . . .' bassist Adam Clayton confessed to *Q*. 'I suppose the hard fact of it is that (first single) 'Get on Your Boots' didn't ignite people's imaginations. That's a bit of a cold slap.' Although Bono observed that *No Line on the Horizon* 'sold very well,' it took eight months to go platinum in the US (Its predecessor – 2004's *How to Dismantle an Atomic Bomb* – had gone triple platinum in three weeks.) As U2's '360°' tour wound its way round the globe for two years, there was repeated talk of a prompt follow-up – and, at one point, *three* follow-ups – but, as Bono admitted, 'It all comes down to tunes. Can we find those tunes?'

NEARLY KILLED THE BAND

'Finding tunes' was precisely the issue when the band began work in 2006 with producer Rick Rubin. He favoured them bringing completed songs to the studio. They preferred the improvisational methods they had established with producers Brian Eno and Daniel Lanois. The sessions yielded two singles – 'The Saints Are Coming', with Green Day, and 'Window in the Skies' – before a parting of the ways. 'Rick strips everything away . . .' Clayton told Sun Media. 'He doesn't like atmospherics and textures.' With Eno and Lanois – whose titles might as well be Atmospherics and Textures – U2 decamped to Morocco to create the genesis of *No Line on the Horizon*. However, producer Steve Lillywhite had to be summoned to marshal the results into a releasable whole, just as he had done with most U2 work from *The Joshua Tree* onwards. At final sessions in London at the end of 2008, with a February release looming, Eno, Lillywhite, and new recruit will.i.am of the Black Eyed Peas toiled on the album in separate studios. 'I don't want to do *that* again,' Bono later grumbled.

Drummer Larry Mullen's observation that the songs were 'good' but 'unfinished' echoed the band's verdict on their 1997 set, *Pop*. Both ultimately sounded like expensive demos – the key difference being the quality of the music. Having opened the 'Popmart' tour playing ten new songs, they closed it still playing seven. In contrast, the '360°' tour began with seven new songs and ended with just three – including, despite its woeful chart showing, 'Get on Your

BONO
'Lots of people have U2 albums,' the star noted to *Q* in 2011. 'Why they would want another one is a reasonable question. I don't know if it's possible for us to make something current that is meaningful, not just to our audience but to the times we live in. But that's kind of the job for me and I'm not ready to give it up. I think it's unlikely that we'll pull it off, but then so has the last twenty years been unlikely.'

U2 R I

Bar The Edge's 1986 soundtrack *Captive,* no U2 member has made a fully-fledged solo album. So it's tricky to gauge whether booze or bravado played the biggest part in Larry Mullen's intention, mooted during the band's 1987 *Joshua Tree* tour, to cut a country album. 'I've had it planned for a long time . . .' the drummer told *Musician,* 'When this tour's finished, I'll get down to it seriously. . . . I did say to Maria (McKee) that, if I did get this country record together, I'd like her to come and help me sing, and maybe write a few songs. Unfortunately, I can't play guitar and, when I did start to learn, I did something to my hand and I couldn't get it round the neck. (The band) think that I didn't bother to try, but it's completely untrue, and I *will* learn how to play.' Over a quarter of a century later, the set has yet to appear.

Boots.' And while the album ultimately sold around five million – spectacular by most standards – not one of its songs became a true live favourite.

On its release in February 2009, however, optimism was running sufficiently high that Bono was already mooting a new album before the end of the year: 'A more meditative album on the theme of pilgrimage,' he told the *Observer.* Its title, *Songs of Ascent,* referred to psalms sung by worshippers or priests. Drawing on the Sufi singing of Muslim prayer they had enjoyed in Morocco, this 'reflective piece' would, the singer told *Rolling Stone,* 'have a clear mood, like (Miles Davis's) *Kind of Blue.* Or (John Coltrane's) *A Love Supreme.'* He even had its first single picked out: the *No Line* offcut 'Every Breaking Wave' (which earned a belated live debut in August 2010). But that wasn't all: he also hoped his bandmates would record a rockier album, based on his and guitarist The Edge's songs for the then yet-to-be-previewed Broadway musical, *Spider-Man: Turn Off the Dark.* 'It could be our *Tommy!'*

Manager Paul McGuinness was skeptical, recalling to *Hot Press* how making *Achtung Baby's* sequel *Zooropa* while still on tour 'nearly killed the band. They should remember that period if they think about doing it again.' Mullen, for his part, wasn't interested, dismissing *Spider-Man* as 'a Bono and Edge project.'

> *'We've got a whole album we started with Rick Rubin . . . a rocking club album with beats and big guitars.'*
>
> Bono

As the '360°' tour wound its way through Europe, plans changed according to who interviewers talked to. 'We've got a whole album we started with Rick Rubin, which is a rocking club album with beats and big guitars,' said Bono. 'I can't wait to get back to that. . . . We have five or six songs on that. We have about twelve on the *Songs of Ascent.'* The Edge allowed that, 'We would love the idea of the next record being sooner rather than later,' but noted, 'It's about whether we have the time.' Clayton, injecting a note of realism, remarked, 'Until there are ten songs finished, mixed, and on a shelf, (an album's) not definite . . . When Bono hears two notes together, he hears a song complete. When anyone else hears two notes together, we hear a starting point.'

NOT ALWAYS OBVIOUS

By the time the tour hit the States in September, Bono had yet to convince Clayton and Mullen to take on *Spider-Man.* 'It's the unfinished songs from (*No Line*) that we should be concentrating on,' the drummer told *Rolling Stone.* 'There is slower, meditative stuff on there, but . . . I don't think it will end up being that kind of record. . . . I would like to think that we would have a song that would end up on the radio.' Bono remained convinced the gentle 'Every Breaking Wave' would do just that, being emblematic of *Songs of Ascent's* 'beautiful love songs, where the object of love is not always obvious.' The Edge mooted 'Kingdom of Your Love' – later rechristened 'Soon', and the song to which U2 took the stage each night – as another contender for the album.

When the tour halted for winter – the elaborate set meaning they could only play stadium shows – Bono and The Edge resumed writing and recording. The former, McGuinness told the *Irish Independent,* 'is always an optimist, but he seems confident of getting a new record out by the end of the next six months. . . . By that time we will be ready to go back on tour and I think that will give it a different flavour.' Accordingly, when the tour restarted in August 2010, only three *No Line* songs remained in the set, and three new ones were debuted (marking the first time in a decade that U2 had played songs live before releasing them). 'Return of the Stingray Guitar', which replaced 'Kingdom of Your Love' as their intro music, was coloured – Bono told *Rolling Stone* – by The Edge 'hanging out with Jimmy Page.' (The pair had formed a summit with Jack White for the 2008 movie *It Might Get Loud.*) 'So now it's Willie Dixon; all those blues guys.' The acoustic ballad 'North Star' – 'A love song for the universe' – preceded a third new song, 'Glastonbury', written in anticipation of their headline appearance at the British festival of that name. (Originally scheduled for 2010, the band instead appeared at the 2011 event, owing to Bono undergoing back surgery.) 'I hear "Glastonbury" like The Chemical Brothers, The Prodigy,' said Bono, still clinging to the idea of a 'club-sounding album,' alongside *Songs of Ascent,* 'a rock album,' and 'the *Spider-Man* stuff.'

A BIT MAD
Even a suggestion from a fan whose sales now eclipsed that of his heroes couldn't change Bono's mind: '(Coldplay's) Chris Martin called me and said, "I hear you've got all these albums going. I have a great idea: why not just pick the best songs from all of them and put them out now?" And I'm like, "Hmm . . ." Because we don't think like that. It's a bit mad. In that sense, we're not as twenty-first century as we think we are, because we'd be putting out more new songs online, involving our audience in the choice, if we were really modern.'

By the end of 2010, three producers were reported to be toiling on U2 music: will.i.am, Brian 'Danger Mouse' Burton, and Nadir 'RedOne' Khayat, a hit-maker for Lady Gaga. As 2011 unfolded, however, the proliferation of projects was whittled down. The *Spider-Man* songs were issued as a cast recording, will.i.am swapped the 'club-sounding album' for his own musical and TV work, and the RedOne sessions were abandoned. 'We have to focus on what we do best,' Clayton observed, 'and the work we did with Danger Mouse came closest to that. We want to be in the clubs and make pop music as well as the thing U2 does but . . . RedOne doesn't feel like the right fit.' Of *Songs of Ascent,* he remarked, 'We now feel a long way from that material.' **BM**

WILL IT EVER HAPPEN?
3/10   *Songs of Ascent* was last discussed by Bono in a January 2012 interview with the band's website, after which his enthusiasm was directed instead to the Danger Mouse material. Assuming it ever neared completion, the album could be made available to fan club members, to whom a variety of remix and live sets have been issued since 1995.

WHAT HAPPENED NEXT . . .
Work with Danger Mouse continued for two years. 'Powerful-sounding,' Daniel Lanois reported to the *Globe and Mail* of the results, as played to him by Bono. 'Some of it was adventurous. There were shades of *Achtung Baby.* A couple of songs I was familiar with, because we worked on them before but had not completed them. Now they're back on the burner. . . . I'm actually glad that I'm not making this record with them. I don't think I'd survive the experiment. It's hard work. . . . and it will be a character-building experience for Danger Mouse.' The first fruit of the latter's work was the 2013 single 'Ordinary Love' (below).

SONG READER

Artist Beck   Year 2012   Country US   Genre Folk/Country/Dance   Label Self-release   What A new *Great American Songbook*

BECK
'Recordings have become definitive for songs over the decades,' Beck told KCRW, 'so we really associate a song with whether Tom Petty did it or Black Sabbath. I thought there was something interesting about the period before recorded music, where there was nobody telling you how to play it, how to hear it, or how to feel it.'

Beck Hansen's shape-shifting genius has never been shackled by the expectations of the music business. A chameleon of near Bowie-esque proportions, he delivered albums of rap-laden noise rock (the double platinum *Odelay*, 1996), country-esque laments (*Mutations*, 1998), and full-on funk (*Midnite Vultures*, 1999) in the space of three years. With that kaleidoscopic burst, Beck established himself as a byword for single-minded projects that transcend both genre and fashion. And that's perhaps why, when he revealed plans to release *Song Reader*, a collection of sheet music published by best-selling author Dave Eggers' McSweeney's imprint, there was such little surprise among his hardcore fans and the music press. The concept of Beck working on such an audacious and unique project, antithetical to the instant access of streaming and downloads, was hardly shocking.

HAPHAZARD AND HAM-FISTED
The idea, says Beck, was to reflect the way in which music was written and consumed before the mass availability of recorded sound. 'I came across a story about a song called 'Sweet Leilani' (by Harry Owens), which Bing Crosby had released in 1937,' he writes in his preface to *Song Reader*. 'Apparently, it was so popular that, by some estimates, the sheet music sold fifty-four million copies. Home-played music had been so widespread that nearly half the country had bought the sheet music for a single song, and had presumably gone through the trouble of learning to play it. It was one of those statistics that offers a clue to something fundamental about our past.'

His interest in sheet music was piqued during the 1990s, the era in which he rose to fame via the hit 'Loser'. 'The idea came out of a time when one of my first records came out – *Mellow Gold* or *Odelay* – and they sent me a sheet music version of it, and it didn't make any sense,' he told Pitchfork. 'They were trying to notate, for piano, various guitar squeals, feedback, me shouting through a distortion pedal, and instruments and synthesisers not even playing notes that are in any kind of scale. It was very haphazard and ham-fisted.'

The aim of *Song Reader*, therefore, was to produce music that was loosely written and could be easily interpreted, so anyone sitting at a piano or

Cover: Heath Killen

BECK'S RECORD CLUB

Beck's Record Club echoes *Song Reader*'s idiosyncrasy. The idea is simple: gather a bunch of musicians, cover classic albums in their entirety, and upload videos of the results. Each track is done in a single take and put on the beck.com/recordclub site. With the likes of Devendra Banhart, MGMT, St Vincent, and Nigel Godrich, he has completed *The Songs of Leonard Cohen* and INXS's *Kick* (above), Yanni's *Live at the Acropolis,* Skip Spence's *Oar,* and *The Velvet Underground and Nico.*

equipped with a guitar could make of it what they wished. 'I realised early on that the songs would have to be different. . . . ' he said in a Q&A with McSweeney's on the book's release in December 2012. 'When you write for your own voice, you have certain constraints you become accustomed to. When you're asking other people to learn songs they've never heard, that puts a different kind of pressure on what the songs should be.'

The project began to come together in 2004. Coming off the back of a heavy touring schedule for the acclaimed *Sea Change,* Beck met with Eggers – best known for the memoir *A Heartbreaking Work of Staggering Genius* – to discuss the concept of releasing an album of sheet music. McSweeney's reputation for its quarterly parcels of literary miscellany, coupled with a dedication to the finer aspects of print, made it a natural fit. (Eggers completed the circle by appearing on Beck's 2006 album *The Information,* as a spoken word contributor with Spike Jonze. 'We were going to have a commentary going through the whole album, almost like the two old men in *The Muppets,*' Beck told the *Guardian.* 'It was hilarious. A heavy beat would kick in and they would go, "Shit! Listen

> *'I know I have friends who will dismiss it as a stylistic indulgence, a gimmick.'*
>
> Beck

to that beat! That drummer is so confident!" But we couldn't fit it all in. I asked them, "What would the ultimate record that ever could possibly be made sound like?" That's what they're going on about [in the concluding third of 'The Horrible Fanfare/Landslide/Exoskeleton']. They're saying it would be like an illuminated manuscript, handmade by monks. Or it would be a record that changed every time you listened to it.' Eggers also contributed entertaining sleevenotes to a 2008 reissue of *Odelay.*)

As Beck and Eggers collected old sheet music, the project's scope quickly changed. The initial plan had been to release a book with the songs notated in a straightforward design, but the pair realised there was far more to the form than simply putting notes and chords on a page. 'As we started to explore the whole world of sheet music – especially from the 1880s through the 1930s – we discovered how it's such a rich, strange world,' Beck told Pitchfork. 'There are so many elements of who we were as a society, which have been completely erased in the postwar era, after rock 'n' roll. So many things have worn away. So it was really interesting to go back to that and engage with it.'

REVEALING ASPECTS

Song Reader is a collection of twenty songs, each presented as a separate sheet in a decorative, book-like case. Like traditional sheet music, it can easily be put on a stand and played. But it's much more than music on a page: each sheet stands alone as a piece of art. Colourful and cutely illustrated, it demonstrates just why this project took the best part of eight years to come to fruition. And, quipped Beck, 'It looks nice on a coffee table.'

In the days leading up to the book's release, tracks from *Song Reader* were played live at London's Rough Trade record store, by musicians including Ed Harcourt, former Beta Band man Steve Mason, and one-time Libertine Carl Barat. Beck then played 'Sorry' and 'Heaven's Ladder' at a solo show in Santa Cruz in May 2013.

That July, the entire album was given the live treatment at a one-off show at London's Barbican, for which Beck (left) enlisted fellow musicians to help him interpret and realise his creations. Pulp's Jarvis Cocker joined him for a dramatic, Bads Seeds-esque take on 'Why Did You Make Me Care?' and Charlotte Gainsbourg (right) added vocals to a sweetly strummed version of 'Just Noise'.

Franz Ferdinand, Villagers' Conor O'Brien, Beth Orton, Joan as Police Woman, The Staves, and James Yorkston were also on hand to add their interpretations, as Beck took the collaborative concept to its logical conclusion.

Importantly, it doesn't feel like an antiquated relic, despite its insistence on looking at music and music consumption from a pre-1950s perspective. The SongReader.net website allows fans and musicians to upload their own take on Beck's tracks. This means the country-tinged ballad 'Don't Act Like Your Heart Isn't Hard' has been reworked as an 'I'm Waiting for the Man' style stomper, while 'They Didn't Believe I Could Do the Foxtrot' has been mixed into a scratch-heavy, freeform jazz piece. That collaborative aspect has confirmed *Song Reader* as a socially interactive music project, when it could so easily have been a hubristic attempt at confounding listeners.

'I know I have friends who will dismiss it as a stylistic indulgence, a gimmick,' wrote Beck at the time of the book's release. 'There's a way of miniaturising and neutralising the past, encasing it in a quaint, retro irrelevancy and designating it as something only fit for curiosity-seekers or revivalists. But although the present moment can exclude the past from relevance, it can't erase its influence entirely. Each era finds something new to return to; things that seemed out of date have a way of coming back in new forms, and revealing aspects of themselves we might not have noticed before.' **JM**

WILL IT EVER HAPPEN?

2/10 While Beck hasn't explicitly discounted the idea of releasing a recorded version of *Song Reader,* all the noises suggest it's unlikely. 'The opening up of the music, the possibility of letting people work with these songs in different ways, and of allowing them a different accessibility than what's offered by all the many forms of music available today, is ultimately what this collection aims for,' he wrote in the book's preface. With new albums – including 2014's *Morning Phase* – and a series of stand-alone twelve-inch releases reportedly lined up, *Song Reader* looks as if it will remain on the page.

IV (1971) Led Zeppelin

It's one of rock's sales blockbusters – twenty-three million and counting in the US alone – but Led Zeppelin's untitled fourth album could have been very different. Between late 1970, when Robert Plant and Jimmy Page undertook writing at a remote cottage in Snowdonia, and February 1971, when sessions wrapped at Island studios in London, Zeppelin nailed thirteen songs. With another three left over from *Led Zeppelin III* ('Poor Tom', 'I Wanna Be Her Man', and 'The Rover'), they had enough for a double album – or, as Page briefly contemplated, four EPs.

It would have been a superb collection, but the guitarist decided 'people can appreciate a single album better'. Most of the cuts found homes: 'No Quarter' on *Houses of the Holy;* 'Boogie with Stu', 'Night Flight', 'Down by the Seaside', 'The Rover' (electrified from its acoustic *III* incarnation) and 'Houses of the Holy' on *Physical Graffiti.* 'I Wanna Be Her Man' was left in the cold, but Page's expanded reissues will hopefully rescue it from obscurity.

THE LAST DAYS OF EASTER (1973) Stevie Wonder

Where I'm Coming From, Music of My Mind, and *Talking Book* heralded Stevie Wonder's blossoming into the 1970s' greatest soul star, being the first albums over which he – rather than Motown – had control.

A fourth album, *The Last Days of Easter,* was to depict 'the horror and hypocrisy in the world' and 'what needs doing – socially, spiritually and domestically.' (Characteristically, he resolved to 'be positive.') He even had artwork lined up: a 'picture of a very old man who's been through it all and can now rest and look back at the confusion. He would have the wisdom and the contentment.'

To writer David Nathan, he played 'a really funky raw blues' (possibly 'Living for the City') and 'an enchantingly beautiful tune entitled "Images"' (possibly, later, 'Visions').

The *Easter* idea was dumped when he realised 'people would only relate it to Easter and not the other things I'll be saying.' But 'the concept of the last days . . . of life, of love, of youth' evolved into 1973's *Innervisions.*

12 HITS FROM HELL (1980) Misfits

12 Hits from Hell, by horror punk pioneers the Misfits, was cut in 1980 but shelved when guitarist Bobby Steele was booted from the band. Steele was a thorn in the side of bassist Jerry Only – who, alongside founder Glenn Danzig, is the best-known Misfit, and had groomed his brother Doyle to take over six-string duties. However, the album's mix featured both guitarists, immortalising Steele's work in a fashion that Only found unacceptable. A handful of songs escaped on an EP and single, while the rest were reworked for 1982's *Walk Among Us.*

In 2001, the Caroline label was set to release the 1980 sessions, only to incur Danzig and Only's wrath. 'The version that was withdrawn was not pleasing to the Misfits . . .' the label grovelled, 'and not a representation of the band's authentic sound as it had two guitars in the mix – the Misfits never had two guitarists.' Forty thousand copies were destroyed, although promo editions sent for review were professionally duplicated by enterprising bootleggers.

UNTITLED (1992) Mick Jagger

Mick Jagger's solo debut *She's the Boss* (1985) was a smash. Yet *Primitive Cool* (1987) was a flop, which doubtless influenced his decision to reunite with The Rolling Stones in 1989. By 1992, the singer was ready to give his solo career another shot. He duly hooked up with Rick Rubin, then riding high on the sales of his Red Hot Chili Peppers production *Blood Sugar Sex Magik.*

Wary of high-gloss sheen, Rubin teamed Jagger with LA bar band the Red Devils. On 18 June 1992, they convened at Hollywood's Ocean Way studio and, in fourteen hours, cut thirteen R&B covers, drawn from records that influenced the formative Stones. However, the star seems never to have regarded the session as anything more than a diversion: with Eric Clapton's platinum-coated blues revival still a couple of years away, Jagger didn't envisage it as likely to revive his fortunes. One cut (Sonny Boy Williamson's 'Checkin' Up On My Baby') graced 2007's *The Very Best of Mick Jagger*, but the rest resides in bootleg form only.

UNTITLED (1992 onwards) The La's

Rock history is littered with reclusive geniuses. Slightly rarer are reclusive geniuses who make a classic album, then effectively vanish. Among them is La's frontman Lee Mavers (above), whose reputation rests on a sole album (which the band disowned the moment it hit shops) and its international hit 'There She Goes'.

The La's disintegrated in the early 1990s. Bassist John Powers formed Cast, while Mavers revived the band name for periodic live outings. Refusing to grant interviews, and restricting airings of new songs, he created a self-mythology that led to M.W. Macefield's meticulously researched 2003 book *In Search of The La's: A Secret Liverpool.* Despite the author's discovery that Mavers was a genial father, not a drug-addled nutter, the legend remained intact.

Mavers and Powers reunited in 2004 and the former occasionally plays clubs and festivals. Of the new and apparently brilliant songs that he has amassed in the past two decades, however, there is no commercially available evidence.

TOO TIGHT (1996) 2Pac & Hammer

Eyebrows lifted when, in 1995, 'U Can't Touch This' star MC Hammer signed to Death Row. His glory years had passed and the gangsta label seemed an odd fit for a man best known for poppy rap. However, friend and label boss Suge Knight, perhaps hoping to exploit the novelty value of this odd coupling, paired him with their biggest star, Tupac Shakur.

'Me and 'Pac became very good friends,' Hammer told bomb1st.com. 'He said, "Now Hammer, I'm gonna make these records (songs) for you, and I want you to speak even more to the streets" . . . Over the course of about a year, almost, we fooled around in places together, we sat down and we mapped out ideas on what to do next. We made records and we dreamed together. It was just devastating when he lost his life.'

Only a couple of cuts surfaced. In 1998, 'Unconditional Love' emerged – minus Shakur – on Hammer's *Family Style,* while 'Pac's demo of it graced his *Greatest Hits.* 'Too Late Playa' (featuring Big Daddy Kane) and 'Too Tight' later appeared online.

DISINFORMATION (1999)
Mad Season

Spawned from meetings in rehab, grunge-era supergroup Mad Season featured Alice In Chains singer Layne Staley, Pearl Jam guitarist Mike McCready, and Screaming Trees drummer Barrett Martin, with bassist John Baker Saunders. Bolstered by their associations and the hit 'River of Deceit', their sole album, *Above* (1995), promptly went platinum.

The four returned to their day jobs, but regrouped – minus Staley, now a reclusive drug addict – in 1997. 'We recorded a second record that we were going to call *Disinformation*,' McCready told premierguitar.com. 'It was about twelve or thirteen songs, eight of which were pretty realised – the rest were just demos.' However, with Staley out of action and plans to recruit Screaming Trees singer Mark Lanegan (who guested on *Above*) faltering, the album was shelved.

After the deaths of Staley (2002) and Saunders (1999), four cuts graced a 2013 reissue of *Above* (including one co-written by R.E.M.'s Peter Buck); three of which featured, at last, lyrics and singing by Lanegan. 'I'd wanted Mark to sing on this stuff forever . . .' McCready enthused. 'I can't think of anybody more perfect.'

A CASE OF JONI (2000) Various

Celebrated in song by Led Zeppelin to Sonic Youth, and covered by artists ranging from Tori Amos to Herbie Hancock, Joni Mitchell is one of rock's best-loved writers. So it was no surprise that a mooted tribute album attracted a diverse cast: Chaka Khan ('Hejira'), Lindsey Buckingham ('Big Yellow Taxi'), kd lang ('Help Me') P.M. Dawn ('Night in the City'), Janet Jackson ('The Beat of Black Wings'), Duncan Sheik ('Court and Spark'), Annie Lennox ('Ladies of the Canyon'), Björk ('The Boho Dance'), Elton John ('Free Man in Paris'), Sarah McLachlan ('Blue'), Elvis Costello ('Edith and the Kingpin'), Etta James ('Amelia'), and Stevie Wonder ('Woodstock').

A Case of Joni was to have followed Wonder's performance of 'Woodstock' at a 1999 ASCAP award show that honoured Mitchell's songwriting achievements. Sadly, it was shelved for unexplained – but presumably contractual – reasons.

By the time it surfaced as the more prosaically titled *A Tribute to Joni Mitchell* (above) in 2007, it had gained Sufjan Stevens, Prince, and James Taylor, but lost Buckingham, Jackson, Wonder, Khan, Elton, James, Sheik, and P.M. Dawn.

UNTITLED (2001 onwards)
Zack de la Rocha

When Rage Against the Machine imploded in 2000, singer Zack de la Rocha seemed a shoo-in for a solo career. But, as he later told the *L.A. Times,* 'I became obsessed with completely reinventing my wheel – in an unhealthy way, to a degree.'

After cutting tracks with hip-hop producer DJ Shadow, de la Rocha hooked up with Nine Inch Nails' guru Trent Reznor. However, as Reznor told *Maximum Ink,* 'He will, eventually, make a great record, but he's going to have to have the balls to do it, which he didn't at the time. He was trapped in a corner that he placed himself in. [He said] "I don't want to do anything that sounds like Rage Against The Machine." Okay, then try this . . . "I can't do that, it doesn't sound like Rage Against The Machine"!'

The Shadow-produced 'March of Death' was released online in 2003, and the Reznor-helmed 'We Want It All' graced 2004's *Songs and Artists that Inspired Fahrenheit 9/11*. But when de la Rocha finally issued his solo debut – the EP *One Day As a Lion* – in 2008, it included nothing with Shadow or Reznor (nor another collaborator, ?uestlove) and he has since focused on the reunited Rage.

Device 1

DEVICE 1 (2003) Flint

After a decade of working together, The Prodigy's Liam Howlett, Keith Flint, and Maxim Reality were sick of each other. And after 2002's divisive 'Baby's Got a Temper', birthed by Flint, Howlett 'called Keith and Maxim down to the studio and basically said, "Right, you're not going to be on the album (2004's *Always Outnumbered, Never Outgunned*)."'

Flint used his downtime to form a band named after himself, featuring Prodigy guitarist Jim Davies, Gary Numan sidekick Rob Holliday, and drummers (and 'Baby's Got a Temper' co-writers) Kieron Pepper and Tony Howlett (no relation to Liam). They debuted at 2003's Download festival and cut an album, whose punky sound met a frosty reception at his label. Enter Nine Inch Nails instrumentalist Danny Lohner. 'Punk rock elements fused with slightly more electronic,' he told movementmagazine.com. 'It's dirty, lo-fi. Like an expensive punk band.'

The finished *Device 1* featured 'NNNN (No Name No Number)', a 'Baby's Got a Temper' prototype. But when the singles 'Asteroids' and 'Aim 4' sank, the group disbanded, and Flint – having made up with Howlett – returned to his day job.

LIVE IN LONDON (2004) The Strokes

The Strokes' 2003 album *Room on Fire* earned a rather less rapturous response than their 2001 debut *Is This It*. Nonetheless, the quintet remained a sufficiently big deal to headline London's prestigious Alexandra Palace in December 2003.

Reviews were mixed. 'Clinically rehearsed retro-indie,' grumbled Drowned In Sound. 'From fashionable indifference to feverish passion,' said the BBC. 'A slew of mid-paced new album tracks doesn't help matters,' noted *NME,* 'and nor does their obvious mid-tour complacency.'

Nonetheless, a record of the event was mooted for release in October 2004. Omitting the evening's cover of The Clash's 'Clampdown' and its Regina Spektor duet 'Modern Girls & Old Fashion Men', it was to include 'Reptilia', 'Under Control', 'Whatever Happened To...', 'Alone, Together', 'The Modern Age', '12:51', 'NYC Cops', 'You Talk Too Much', 'Someday', 'Hard to Explain', 'The End Has No End', 'Automatic Stop', 'Soma', 'Take or Leave It', and 'I Can't Win'.

Ultimately, however, it was pulled, reportedly owing to sound problems – specifically, presumably, 'the sound of a band not giving a shit.'

KORN KOVERS (2005–2010) Korn

Covers tackled by nu-metal pioneers Korn range from Radiohead's 'Creep' to War's 'Low Rider', via Metallica's 'One' and Ice Cube's 'Wicked'. Their plans for an entire covers collection revolved around similarly far-flung favourites. 'We've already done "Love My Way" from Psychedelic Furs,' singer Jonathan Davis (above) told *Billboard* in 2007. 'We've done "We Care a Lot" from Faith No More, (and Nine Inch Nails') "Head Like a Hole."' (The latter boasted guest vocals by Linkin Park's Chester Bennington.)

Korn Kovers was first mooted in 2005, when the track list included Mötley Crüe's 'Shout at the Devil', Public Enemy's 'Fight the Power' (with Lil' Jon), and Black Sabbath's 'Paranoid'. Davis's own wish list ranged from Ozzy Osbourne's 'Diary of a Madman' to Prince's 'Erotic City' and Debbie Deb's 1984 electro gem 'Lookout Weekend'.

'I would love to get that finished,' bassist Fieldy assured New York's Hard Rock Examiner in May 2010. 'A bunch of covers tunes would be cool. . . . We just gotta get back in and do some more.' That summer, however, Davis announced that *Kovers* had been kiboshed owing to pesky 'unforeseen circumstances.'

THE GREATEST ALBUMS . . . you heard eventually

3rd/SISTER LOVERS (started 1974, released 1978) Big Star

When the Box Tops, best known for 'The Letter', splintered, singer Alex Chilton soaked up influences from Stax soul to Roger McGuinn. The result was power pop pioneers Big Star, co-founded with guitarist Chris Bell (writer of the classic 'Thirteen').

After two albums sold in negligble quantities, Bell and bassist Andy Hummel quit. Chilton and drummer Jody Stephens staggered on, creating *Sister Lovers* (the pair were dating sisters at the time). Review copies earned verdicts including 'essential listening for any Chilton devotee but be warned of its utterly hopeless atmosphere and morbid contents' (*NME*) and 'a maelstrom of conflicting emotions' (*Rolling Stone*). Record labels lined up for the then deal-free band were also perplexed. 'We'd go in and play it,' recalled band rep John Fry, 'and these guys would look at us like we were crazy.'

The band broke up, but Chilton's cult reputation eventually led to *Sister Lovers'* belated release, its title augmented by the prosaic *3rd*.

DIANA (Chic mix) (started 1979, released 2003) Diana Ross

Spawned from a Studio 54 summit, *Diana* was the crashing together of R&B juggernauts. Ross's *The Boss* (1979) had revived her commercial fortunes, while Nile Rodgers and Bernard Edwards were basking in glory from two platinum Chic albums.

Thrilled to be producing one of their heroines, Rodgers and Edwards conceived *Diana* as a documentary: a statement about her rather than a vehicle for conventional Motown fare. The singer was on board until influential DJ Frankie Crocker warned her that 'I'm Coming Out' might lead listeners to think she was gay. Motown, too, were less than thrilled by the gritty, funky sound. The album was remixed and sped up without Rodgers' and Edwards' knowledge or consent, and – thanks to the hits 'Upside Down' and 'I'm Coming Out' – became her biggest ever seller.

'It's not hugely different,' Rodgers admitted, 'but ours *is* better.' Fans finally got a chance to judge for themselves when both versions were included in a 2003 deluxe reissue.

'THE BLACK ALBUM' (started 1986, released 1994) Prince

Officially untitled and uncredited, *'The Black Album'* was created after the collapse of The Revolution (see page 141). Prince's mid-1980s work had drifted from his X-rated funk of old, and cuts like 'Bob George' and 'Superfunkycalifragisexy' were clear bids to redress the balance. ('Dead On It', in contrast, was an ill-advised slight at the rappers who had stolen his crossover crown.)

The album was scheduled for a December 1987 release. A minimal cover, bearing neither a title nor the artist's name, was prepared, and thousands of discs were pressed. Then Prince had a change of heart, attributing the hard-hearted set to the malign influence of 'Spooky Electric' (an apparent euphemism for Satan).

By way of repentance, he created 1988's uplifting *Lovesexy* (which reused *'The Black Album'*'s 'When 2 R in Love), while its predecessor lined bootleggers' pockets. It eventually limped out to fulfil Prince's contractual obligations to Warner during his 1990s war with them.

MODERNISM: A NEW DECADE
(started 1989, released 1998)
The Style Council

Jam fans were horrified when leader Paul Weller split the new wave chart-toppers in 1982. But he either won them over or attracted fresh legions of fans, as his new, soul-flavoured band The Style Council scored three gold-selling albums and a series of hits (two of which achieved the US success that had eluded The Jam).

In 1989, however, even the faithful were appalled when Weller bravely adopted house music as his new holy grail. This disdain extended to Polydor, for whom The Jam and The Style Council were flagship acts: when he turned in *Modernism: A New Decade,* the label rejected it.

Weller was indignant, pointing out, 'I've made all you fuckers millions of pounds.' However, as he admitted to *Uncut,* 'It taught me a good lesson.' He returned to guitar-oriented rock, with increasingly successful results, and *Modernism* languished in the vault for nearly a decade until its inclusion in the box set *The Complete Adventures of The Style Council.*

STONE OF SISYPHUS (started 1993, released 2008) Chicago

By 1993, AOR gods Chicago were in a slump. Their most recent album, 1991's *Twenty 1,* was their first in a decade not to go gold. Its opening single scraped into the top forty, but two further ones failed even to chart – a dismal result after two decades of smashes. New blood was needed.

Enter Peter Wolf, a keyboardist who had graduated from Frank Zappa's band to become a platinum-pulling producer for the likes of Starship. 'It's hard when you have $20 million in the bank and you don't have to think and you can do whatever the hell you want,' he observed to writer Dan LeRoy. 'To motivate yourself is kind of hard! And that was my job.'

With few concessions to the syrupy AOR that had become their stock-in-trade, *Stone of Sisyphus* returned to Chicago's more adventurous sound of the 1970s. To their bewilderment, the Reprise label rejected it, and the two sides parted ways. A few tracks were revamped on solo albums until the band's new label, Rhino, finally unleashed *Sisyphus* itself in 2008.

CHINESE DEMOCRACY (started 1994, released 2008) Guns N' Roses

Led Zeppelin created eight classics, became hard rock's biggest band, split, and put out a posthumous outtakes collection in the same time it took Axl Rose to make one album.

Along the way, he lost or fired the musicians who helped make Guns N' Roses one of rock's greatest acts – notably Slash in 1996 and Duff McKagan in 1997. A raft of talent emerged in their place as Axl tinkered, including Zakk Wylde, Dave Navarro, Brian May, producers Youth and Moby, ex-Replacement Tommy Stinson, and Nine Inch Nailers Robin Finck and Josh Freese. With the album assuming mythical status, The Offspring mockingly threatened to call *their* 2003 set *Chinese Democracy (You Snooze, You Lose).*

In March 2008, Dr Pepper offered a free can of the drink to 'everyone in America' if Axl issued the album that year. Eight months later, he did just that. Preposterously overproduced, at a reported cost of $13 million, it crawled to platinum status before descending into bargain bins.

mbv (started 1996, released 2013)
My Bloody Valentine

'I honestly thought it was going to be the next *Nevermind* and it was going to change everything,' Creation label boss Alan McGee said of My Bloody Valentine's 1991 album. 'It sort of did, but . . . twenty years later.'

Loveless did indeed prove vastly influential, its disciples ranging from leading lights of grunge like Billy Corgan and Trent Reznor to Brian Eno (hence Coldplay's Valentines homage 'Chinese Sleep Chant' on 2008's *Viva la Vida or Death and All His Friends,* which he produced).

At the time, however, acclaim failed to translate into sales. And, having nearly bankrupted Creation with *Loveless,* the Valentines petered out during attempts at a third album. (By the time sessions ended in 1997, half the band had left.)

Main man Kevin Shields resumed work on it in 2006 and the group reunited in 2008, but few expected the third album would ever appear. Even when, at a January 2013 show in London, Kevin Shields announced it would come out 'in two or three days,' it was assumed that he was joking. In fact, *mbv* appeared six days later, its unexpected arrival causing the band's website to crash.

OUR SECRETS ARE THE SAME
(started 1999, released 2004)
Simple Minds

By 1998, Simple Minds' star had dimmed so drastically that *Neapolis* went unreleased in the US. At home, it briefly crept into the top twenty.

Consequently, when they turned in its successor, as frontman Jim Kerr explained to earcandymag.com, 'The album was not a priority for EMI. But they said that they would find a release day soon. Unfortunately, EMI was then supposed to join with Warner Bros, BMG, or someone else. Because of that everyone apart from big names were put on hold.'

Kerr and guitarist Charlie Burchill – sole survivors of the band's original incarnation in 1978 – fought to regain control of the album. But by the time lawyers had picked at the case, 'We didn't want to release it. It had already appeared on the internet and we already had a new album.'

Our Secrets Are the Same finally emerged as part of the retrospective *Silver Box.* 'The best music the band have made in twenty years,' enthused the *Guardian.*

'When you have a long career,' Kerr observed, 'there will be periods when not all things go right. This was just one of those periods.'

KAMAAL/THE ABSTRACT (started 2001, released 2009) Q-Tip

'Clive Davis signed me to Arista . . .' Q-Tip told MTV. 'He put out an album with Miles Davis called *Bitches Brew* in the seventies. It's considered to be the first fusion album of its kind. I said to Clive, "I want to do the hip-hop album that's kind of like fusion in that way." He co-signed it. In 1999, I started putting it together.'

Unfortunately for the former star of A Tribe Called Quest, Davis and Arista parted company, and the former's successor, L.A. Reid, blew hot and cold. 'He dug it,' Tip recalled. 'We passed it out to press. L.A. was like, "I need a single . . ." I went in, worked on some songs. Played it for him. He kinda didn't say anything.'

Unable to reconcile his approach with corporate demands, Tip left Arista. Three years later, to his wry amusement, the label sold millions with André 3000's *The Love Below,* the fusion-esque half of OutKast's *Speakerboxxx/The Love Below* set. 'I might have been a little too early,' Tip noted, 'but at least I know I wasn't wrong, because dude did it and rocked with it and it was great.'

In 2006, he opened negotiations to win back control of the album, and it belatedly emerged three years later.

YANKEE HOTEL FOXTROT (started 2000, released 2002) Wilco

'I'm still really curious about that . . .' mused Wilco main-man Jeff Tweedy, when *The Wire* asked why his label turned down *Yankee Hotel Foxtrot,* mixed and influenced by then Sonic Youth bassist Jim O'Rourke. 'Every record we made for Reprise has been problematic for them. *A.M.* was too country. *Being There* was a double album – that's a problem. *Summerteeth* – "Why isn't it country any more?" *Yankee Hotel Foxtrot* – "That's it! We can't work with you guys any more." Their goalposts were constantly shifting.'

Wilco accepted a $50,000 pay-off and streamed *Yankee Hotel Foxtrot* for free online in September 2001 – unwittingly creating a soundtrack for a post 9/11 America. In the aftermath, they secured a deal with Nonesuch (like Reprise, a subsidiary of Warners). A 2002 physical release of the album soared into the US top twenty, earning them a first gold disc.

Even guitarist Jay Bennett, ousted during the album's creation, shared the last laugh. 'That record was not rough to make,' he told rockzilla.net. 'It was a joyous experience, really. No rougher or less rough than any other record we ever made.'

EXTRAORDINARY MACHINE (started 2002, released 2005) Fiona Apple

Fiona Apple has long been a square peg in pop's round hole: publicly dismissive of hype, prone to wordy album titles, and reluctant to fit the female singer-songwriter stereotype.

Nonetheless, it was a surprise when Epic rejected *Extraordinary Machine,* given that its predecessors *Tidal* and *When the Pawn . . .* had sold a combined four million in the US. The problem, according to Apple's producer Jon Brion, was a lack of obvious hits. Even when he and the singer returned to the studio to cook up something radio-friendly, Epic remained unmoved.

An online 'Free Fiona' campaign urged supporters to send 'a fake apple, a photo of an apple, a piece of paper with an apple sticker, a sketch of an apple, even an apple pie' to the label. The fire was fuelled by leaks of the album's songs.

Meanwhile, Apple revisited it with Mike Elizondo, an associate of Dr. Dre and co-producer of 50 Cent's hit 'In Da Club'. 'I remain a fan . . .' Brion told MTV loyally, 'and she shouldn't have to meet too much resistance.' Indeed, when the revamped album saw the light of day, it soared into the US top ten.

LOST SIRENS (started 2003, released 2013) New Order

'Really weird,' declared former New Order bassist Peter Hook to *Billboard* of the band's lost album. 'It reminded me of the good times. After the year I have had, and the legal wrangling that I'm going through with them lot, it was nice to be able to listen to *Lost Sirens* and go, 'Oh my god, we did do some really good work, despite all the arguing.' Even though we were at each other's throats, there was still chemistry between us that was absolutely fantastic.'

The fragile relationship between Hook and frontman Bernard Sumner had splintered at the close of work on *Waiting for the Sirens' Call* (2005). 'I missed the last week because I went into rehab,' the bassist said. On his return a month later, Sumner declared him 'a worse person, in my opinion.' That, Hook responded, was 'because I was sober and I couldn't get drunk anymore to put up with his outrageous behaviour, so I was standing my ground.' 'Very Spinal Tap,' noted drummer Stephen Morris.

As the dispute descended into bitter legal wrangling, outtakes from the sessions were bound in red tape, but emerged after a decade to respectable reviews and sales.

ALBUM COVER DESIGNERS

Natalie Abadzis is an artist, author, and teacher from South London. Her career as a commercial artist informs both her own practice and work as a teacher. Her work archives the profound and absurd of the everyday, creating flow between practice, teaching, and her commercial work.
natalie-abadzis.tumblr.com

Steve Clarke worked for the BBC and now designs magazines including *Kerrang!* and *Mojo*.
phoresttphyre.com

Isabel Eeles achieved first class honors in graphic design at Central Saint Martins School of Art and Design. In 2012, she won a competition to create designs for L'Oréal Professionnel styling products. She also contributed to *The Greatest Movies You'll Never See*.
isabeleeles.com

Jayne Evans is a freelance artist, paper engineer, and graphic designer. Her work ranges from designing and making children's pop-up books and 3D models, to album covers and painting from her North London studio.
jayneevansart.co.uk

Louise Evans is a graphic designer who, while a student at Norwich University of the Arts, won Best Student Book at the British Book Design and Production Awards in 2010. Soon after graduating, she joined Grade Design in London to work on print, publishing, and branding projects.
gradedesign.com

Gerry Fletcher is a user experience designer for the BBC. He is also an illustrator, designing products, album covers, and websites. Music plays an important part in his life, whether it is playing gigs with his band Propel or working on artwork for other local acts.

Simon Halfon works as an art director in London and Los Angeles. He has designed album covers and campaigns for acts including George Michael, Frank Sinatra, and Oasis.
simon-halfon.com

Sarah Holland is a London-based graphic designer who graduated from Central Saint Martins.
sarahhollanddesign.co.uk

Tom Howey lives and works in London as a designer of popular illustrated reference books.

Damian Jaques trained in printmaking at Wimbledon College of Art and Portsmouth Polytechnic before becoming involved in graphic design. He was a co-founder and designer of *COIL, Journal of the Moving Image,* and designer of *Mute* magazine from 1997 to 2005. His work has been published in *Typography Now Two – Implosion, Mapping* (2008), and *magCulture: New Magazine Design* (2003).

Heath Killen is a designer, art director, and design consultant from Newcastle, Australia. Represented by The Jacky Winter Group creative agency, he has worked on high-profile projects for clients as diverse as Smirnoff, Paramount Pictures, Art Gallery of New South Wales, and Tropfest. Most recently, he was the managing editor of Australian design magazine *Desktop*.

Herita MacDonald created the media's most requested poster (the Dali/Marx Brothers tribute *Giraffes on Horseback Salads*) for *The Greatest Movies You'll Never See*. Her publishing, packaging, web design and corporate identity work includes illustration, painting, 3D modelling, and stained glass.
heritamacdonald.com

Dean Martin is a London-based graphic designer and illustrator.
deangmartin@me.com

Vaughan Oliver is one of the most innovative and prolific album cover designers of the past thirty years. His work for London record label 4AD won him an international following among fellow designers and music fans. He has designed covers for many different artists, including Pixies, Bush, Cocteau Twins, Dead Can Dance, The Breeders, This Mortal Coil, Pale Saints, Lush, and Throwing Muses. Recognition for his work has led to Grammy nominations, a Visiting Professorship at University of Greenwich, and election into the AGI, an elite club of international graphic designers with 400 members.

Paul Palmer-Evans combines a love of design with a love of music. While pasting up ads and covers for EMI in the 1970s, he performed with several bands. In the 1980s, he worked for design companies and gigged around London, until hanging up his guitar to concentrate on design. In 2000, he co-founded Grade Design, specialising in publishing, and has since worked on many award-winning projects.

John Pasche is best known for his collaboration with The Rolling Stones. After designing the poster for a 1970 European tour, he was asked to create a new logo for them. The result was the famous 'Tongue and Lip', originally

CONTRIBUTORS

reproduced on *Sticky Fingers*. John went on to become art director at United Artists' music division, before moving to Chrysalis as creative director. In his various roles, he has worked on sleeve and poster projects for artists including The Who, Jimi Hendrix, Paul McCartney, Sinéad O'Connor, Debbie Harry, and Jethro Tull. Limited edition prints of his posters from the Seventies are available at johnpasche.com

Matt Reynolds is a London-based designer and publisher of *Umbrella* magazine (umbrellamagazine.co.uk). When not photographing disused tube stations or listening to Morrissey, he can be found buying expensive shoes – and then hiding them from his girlfriend. matthewdavidreynolds.wordpress.com

Bill Smith set up Bill Smith Studios in 1978, and was creative director for acts including The Jam, Rolling Stones, Kate Bush, Genesis, Van Morrison, and Mike Oldfield. He has written and directed videos and TV spots for acts including Mike Oldfield, The Jam, Clannad, Paul Young, Elaine Paige, and Alison Moyet. Bill's work for Led Zeppelin's box set was nominated for a Grammy and his box set for King Crimson's *Frame by Frame* won a US industry award.

Akiko Stehrenberger is an award-winning movie poster designer and illustrator, based in Los Angeles. She was dubbed 'poster girl' by *Interview* and *Creative Review* dedicated their entire *January Monograph* zine to her posters. Her work was personally approved by directors Michael Haneke, David Lynch, Todd Solondz, and Roman Polanski. akikomatic.com

Theunis Bates (TB) is a senior editor at *The Week* magazine in New York City, and has written for *Time, Playboy, Fast Company,* and AOLNews.com. A former metalhead, he now listens almost exclusively to depressing country music.

Mark Bennett (MB) lives in London until further notice.

Chris Bryans (CB) has written for several entries in the *1001* series, from songs to albums to guitars, plus *Rock Chronicles, Rock Connections, The Observer, Radio Times,* and *Time Out*. He seeks the holy grail of lost albums: a Mogwai project with Céline Dion.

David Crawford (DC) has written for titles such as *Radio Times* and *Screen International,* on subjects ranging from Smokey Robinson and Mozart to music in Communist Berlin. He contributed to *1001 Songs* and *1001 Albums You Must Hear Before You Die*.

James Forsyth (JF) is a freelance journalist and reviewer who has worked in America and the UK, including writing for *Q* magazine and BBC Online.

Andrew Greenaway (AG) wrote *Zappa the Hard Way* and *The Beatles . . . The Easy Way*, helped ghostwrite *King of Clubs* for Anton Johnson, and contributed to *We Are the Other People – 25 Years of Zappanale* and *1001 Songs You Must Hear Before You Die*. He runs the website idiotbastard.com.

Matthew Horton (MH) is a freelance journalist. He writes about music and *Doctor Who* for Virgin Media, and about music for *NME* and *Esquire* Middle East. He has contributed to books including *1001 Albums You Must Hear*

Before You Die, 1001 Songs, and *Rock Chronicles*. He lives in Dartford with his wife, three daughters, and an excessive number of Beach Boys records.

Johnny Law (JL) works for Channel 4. He's three quarters Scottish, one quarter Danish, and entirely a dad. Having evaded musical success in Erotic Utensils and Johnny Law and the Love Commandos, he now writes about music in such weighty tomes as *1001 Songs You Must Hear Before You Die*.

Bruno MacDonald (BM) project-edited *The Greatest Movies You'll Never See*.

Joe Minihane (JM) is a London-based freelance journalist, writer and vinyl obsessive. His favourite music includes Ryan Adams, Bob Dylan, Beck, and New Order. Joe's writing has appeared in *1001 Albums You Must Hear Before You Die, 1001 Songs You Must Hear Before You Die,* and *Record Collector*.

David Roberts (DR) is author of *Rock Atlas*. He managed music projects at Guinness World Records, including *British Hit Singles* and *Hit Albums*. In 2006 he was made consultant, writer, and filmmaker to the London's O2's British Music Experience. He edited *Rock Chronicles* and wrote for *1001 Songs You Must Hear Before You Die*.

Rod Yates (RY) is a Sydney-based journalist who has written about music and film for the past twenty years. Now editor of *Rolling Stone* Australia, he has edited Australian editions of *Kerrang!* and *Empire*. Rod is a regular contributor to *Classic Rock, Mojo, Kerrang!* (UK), and myriad Australian titles. He has a weakness for hair metal, perhaps because he has no hair. Or taste.

SELECTED BIBLIOGRAPHY & WEBSITES

Brannigan, Paul *This Is a Call: The Life and Times of Dave Grohl* (HarperCollinsPublishers, 2011)

Bussy, Pascal *Kraftwerk – Man, Machine and Music* (SAF Publishing, 1993)

Carlin, Peter Ames *Bruce* (Simon & Schuster, 2012)

Cross, Charles R. *Backstreets – Springsteen: The Man and His Music* (Harmony Books, 1989)

Geldof, Bob *Is That It?* (Sidgwick & Jackson, 1986)

Goldsmith, Lynn, *PhotoDiary* (Rizzoli International Publications, 1995)

Gooch, Curt; Suhs, Jeff *Kiss Alive Forever* (Billboard Books, 2002)

Heylin, Clinton *Still on the Road: The Songs of Bob Dylan Vol. 2: 1974–2008* (Constable, 2010)

Hoskyns, Barney *Waiting for the Sun – Strange Days, Weird Scenes, and the Sound of Los Angeles* (St. Martin's Press, 1996)

Leaf, David; Sharp, Ken *Kiss – Behind the Mask* (Warner Books, 2003)

LeRoy, Dan *The Greatest Music Never Sold* (Backbeat Books, 2007)

Lewisohn, Mark *The Complete Beatles Recording Sessions* (Hamlyn, 1988)

Mason, Nick *Inside Out – A Personal History of Pink Floyd* (Weidenfeld & Nicolson Illustrated, 2004)

McKagan, Duff, *It's So Easy (And Other Lies)* (Orion, 2011)

Miles, Barry *Paul McCartney: Many Years from Now* (Martin Secker & Warburg Ltd, 1997)

Pegg, Nicholas *The Complete David Bowie* (Reynolds & Hearn Ltd, 2009)

Pidgeon, John *Classic Albums* (BBC Books, 1991)

Rees, Dafydd; Crampton, Luke *Q Rock Stars Encyclopedia* (Dorling Kindersley, 1996)

Rogan, Johnny *Neil Young – Zero to Sixty* (Rogan House, 2000)

Rosen, Craig *The Billboard Book of Number One Albums* (Billboard Books, 1996)

Schaffner, Nicholas *The British Invasion* (McGraw-Hill, 1982)

Slash; Bozza, Anthony *Slash* (HarperCollinsPublishers, 2007)

Spitz, Marc *Nobody Likes You – Inside the Turbulent Life, Times and Music of Green Day* (Sphere, 2006)

Spizer, Bruce *The Beatles Solo on Apple Records* (Four Ninety-Eight Productions, 2005)

Strauss, Neil *Everyone Loves You When You're Dead* (HarperCollins, 2011)

Thompson, Dave *In Between Days – An Armchair Guide to The Cure* (Helter Skelter Publishing, 2005)

Tobler, John; Grundy, Stuart *The Record Producers* (BBC, 1982)

Townshend, Pete *Who I Am* (HarperCollinsPublishers, 2012)

Trynka, Paul *Starman: David Bowie – The Definitive Biography* (Sphere, 2011)

Wall, Mick *AC/DC – Hell Ain't a Bad Place to Be* (Orion, 2012)

Zimmer, Dave *Crosby, Stills & Nash – The Authorized Biography* (Da Capo Press, 2000)

Classic Rock (classicrockmagazine. com), *Q* (qthemusic.com), *Rolling Stone* (rollingstone.com), and *Uncut* (uncut.co.uk) magazines

- angelfire.com/darkside/misfits12hits (Misfits)
- atu2.com (U2)
- beastiemania.com (Beastie Boys)
- beatlesbible.com (Beatles)
- beatlesinterviews.org (Beatles)
- bowiegoldenyears.com (Bowie)
- brucebase.wikispaces.com (Bruce Springsteen)
- chainofflowers.com (The Cure)
- complex.com
- daytrippin.com (Beatles)
- discogs.com
- dustyspringfield.org.uk (Dusty Springfield)
- eazy-e.com (Eazy-E)
- genesis-news.com (Peter Gabriel)
- goldminemag.com
- greendayauthority.com (Green Day)
- heretodaygonetohell.com (Guns N' Roses)
- heyheymymy.com.au
- jimdero.com
- jonimitchell.com (Joni Mitchell)
- kissfaq.com (Kiss)
- maccafan.net/Vaultquiz/SecretVault/ secretVault.htm (Paul McCartney)
- mega-superior-gold.blogspot.co.uk (Ryan Adams)
- members.shaw.ca/fz-pomd/ (Zappa)
- mtv.com
- ninwiki.com (Nine Inch Nails)
- prefabsprout.net (Prefab Sprout)
- princevault.com (Prince)
- rapgenius.com
- rocksbackpages.com
- rollingstone.com
- shutemdown.com (Public Enemy)
- spfc.org (The Smashing Pumpkins)
- springsteenlyrics.com (Springsteen)
- teenagewildlife.com (Bowie)
- thesmokinggun.com
- thrasherswheat.org (Neil Young)
- u2setlists.com (U2)
- vhnd.com (Van Halen)
- weezerpedia.com (Weezer)

INDEX

PICTURE CREDITS

Every effort has been made to trace all copyright owners, but if any have been inadvertently overlooked, the publishers would be pleased to make the necessary corrections at the first opportunity.
(Key: **t** = top; **c** = centre; **b** = bottom; **l** = left; **r** = right; **tl** = top left; **tr** = top right; **bl** = bottom left; **br** = bottom right)

2 Keystone/Hulton Archive/Getty Images **6** Ken Regan/Camera 5/Contour by Getty Images **13** Michael Ochs Archives/Corbis **15 t** Michael Ochs Archives/Corbis **15 b** Michael Ochs Archives/Corbis **18** Michael Ochs Archives/Getty Images **22** Petra Niemeier - K & K/Redferns/Getty Images **25** Daily Sketch/Rex Features **26** Duffy/Getty Images **27 t** Richard Keith Wolff/Retna **32** Michael Putland/Retna **35** Walter Iooss Jr./Getty Images **36 b** Good Times/Vanit/Retna **37** Fred W. McDarrah/Getty Images **38** Chris Walter/Retna **42** Mirrorpix **45** Chris Morphet/Redferns/Getty Images **47** Chris Morphet/Redferns/Getty Images **48 b** Jan Olofsson/Redferns/Getty Images **48** Michael Putland/Getty Images **50** Michael Putland/Retna **53 b** Jack Robinson/Hulton Archive/Getty Images **55** Ginny Winn/Michael Ochs Archives/Getty Images **58** Peter Mazel/Sunshine/Retna **61** Sunshine/Retna **65** Mick Gold/Redferns/Getty Images **66 tr** David Warner Ellis/Redferns/Getty Images **69** Photo Features **71 t** Globe Photos/ZUMA Press, Inc./Alamy **72** ABC/The Kobal Collection **75** DAGMAR **76** Ron Galella/WireImage/Getty Images **78** A. Spanjaard/Retna **80** Gijsbert Hanekroot/Sunshine/Retna **84** Gijsbert Hanekroot/Sunshine/Retna **87** Chris Morphet/Redferns/Getty Images **88** Peter Noble/Redferns/Getty Images **88** Ray Stevenson/Rex Features **90** Michael Putland/Retna **94 b** Gijsbert Hanekroot/Redferns/Getty Images **96** Time & Life Pictures/Getty Images **98** Neal Preston/Corbis **100** Philip Morris/Rex Features **103** Neal Preston/Retna **104 b** Michael Ochs Archives/Getty Images **106** MUSE/The Kobal Collection **108** Muse/The Kobal Collection **113** ITV/Rex Features **114** David Montgomery/Getty Images **116** Ebet Roberts/Redferns/Getty Images **118 t** AF archive/Alamy **121** MGM/Photofest/Retna **122 b** David Appleby **124 b** MGM/Photofest/Retna **126** Photo Features **128 t** Paul Bergen/Redferns/Getty Images **130** MARKA/Alamy **140** Ross Marino/Sygma/Corbis **142** ZUMA Press, Inc./Alamy **145** Jeff Kravitz/FilmMagic/Getty Images **148** Chris Taylor/Retna **150** Neal Preston/Corbis **152** RB/Redferns/Getty Images **157** Raymond Boyd/Michael Ochs Archives/Getty Images **158** Kevin Winter/ImageDirect/Getty Images **159** Ke.Mazur/WireImage/Getty Images **161** Tim Mosenfelder/Getty Images **164** Benjamin Oliver/Acceleration/Retna Ltd USA **166 tl** Mick Hutson/Redferns/Getty Images **166 tr** Patti Ouderkirk/WireImage/Getty Images **166 b** Tim Mosenfelder/Getty Images **168** Alastair Indge/Photoshot/Getty Images **170** Retna **172** Ian Dickson/Redferns/Getty Images **174** ZUMA Press, Inc./Alamy **176** Tina Korhonen/Retna **178** Tim Mosenfelder/ImageDirect/Getty Images **179 r** Steve Granitz/WireImage/Getty Images **182** Steve Jennings/Retna **185** Cent Productions/Paramount Pictures/The Kobal Collection/Gibson, Michael **188** Bob Berg/Getty Images **189** Cent Productions/Paramount Pictures/The Kobal Collection/Gibson, Michael **190** Sean Gallup/Liaison/Getty Images **192 t** Brink/Little Magic/Muse/The Kobal Collection **192 b** Paul Drinkwater/NBC/NBCU Photo Bank via Getty Images **195** Tina McClelland/Retna **198** Ralf Collaris/SUNSHINE/Retna **200 b** Theo Wargo/WireImage/Getty Images **203** S.I.N./Alamy **205** Dave Hogan/Getty Images **206** Mirrorpix **210** Joseph Cultice/Corbis **213** Mathew Hayward/Alamy **214 b** Timothy A. Clary/AFP/Getty Images **216** Richard Ecclestone/Redferns/Getty Images **218** Samir Hussein/Getty Images **220** Andy Sheppard/Redferns/Getty Images **226** Allstar Picture Library/Alamy **228 b** Jeff Kravitz/FilmMagic/Getty Images **230** Shirlaine Forrest/WireImage/Getty Images **233** Kevin Mazur/WireImage/Getty Images **234** Peter Still/Redferns/Getty Images **236** Douglas Mason/Getty Images **239 l** Douglas Mason/Getty Images **239 r** Robin Little/Redferns via Getty Images **240 l** Michael Putland/Getty Images **240 r** Echoes/Redferns/Getty Images **241 l** D.Pilkington/Lebrecht Music & Arts **241 r** Echoes/Redferns/Getty Images **243** Dosfotos/Lebrecht Music & Arts **243** Jon Stark/Lebrecht Music & Arts

The copyright for the album covers is held by the designers who created them. However, for some of the covers, third parties supplied images that were incorporated into the designs: **19** Michael Ochs Archives/Getty Images **24** Mirrorpix **39** Keystone Pictures USA/Alamy **40** Chris Walter/Retna **41** Chris Walter/Retna **68** Michael Putland/Getty Images **79** Michael Ochs Archives/Getty Images **91** OJO Images/Getty Images **107** Michael Ochs Archives/Getty Images **131** Michael Ochs Archives/Getty Images

Thanks to: Alison Hau (original book design), Dominic Nolan and Simon Ward (original book concept), Isabel Eeles (inexhaustible patience), Herita MacDonald, Siobhan O'Neill, Roger Griffin, Jamie Healy, and all the writers and designers.